THE CORPORATE
ASSAULT ON YOUTH

AC Adolescent
Cultures,
SS School &
Society

Joseph L. DeVitis & Linda Irwin-DeVitis
GENERAL EDITORS

Vol. 44

PETER LANG
New York • Washington, D.C./Baltimore • Bern
Frankfurt am Main • Berlin • Brussels • Vienna • Oxford

THE CORPORATE ASSAULT ON YOUTH

Commercialism, Exploitation, and the End of Innocence

EDITED BY Deron Boyles

PETER LANG
New York • Washington, D.C./Baltimore • Bern
Frankfurt am Main • Berlin • Brussels • Vienna • Oxford

Library of Congress Cataloging-in-Publication Data

The corporate assault on youth: commercialism,
exploitation, and the end of innocence / edited by Deron Boyles.
p. cm.—(Adolescent cultures, school and society; v. 44)
Includes bibliographical references and index.
1. Business and education—United States. 2. Commercialism in schools—
United States. I. Title. II. Boyles, Deron.
LC1085.2.B695   371.19'5—dc22   2008000231
ISBN 978-1-4331-0084-0
ISSN 1091-1464

Bibliographic information published by **Die Deutsche Bibliothek**.
Die Deutsche Bibliothek lists this publication in the "Deutsche
Nationalbibliografie"; detailed bibliographic data is available
on the Internet at http://dnb.ddb.de/.

© 2008 Peter Lang Publishing, Inc., New York
29 Broadway, 18th floor, New York, NY 10006
www.peterlang.com

Printed in the United States of America

Contents

Acknowledgments

This work emerged from a conversation I had with Joe DeVitis at a state-wide meeting to overhaul undergraduate core courses in teacher education in Georgia. As advocates of interpretive and critical inquiry, we worked together with other scholars to craft courses that enable future teachers to read between the lines and examine the everyday and the taken for granted. The influence of corporations on schools is one area where teachers, and others, rarely critique, given the ubiquitous nature of commercialism in the U.S. and, inseparably, schooling. From advertising on buses to providing teachers with "ready-made" curricula, businesses are continuing to expand their reach into schools. Their reach is increasingly seen in younger and younger grades, too. Joe's idea, then, was to craft a work that focuses on the influence of commercialism and youth—a focus too often overlooked. Without his vision and support, this work would not have come to fruition and I thank him.

In addition to Joe's vision, the nuts and bolts work of publishing an edited book can be overwhelming. Tony Carusi was central in bringing together the different authors whose works constitute this volume and provided crucial technical expertise. Beyond his technical skill, which is vast, Tony brings his own critical eye to this work. His contribution was important and significant enough to warrant his authoring the introduction and being the Associate Editor of the book. Sophie Appel, of Peter Lang, was also vital to this project and I appreciate her patience, attention to detail, and support. I also thank the staff members at Peter Lang who are responsible for the cover art, proofreading, and other important aspects necessary for publishing this work.

A version of Chapter Five first appeared in JCT: *Journal of Curriculum Theorizing*, 21: 2, Summer 2005. Reprinted with permission of the publisher. All rights reserved.

A version of Chapter Eight first appeared in *Educational Studies: Journal of the American Educational Studies Association*, 37: 3, June 2005. Reprinted with permission of the publisher. All rights reserved.

A version of Chapter Nine first appeared in *Teacher Education Quarterly*, 34: 2, Spring 2007. Reprinted with permission of the publisher. All rights reserved.

Introduction

There is a certain difficulty in writing an introduction for a work such as the one contained here. The diversity of topics covered, audiences addressed, and questions asked throughout each chapter vary to such an extent that a glance at the table of contents may leave readers wondering how such diverse titles came together in one edited text. It is with this in mind that I will attempt to not only outline the chapters presented here, but also to stress the importance of this text in both its breadth and depth. Given the wide range of topics discussed in these pages, one may assume this collection is a hodge-podge of miscellaneous articles related only in their binding. However, after reading these chapters, it will be difficult to leave this book without a better understanding of how pervasive, multi-faceted, and endemic the work of neoliberalism has become in shaping the youth of the United States, especially through the institutions of public education. Said directly, it is the overarching purpose of this book to exemplify the ways in which adolescents are interpellated into the dominant ideology of neoliberalism and suggest subversions and resistances to such interpellation that youth enact.[1] With this aim set forth, it will be helpful to address briefly what is meant by neoliberalism considered ideologically.

The role of neoliberalism as ideology has been taken up critically by several researchers.[2] According to Michael Apple, as an ideology, neoliberalism in education maintains "that the invisible hand of the market will inexorably

---

[1] For a more in-depth look at the process and meaning of interpellation as it relates to ideology, see Louis Althusser, "Ideology and Ideological State Apparatuses: Notes Toward an Investigation," in *Lenin and Philosophy and Other Essays* (New York: Monthly Review Press, 2001): 127-186.

[2] Some critical research done on educational policy, schools, and neoliberalism includes Michael Apple, "Creating Difference: Neo-Liberalism and Neo-Conservatism and the Politics of Educational Reform," *Educational Policy* 18, no. 1 (2004): 12-44; Deron Boyles, *American Education and Corporations: The Free Market Goes to School* (New York, NY: Falmer Press, 2000); and Alex Molnar, *School Commercialism: From Democratic Ideal to Market Commodity* (New York, NY: Routledge, 2005).

lead to better schools."[3] How this connection is made, between the market and better schools, takes several steps. First, the market must be understood as a neutral entity, open to all individuals regardless of race, gender, ability, or creed. These individuals are all equally capable of making rational decisions based on the information from the market available to everyone. Moreover, the attainment of information is a positive, measurable feature of the individual. Thus, all that remains in achieving the gains the market offers individuals is exerting the work necessary to attain them. As Apple joins them, "markets and the guarantee of rewards for effort and merit are to be coupled together to produce 'neutral,' yet positive results."[4] These three elements (neutrality, measurability, and rewarded effort) work together to produce a neoliberal vision of education. One example of the result of neoliberalism manifests through federal policy for public education in the United States, which considers students as future workers in the globally competitive marketplace. This goal is sought through an accountability scheme based on neutral measurements of knowledge in the form of standardized test scores. And, through current policy measures, public schools are conceived as enterprises which are closed for business, if they fail to serve the market of students and parents.

Another dimension that upholds the dominant ideology is its appeal to common sense. In fact, the dominance of neoliberalism can be gauged by the degree to which its claims are accepted as common sense by the subjects within it. For instance, the link between economic prosperity and level of education has been reiterated to such a point that the primary purpose of education is directly related to obtaining employment or promotion within one's workplace. In other words, common sense dictates that going to school means getting a job.

While tracing all the ways that the tenets of ideology transform into the common sense of a population is beyond the scope of this introduction, it may be helpful to provide a historical example of how the link between education and the workplace was reinforced from a particularly neoliberal tack, in this case, through relatively recent educational policy. The rhetoric of neoliberalism in education grew dramatically during the 1980s with the election of Ronald Reagan as president.[5] Education was specifically influenced by the

---

[3] Apple, 2004, 18.

[4] Ibid., 18.

[5] While an occupational emphasis in educational policy can be traced through to the Smith-Hughes Act of 1917, which provided federal funding to public schools for vocational education to train farm workers, recent educational policy, such as the No Child Left Behind Act

Reagan administration in a number of ways. Reagan, in an effort to reduce government regulation, vowed to eliminate the U.S. Department of Education, though this effort proved unsuccessful. However, convened in 1981 at the behest of President Reagan by the Secretary of Education, Terrel H. Bell, the National Commission on Excellence in Education released its report, *A Nation at Risk* in 1983.[6] The popularity of this report is attested to by the educational historian Joseph Newman, who calls the report "*the* educational document of the late twentieth century."[7] This report famously warns that "the educational foundations of our society are presently being eroded by a rising tide of mediocrity that threatens our very future as a Nation and a people."[8] The threats were being realized through the global market in that "our once unchallenged preeminence in commerce, industry, science, and technological innovation is being overtaken by competitors throughout the world."[9] Competition was found in the efficiency of Japanese automobile manufacturing, South Korean steel mills, and German tool manufacturing. And the cause of the United States' losing economic ground to these other nations was located in the public schools. The report lists thirteen educational indicators of risk, focusing on low literacy rates, standardized test scores, and complaints from business and military leaders about the workers they receive from public schools.

This report marks a pivotal point in the federal government's involvement in public schooling, because it establishes a commonsense link between public schooling and the economic success of the United States. As the report states, "the public understands the primary importance of education as the foundation for a satisfying life, an enlightened and civil society, a strong economy, and a secure Nation."[10] Simply put, everyone knows that if public schools per-

---

of 2001, takes a more direct cue from Reagan-era economic concerns emanating from neoliberal theories of free market rule. As such, the example provided below is taken from policy generated during Reagan's presidency.

[6] National Commission on Excellence in Education, *A Nation at Risk: The Imperative for Educational Reform* (Washington, DC: U.S. Department of Education, 1983). Available at http://www.ed.gov/pubs/NatAtRisk/risk.html. This work will be cited as *ANR* for all subsequent references.

[7] Joseph Newman, *America's Teachers*, 5th ed. (Boston, MA: Pearson, 2006): 352. Emphasis in original.

[8] *ANR*, 5.

[9] Ibid.

[10] Ibid., 17.

sist in their "mediocrity," the United States cannot compete in the global market.

The focus on schools as sites which train future workers for a global economy has several effects. Through the workplace emphasis in the purpose of schooling, corporations can justify their influence on and presence in schools. Examples run from corporate sponsorship of schools, allowing companies to advertise on school walls, to commercial-curricular projects that place company logos and slogans throughout corporate-donated technologies and texts. The overarching message from these partnerships between the private corporate world and public schools is that corporations support schools through schools' consumption of brand-name products. From within a neoliberal framework, such consumption fosters the free market; therefore corporations must compete for the youth market share.

This is but a brief example of the workings of neoliberal ideology in public schooling. Should this example be read as a digression, the point must be emphasized that neoliberalism, as an ideology, is a multifaceted phenomenon, and, as such, the ways in which it influences the make-up of youth experiences must be addressed from a variety of angles in order to provide a more comprehensive critique. Given that public schools are a site populated by youth, the importance of this institution in relation to how the youth of the United States identify themselves can hardly be overstated. The chapters that follow this introduction, from the ideological point of view outlined above, take youth as a central population targeted and interpellated by neoliberal corporate interests in ways that shape youths' identities and understandings of their position in society.

In the first chapter, Carolyn Vander Schee examines health education and the marketing efforts done by schools in order to combat obesity and encourage students to make healthy choices. At first blush, such an effort seems quite in line with common sense. Given the media representation of an "obesity epidemic" plaguing U.S. youth, one may conclude that schools seeking to fight this epidemic should be lauded for their efforts. However, Vander Schee's analysis reveals many of the problems inherent to the consumerist approach schools take in their health education programs. When schools define "good health" monolithically, as though each youth's health goal is identical, and present "being healthy" to youth, via marketing strategies, as a commodity to be obtained, consumerism is further instantiated as the path to happiness.

In Chapter Two, Jennifer Esposito and Bettina Love consider female rappers and the potential liberatory influence their music holds for young females. They argue that traditional sex education programs currently found in schools promote a "wait until you are married" message for girls which neglects sexual desires young girls experience. Because of this, girls look elsewhere to express and come to terms with those desires. In examining the lyrics of female rappers, Esposito and Love locate a field in which female sexual expression surfaces as an alternative site of sex education. The project of re-identifying women's sexuality outside of male domination is one example of the ways in which youth resist their interpellation by neoliberalism, a historically patriarchal ideology that assigns women a subordinate role to the male actors in the free market.

Dennis Attick provides this volume with two chapters, both of which look at the nexus of media, commercialism, and youth. His first contribution, Chapter Three, considers television advertising directed specifically to the "youth market," and the consumer culture that results in the conflation of consumer and citizen. His second offering, Chapter Seven, examines a specific use of corporate media, BusRadio, and its implications for youth when they are conspicuously subjected to commercialism. While each chapter explores a different medium through which youth are exposed to advertising, together they highlight the pervasiveness of consumerism in youth experience. Understanding product consumption as a key mechanism within the free market, youth are interpellated by neoliberal ideology through desiring the product offered in the television commercial or sitting on the bus listening to BusRadio.

Chapter Four, by Permeil Daas, investigates the automobile marketing industry and its targeting of youth. After providing a history of the rise of the automobile as a consumer product in U.S. society, Daas shows how automobiles marketed to youth overlook the environmental and safety risks involved when promoting youth ownership of cars. By connecting car ownership with social status, automobile advertisement manufacturers appeal to youth by equating having a car with being desirable. The success of these efforts routes youth deeper into the consumptive practices of material acquisition, which, in turn, provides one more process of interpellation that youth encounter.

Deron Boyles also provides two chapters to this volume. His first, Chapter Five, examines Chick-fil-A and their character education program for public schools. Here he inquires into the broader implications of a corporate-Christian fundamentalist organization providing lessons on character within the U.S. public school system. His second contribution, Chapter Eight, dis-

cerns a meta-narrative from commercial book covers given to youth and wonders what messages the product branded images of the free book covers relay.
Together these chapters expose a larger project in which corporations are already doing the work of neoliberalism inside schools. When corporations provide free, branded character education materials and advertisement-laden
book covers, schools, already underfunded, invite the use of these items, often
without consideration of the larger, business-friendly messages that come with
them. Without critical engagement of schools directed toward advertising in
the classroom, the free market encroaches further into the everyday experiences of youth, making consideration of its consequences increasingly difficult.

Chapter Six is a combined effort by Carly Stasko and Trevor Norris to
show the breadth of marketing to youth culture in ways that promote the values of consumption. The authors have coined the term "marketalkracy" in
order to name the dominion of market-rule and emphasize the ways which
such a regime interpellates youth as participating in market discourse. Focusing in on the continually growing domain of the market, particularly directed
at youth, they wonder how U.S. society can empower, rather than profit from,
youth.

The final chapter presented by Kenneth Saltman looks at the phenomenon of disaster capitalism through the response of corporate representatives
offering profit-making relief efforts to communities recovering from disasters,
and how policies, such as No Child Left Behind, foster the privatization of
public schools at the expense of democratic culture. By capitalizing on the
vulnerability of communities which suffer from disaster, such as the Gulf
Coast after Hurricane Katrina, Saltman reveals the profit motivation of corporations claiming to offer help to victims of flood, war, and other crises. With
political backing from current educational policy, for-profit endeavors are better able to remove schools from their public setting and render education into
a neoliberal enterprise of market survival. The dangers of such a shift become
apparent when education is made to serve the demands of the market instead
of promoting a democratic citizenry.

In total, these chapters represent many different viewpoints on the effects
of neoliberalism on youth, particularly in public education settings. They each
urge for a critical response to this development, but, depending on the manifestation they address, these critical responses take different forms. Collectively, these chapters present readers with a clear statement of the problems
neoliberal ideology brings with it when interpellating youth. As the free mar-

ket permeates the very public institutions it seeks to nullify, public schools and services dedicated to youth development are in dire need of support from people seeking to nourish and invigorate the democratic ethos the United States is purportedly based upon. Until educators, parents, civic organizations, and youth take a critical stance against the dominance of neoliberalism, public institutions, and the youth who take part in them, will remain under attack from the powerful ideologues seeking to abolish them.

Tony Carusi, Associate Editor

CHAPTER ONE

Consuming Health
Health Curricula and the
Production of a *Healthy* Student

Carolyn Vander Schee, Northern Illinois University

The problem of poor health related to overweight children and adolescents has received tremendous attention in academic, biomedical, and popular discourses.[1] *The Surgeon General's Call to Action to Prevent and Decrease Overweight and Obesity* considers the problem "the most burdensome faced by the Nation."[2] According to the American Heart Association (AHA) nearly 16 percent of all adolescents are considered clinically overweight.[3] Compared to 20 years ago these figures have doubled among children aged 6-11 and tripled

---

[1] In many ways the problem of obesity has undergone a discursive explosion, creating a kind of fusion between scientific and popular presses. For example, various reports published by the CDC, AMA, Department of Health and Human Services, and AHA proclaiming the problem of obesity resulted in feature publications disseminated by popular news outlets. For example, see the following feature articles: Catherine Arnst and David Kiley, "The Kids Are Not All Right: Child Obesity a Fast-Growing Problem," *Business Week* 3903 (2004): 56; Amanda Spake, "The Future of Fatness," *U.S News and World Report* 136, no. 5 (2004): 56; Peg Tyre and Julie Scelfo, "Helping Kids Get Fit," *Newsweek*, 22 January 2003, 60-64; Time Magazine Incorporated, "Critical Condition: America's Obesity Problem," *Time Magazine*, 7 June 2004.

[2] David Satcher, U.S. Department of Health and Human Services, *The Surgeon General's Call to Action to Prevent and Decrease Overweight and Obesity*. (Rockville, MD: U.S. Department of Health and Human Services, Public Health Service, Office of the Surgeon General; 2001, accessed 1 June 2005); available http://www.surgeongeneral.gov/topics/obesity/calltoaction/ CalltoAction.pdf.

[3] American Heart Association, "Overweight in Children" (Dallas, TX: American Heart Association, accessed 15 June 2005); available from http://www.americanheart.org/presenter.jhtml? identifier=4670. A diagnosis of overweight is given to those whose weights measure beyond the 95th percentile of the CDC's Body Mass Index-for-Age ideal weight.

among youth aged 12-19.[4] In an effort to counter these trends a number of agencies such as the Centers for Disease Control and Prevention (CDC), the AHA, and the American Medical Association (AMA) work diligently with schools to design health education curricula and implement programmatic initiatives for the purposes of educating youth about the importance of *healthful* living.

The "obesity epidemic," as it is commonly dubbed, is likened to a public health crisis engendered by the "conditions of a post modern world: too much television, and computer games, sedentary life-styles, and bad diets": in other words, laziness, overconsumption and overindulgence.[5] It is said to be the product of an apathetic Western existence that rejects physical activity and dietary moderation.[6] In contrast to discourses that attribute ill health as a consequence of *over*consumption, this chapter examines the ways in which the pursuit of "good health" has (also) become a consumerist activity in need of critical analysis. The chapter draws on the work of scholars from various fields that describe the emergence and influence of school-based social marketing efforts aimed at curbing the epidemic of fatness through the production *healthy* students.

The "New" Public Health and Contemporary Health Promotion Activities in Schools

Over the last 30 years health education has become a central aspect of school curricula.[7] In part, these shifts have occurred in response to philosophical changes occurring in the fields of medicine, epidemiology, and public health and the emergence of what is referred to as the "new" public health or,

---

[4] Food and Nutrition Service, U.S. Department of Agriculture, Centers for Disease Control and Prevention, U.S. Department of Health and Human Services, *Making It Happen! School Nutrition Success Stories* (Alexandria, VA: United States Departments of Agriculture and Health and Human Services, January 2005, accessed 10 June 2006); available from http://www.cdc.gov/healthyyouth/nutrition/Making-It-Happen/pdf/background.pdf

[5] John Evans, Bethan Evans, and Emma Rich, "The Only Problem Is, Children Will Like Their Chips: Education and the Discursive Production of Ill-Health," *Pedagogy, Culture and Society* 11, no. 2 (2003): 215-240, 232.

[6] Michael Gard and Jan Wright, *The Obesity Epidemic: Science, Morality, and Ideology* (Routledge, New York, 2005), 2.

[7] Deana Leahy and Lyn Harrison, "Risky Business: The Limits of Risk Discourse," *Education Links* 64 (2002): 17-19, 17.

more generally, health promotion.[8] The new public health refers to a specific ideology underpinning contemporary health initiatives taken on by various public and private health agencies in an attempt to counter "lifestyle diseases" engendered by smoking, obesity, and unsafe sex. The new public health is based on the premise that individuals will make healthy choices when provided knowledge about their individual susceptibility, the causes of illness, and ways in which they can personally alter their lifestyle to counter the disease process.[9] The model assumes that rationally acting individuals will pursue a specific sequence of reasoning to achieve certain desirable ends. As Lupton points out, the new public health presupposes the

> inherent coherence of the chain of reasoning itself and seeks to explain departures from rationality by a variety of internal and external obstacles. It reflects the belief that...views the very essence of humanity as being based on the notion of the ideal self as autonomous from the body.[10]

Petersen and Lupton claim that at the heart of the new public health is a "moral enterprise that involves prescriptions about how we should live our lives and conduct our bodies."[11] While notions of proper bodily care and hygiene have long been bound up with various moral, self, or society bettering endeavors (e.g., as in the Progressive era), the new public health codifies these efforts in novel ways. As such, health initiatives no longer focus on treating discrete illnesses per se, but engage the public through various health promotion and social marketing tactics to take preventative action to promote their own health.

A central component of the new public health agenda involves social marketing and the utilization of various media outlets to increase public awareness of health issues. To be sure, the media has long been implicated in a variety of social services messages.[12] Recall the government-sponsored public service an-

---

[8] Alan Petersen and Deborah Lupton, *The New Public Health: Health and Self in the Age of Risk* (Thousand Oaks, CA: Sage, 1996); Deborah Lupton,*The Imperative of Health: Public Health and the Regulated Body*,(Thousand Oaks, CA: Sage, 1995).

[9] Lupton, *The Imperative of Health*, 57.

[10] Ibid.

[11] Petersen and Lupton, *The New Public Health*, 174.

[12] Ilona Kickbusch and Lea Payne, "Twenty-first Century Health Promotion: The Public Health Revolution Meets the Wellness Revolution," *Public Health International* 18, no. 4 (2003): 275-278, 278.

nouncements marked by the popularized slogan "Uncle Sam Wants You!"[13] Not until the 1960s, however, has social marketing been applied so conspicuously to public health efforts. In essence, social marketing attempts to convince a target audience to adopt a certain philosophy, behavior, product, or all three.[14] It is an approach to marketing that blends psychologically oriented behavioral change models with a business-oriented marketing mix. In the case of health, this includes marketing anything from encouraging individuals to perform regular breast self-examinations, wear sunscreen, or consume fat-free potato chips. Importantly, however, just like traditional marketing practices, social marketing is not always effective. While anti-tobacco campaigns have been deemed successful, antidrug efforts typified by the "just say no" campaign experienced limited success.[15]

Because schools are viewed as a widely available venue in which children and youth can learn healthy behaviors, the school curriculum has increasingly become an important site of entry for health marketers.[16] Moreover, when it comes to marketing health, efforts are, for the most part, uncritically accepted as part and parcel of contemporary health education curriculum. Take, for example, the CDC document *Making It Happen: School Nutrition Success Stories* (*Making It Happen*).[17] Within the document, school health personnel are warned of the problem of poor nutrition and the multifarious health consequences associated with it. School personnel are further told, in rather unambiguous terms, that children will innately choose unhealthy foods but that they can "help" students make healthy choices by "adopting some of the effective [marketing] techniques used by the food industry."[18] In fact, the CDC advises school personnel to design health campaigns that mirror corporate marketing schemes. Consider the following passage taken from the document:

---

[13] Jack C. Ling, Barbara A. K. Franklin, Janis F. Lindsteadt, and Susan A. N. Gearon, "Social Marketing: Its Place in Public Health," *Annual Review of Public Health*, 13 (1992): 341-362, 342.

[14] Ibid.

[15] Proponents of social marketing argue that the market model approach to health advertising holds the potential to remedy health inequities by making health information more accessible to health-marginalized populations such as women, children, and the elderly. Kickbusch and Payne, "Twenty-first Century Health Promotion," 278.

[16] David Johns, "Recontextualizing and Delivering the Biomedical Model as a Physical Education Curriculum," *Sport, Education and Society* 10, no. 1 (2005): 69-84, 70.

[17] Food and Nutrition Service, et al., *Making It Happen! School Nutrition Success Stories*.

[18] Ibid., 113.

Effective marketing involves more than just communication. Marketing means focusing on the target audience and learning how to satisfy its needs and wants. Effective marketing centers on designing the best marketing mix, also known as the 4 Ps:

- Identifying and offering **PRODUCTS** that meet student needs.
- **PLACEMENT** of products in locations so they are easy to choose.
- **PROMOTION** of products so that students know about them and are motivated to try them.
- Setting the **PRICE** of products so that students will want to buy them.[19]

The preceding excerpt provides an example of the ways in which school health marketers have not only co-opted the discourse of corporate marketers, but their business tactics as well. In the same way that corporate marketers do, school personnel are encouraged to invoke the instrumental logic of consumption and consumerism through the *selling* of health, nutrition, fitness, and body image. In doing this, I argue that contemporary health education efforts represent strategic attempts to market not a benign conception of health, but a particular *brand* of health—namely one that confounds health with morality and bodily perfection, and is ultimately connected to a consumer culture. In the following pages I will show how the CDC's *Making It Happen* document is emblematic of how students have become both the objects and subjects of a consumer-oriented health curriculum. Students are objects in the sense that they are, through such health-related discourses, used by schools to bolster profits—in the name of health. They are subjects because these same health messages are also directed at their bodies, enticing students to embrace certain products and/or ways of living and being in the world.

For the most part, little attention is paid to the unintended consequences of marketing health in schools. However, it is important for both educational theorists and practitioners to carefully consider whether health initiatives are uncritically embraced simply because they are advocated in the name of health and wellness. In this chapter I argue that marketing health in schools holds the potential to engender materialism, competition, cynicism, and anxiety through its preoccupation and promotion of the perfectible self.

Crawford coined the term "healthism" to describe contemporary Western culture's hegemonic ideation epitomizing the slim and lean body as the ideal one.[20] Through this discourse, slenderness is portrayed as an ultimate physical

---

[19] Ibid.

[20] The term "healthism" was originally coined by Robert Crawford in his article "Healthism and the Medicalization of Everyday Life," *International Journal of Health Service* 10 (1980): 365-388.

state that everyone, through practicing strict body control, can and should achieve.[21] According to Dutton, healthism acts as a specific form of "body-ism" in which "a hedonistic lifestyle is (paradoxically) combined with a preoccupation with ascetic practices aimed at the achievement or maintenance of appearance of health, fitness, and youthfulness."[22] By analyzing various health initiatives and curricula, the chapter considers how specific notions of health, consumption, morality, and bodily perfection are increasingly and impetuously advocated in schools.

It is important to note that responses to the *problem* of youth health, specifically as this relates to issues of nutrition and obesity, are merely a reflection of discourses and practices defined and embodied in popular culture regarding what is considered healthy. These discourses set the conditions for schools to advocate certain messages in the name of "healthy living" about food, self, the body, and appropriate modes of consumption. Thus, I examine how the world of commodified popular culture bears on school health curricula where healthful living and its antithesis, the unhealthy body, are perennial themes. I position school health practices as a consumerist activity in which adolescents, through the social marketing of health, are incited to pursue healthism and achieve a healthy body for *their* own best interest.

Since then a number of authors have investigated the nature and influence of healthism in society. See, for example, Alan Peterson and Deborah Lupton, *The New Public Health: Health and Self in the Age of Risk* (Thousand Oaks, CA: Sage, 1996); Deborah Lupton, "Developing the Whole Me: Citizenship, Neoliberalism and the Contemporary Health and Physical Education Curriculum," *Critical Public Health* 9, no. 4 (1999): 287-300; Deborah Lupton, *The Imperative of Health: Public Health and the Regulated Body* (Thousand Oaks, CA: Sage); Rose Galvin, "Disturbing Notions of Chronic Illness and Individual Responsibility: Toward a Genealogy of Morals," *Health: An Interdisciplinary Journal for the Study of Health, Illness and Medicine* 6, no. 2 (2002): 107-137; Richard Tinning and Trish Glasby, "Pedagogical Work and the Cult of the Body: Considering the Role of the HPE in the Context of the 'New Public Health,' " *Sport, Education and Society* 7, no. 2 (2002): 109-119,109.

[21] Evans, Evans, and Rich, "The Only Problem Is, Children Will Like Their Chips," 218.

[22] Kenneth R. Dutton, *The Perfectible Body: The Western Ideal of Physical Development* (London: Cassel, 1995), 273.

Foucault and Governmentality

Michel Foucault's work on governmentality provides the theoretical basis from which this examination materializes.[23] The literature on governmentality can help illumine how a "particular mode of being [unhealthy], and a particular mode of managing this way of being" is regulated and produced by schools through various curricular activities.[24] The purpose in using the literature on governmentality is to problematize notions of health to understand the ways in which students are regulated and managed by school leaders and by the self and the possible consequences of these actions. Theories in governmentality also function to elucidate the methods that governments (broadly conceived) intentionally or unintentionally utilize to achieve certain outcomes. Foucault's work assists in realizing "the kinds of individual and collective identity, and the forms of subjectivity and agency" constructed through various rationalities, dispositions and technologies.[25] In many ways, then, the interest is not solely philosophical or theoretical in nature; rather, it is about examining the intelligibility of certain health practices, strategies, and outcomes.[26]

Foucault's work highlights the productiveness of knowledge: "it produces, among other things, normative categories, prescriptions for proper conduct, and relations of power."[27] Through the lens of governmentality, school health

---

[23] Michel Foucault, "Governmentality," in The Foucault Effect: Studies in Governmentality, ed. Graham Burchell, Colin Gordon, and Peter Miller (Chicago: University of Chicago Press), 93-96.

[24] Peter Kelly and Derek Colquhoun. "Governing the Stressed Self: Teacher 'Health' and 'Wellbeing' and Effective Schools," Discourse: Studies in the Cultural Politics of Education 24, no. 2 (2003): 191-204, 192.

[25] Mitchell Dean. "Powers of Life and Death Beyond Governmentality," Cultural Values 6, no. 1 & 2 (2003): 119-138, 119-120. The literature on governmentality encourages analysis on how these government and nongovernment entities emerge, coalesce, govern, and function as various apparatuses of the state. See Michel Foucault, "The Subject and Power," in The Essential Foucault: Selections from the Essential Works of Foucault, 1954-1984, ed. Paul Rabinow and Nikolas Rose (New York: The New Press, 2003), 139. Foucault writes: "The forms and specific situations of government of some by others in a given society are multiple; they are superimposed, they cross over, limit and in some cases annul, in others reinforce, one another. It is certain that, in contemporary societies, the state is not simply one of the forms of specific situations of the exercise of power – even if it is the most important – but that, in a certain way, all other forms of power relation must refer to it."

[26] Dean, "Powers of Life and Death" 119.

[27] Jeremy Packer, "Disciplining Mobility: Governing and Safety," in Foucault, Cultural Studies and Governmentality, ed. Jack Z. Bratich, Jeremy Packer, and Cameron McCarthy (Albany: State University of New York Press, 2003), 135-161,139. See also Foucault, "The Birth of So-

programs can be seen as a neoliberal strategy of governance bound up with the tenets of the new public health. As such, these programs are dependent on systems of knowledge and truths that are used to "constitute and define the object of its activities and continually monitor its progress."[28] In this case the object is the postmodern student and the system of knowledge that surrounds the constitution of a healthy self. Through the reconstitution and amalgamation of biomedical and epidemiological knowledge, students are enticed and rewarded for embracing self-responsibility through mass public health educational initiatives that warn of the danger of bodily misuse or neglect.[29] Ultimately, it is a neoliberal approach that seeks to reduce health care expenditures while simultaneously instilling within individuals a desire to achieve biological self-betterment. Thus, rather than situating students as passive recipients of health care, social marketing efforts endeavor to persuade individuals to take preventative care of their bodies through exercising self-control, self-denial, and strict bodily discipline.[30]

For clarity, the term *discourse* is used consistently with Foucault's definition of the term. Foucault claimed that discourses are practices, that is, thoughts, actions, and writings that are intrinsically bound together through various webs of connection. Discourses shape ways of thinking, speaking, and acting; they influence the very nature of the body itself, the unconscious and

---

cial Medicine" in *The Essential Foucault: Selections from the Essential Works of Foucault, 1954-1984*, ed. Paul Rabinow and Nikolas Rose (New York: The New Press, 2003), 329. Foucault describes how illnesses were managed in the eighteenth-century urban environment. He writes that a growing body of medical knowledge brought about new methods of categorization and containment for those inflicted with disease. The production of descriptive categories of illness and wellness meant that one's health could be managed but, more importantly, should be managed by the state to secure the health of the city. Foucault writes: "Medicine's political power consisted of distributing individuals side by side, isolating them, individualizing them, observing them one by one, monitoring their state of health, checking to see whether they were still alive or had died, and, in this way maintaining society in a compartmentalized space that was closely watched and controlled by means of a painstaking record of all the events that occurred."

[28] Lupton, *The Imperative of Health*, 10.

[29] Samantha J. King, "Doing Well by Running Well," in *Foucault, Cultural Studies and Governmentality*, ed. Jack Z. Bratich, Jeremy Packer, and Cameron McCarthy (Albany: State University of New York Press, 2003): 295-316, 309.

[30] David Goss, "Healthy Discipline? Health Promotion at Work," *The Electronic Journal of Radical Organizational Behavior* 3, no. 2 (1997): 1-8, 2.

conscious mind and soul of the individuals they govern.[31] Relying on Foucault's description, this research affirms that discourses can impose specific meanings and invoke particular dispositions through knowledge, interpretive and conceptual schema, and signs.[32] Moreover, this phenomenon is typically suppressed in such a way that neither its manufacturing nor the discourse itself is necessarily recognizable or deemed problematic.

Following the work of Deborah Lupton, I investigate the ways in which adolescents are constructed within and in contrast to discourses of health via health education curricula.[33] Specifically, I am looking at the presence of key phrases, ideas, and words and the appearance of such items as they connect to larger discourses (those occurring outside the text, i.e., media constructions). Moreover, texts will be read considering the following questions: How do they represent the objectives and concerns of health? What kind of consumerist health ethic do the texts espouse? What activities, dispositions, or notions of health and/or consumerism are privileged in the text?[34] Thus I examine health education curricula to show how these materials symbolically and materially advance a particular consciousness that, at its core, presupposes a one-dimensional, moralistic, and consumer-oriented conception of health.[35]

In the following pages I examine health education curricula by paying particular attention to the ways in which these health-related discourses are promoted and produced in schools and, concurrently, how these messages are drawn upon as scripts for understanding youth health.[36] Consistent with Foucault, I argue that knowledge actively works to define subjects, and in line with Bacchi, that these discursive practices have material effects.[37] In this chapter I seek to disentangle some of these discursive practices by describing knowledge articulated in health education curriculum and, in light of this,

---

[31] Michel Foucault, *The Archaeology of Knowledge and the Discourse on Language*, trans. A.M. Sheridan Smith (New York: Harper Colophon Books, 1972), 33-49.

[32] Carol Bacchi, "Policy as Discourse: What Does It Mean? Where Does It Get Us?" *Discourse: Studies in the Cultural Politics of Education* 21, no. 1 (2000): 45-57, 48.

[33] Lupton, "Developing the Whole Me," 289.

[34] Ibid.

[35] David Kirk and Derek Colquhoun, "Healthism and Physical Education" *British Journal of Sociology of Education* 10, no. 4 (1989): 417-434, 419.

[36] Jan Wright and Lisette Burrows, "'Being Healthy': The Discursive Construction of Health in New Zealand Children's Responses to the National Education Monitoring Project," *Discourse* 25, no. 2 (2004): 211-230, 212.

[37] Bacchi, "Policy as Discourse," as cited in Wright and Burrows, "Being Healthy," 212.

speculating on the ways in which youth are encouraged "to make sense of their health and their lives."[38]

Making It Happen: Marketing Nutrition, Morality, and Profits

Making It Happen, the document mentioned earlier in this chapter, is a curricular piece co-authored and sponsored by the CDC's Division of Adolescent and School Health and the USDA's Child Nutrition Division. The document chronicles the experiences of 32 schools in establishing nutrition policies. I examine this document in terms of its intertextuality - that is, how it resonates with, incorporates, or recontexualizes other narratives or discourses, both implicitly and explicitly.[39] In so doing, attention is paid to the ways in which moralistic concerns regarding the so-called obesity epidemic are deployed in order to convince school personnel to "take action" on issues regarding nutrition and overweight among youth. It is then revealed how health initiatives, particularly as they connect to issues of nutrition, are embedded in discourses of consumption that are fundamentally dependent on the commodification of youth.

In many ways, the CDC's document, *Making It Happen*, is characteristic of the genre of curricular resources available to school health personnel. The guide is attractive, containing colorful photos of happy children exercising and consuming foods considered healthy: foods such as apples, oranges, broccoli, carrots, and corn. The document presents school nutrition policies as anodyne initiatives that are rational responses to the problem of youth overweight and obesity. Individuals who choose to follow the step-by-step instructions in the guide are heralded as youth advocates, "champions of change." As the document points out, "anyone can be a champion for changing school nutrition environments—anyone can make it happen!"[40]

According to the CDC the purpose of the document is to "provide inspiration—and a wealth of practical ideas—for anyone who wants to make healthy nutrition environments happen for students and schools everywhere."[41] The report begins with the following statement:

---

[38] Wright and Burrows, "Being Healthy," 212.

[39] Norman Fairclough, *Analyzing Discourse: Textual Analysis for Social Research*, (New York: Routledge, 2003), 17.

[40] Food and Nutrition Service et al., *Making It Happen! School Nutrition Success*, 3.

[41] Ibid, 1.

Parents, students, teachers, school administrators, foodservice staff, and concerned citizens across the nation are taking action to promote healthy eating in schools. Their motives are simple. They know that many American children have poor eating habits that are contributing to the epidemic of childhood overweight and other health problems.[42]

While the CDC's goal of improving student nutrition may appear on the surface a value-free and a noble endeavor, the political and moral undercurrents of the initiative are unambiguously transparent.[43] Even within this short excerpt, for example, the CDC is able to accomplish a number of tasks. First, individuals interested in school nutrition issues are validated. In a congratulatory way the CDC situates interested individuals as being responsible, "concerned" persons. Their collective motives are "simple"—said differently, pure and intuitive. The statement "across the nation" connotes that this is a pressing national issue, that schools are not alone in addressing the issue, and that a responsible school should take part in this *national* initiative. The genesis of the problem as well as the unidirectional sequence of events is clear: youth have innately poor eating habits that, left to their own desires, will eventually cause them to experience overweight. There is no ambiguity in the relationship; the problem of poor eating is directly and positively related to an even greater problem of youth overweight and other associated health consequences.

Running alongside this redemptionist discourse is a subtext surrounding profits and capital. Schools are told, for example, that they can generate profits despite removing high revenue, unhealthy, a la carte items from the menu. Healthy foods, schools are told, such as fruit, yogurt, water, and low-fat snacks, can be just as lucrative as their unhealthy counterparts. Thus, "advocating" for students—in the name of health—can be a rewarding endeavor: good for soul and pocketbook. To illustrate, in the "Introduction" the document summarizes several themes that emerged from the stories of the 32 schools chronicled in the text. The very first theme presented in the document reads as follows:

> *Students will buy and consume healthful foods and beverages—and schools can make money from healthful options.* Schools across the country have proved that they can make money by selling more nutritious foods and beverages. Of the 17 Making It Happen!

---

[42] Ibid.

[43] John Evans, Bethan Evans, and Emma Rich, "The Only Problem Is, Children Will Like Their Chips: Education and the Discursive Production of Ill-Health," *Pedagogy, Culture and Society* 11, no. 2 (2003): 233.

schools and districts that reported sales data, 12 made more money and four made the same amount of money after making nutrition improvements.[44]

Within the text school personnel are again reassured, "The good news is that many schools and districts across the United States are improving their nutrition environments—while maintaining a profitable bottom line."[45]

It is necessary to consider the importance of profits. Why, for example, is the issue of profit given attention at all, much less primacy within the document? If the problem of nutrition is so compelling on its own accord, as suggested in the didactic tone of the text that preceded the thematic summary, why must the CDC use market logic to convince school personnel to adopt such policies? Would, for example, nutrition policies outlined in the document be important if they did not result in profitable situations for schools?

Fairclough argues that texts engage in ideological work by making certain assumptions and universalizing particular meanings and representations.[46] In assuming that schools have certain values, namely, a concern for profits, production, and efficiency, the text instates corporate ideology. *Making It Happen* does not make the case that school health initiatives *can* make money for schools, but that they *should*. In committing to consumer-oriented values, the text identifies not only the sorts of activities that schools should be engaged in, but also speaks to the kinds of places that schools should become—that of capitalist projects. Moreover, because the text connects the "concerned" school personnel as taking such action, it imbues the argument with a kind of moral authority that serves to further bolster unidirectional support for the health initiative.

VERB: Marketing Fitness

In 2002 the CDC introduced VERB, a social marketing campaign designed to stimulate physical activity among what the CDC has designated as "tweens" or, youth between the ages of 9 and 13. The campaign utilizes a variety of paid advertising venues, including television commercials as well as radio and magazine ads, to reach this particular demographic. The CDC proudly claims that VERB "strategically addresses both the general U.S. population,

---

[44] Food and Nutrition Service et al., *Making It Happen! School Nutrition Success,* 14 (emphasis in original).

[45] Ibid., 13.

[46] Fairclough, *Analyzing Discourse,* 4-7.

and ethnic-specific audiences."[47] While the *general market* media strategy delivers messages to tweens who can be reached through "mainstream media," the ethnic media strategy attempts to reach *African Americans, American Indians/Alaska Natives, Asian Americans/Pacific Islanders* and *Hispanics/Latinos* through "targeted media outlets" (i.e., cultural festivals and print media geared for a specific ethnic audience). According to the CDC this multimedia multi-ethnic approach ensures that all tweens are "likely to see them [health messages]—and be inspired to be physically active."[48] According to the CDC:

> VERB surrounds tweens — at home, at school, and in the community — through television, radio, print, the Internet, and out-of-home outlets such as movie theaters, billboards, and city buses. The result is an impressive level of brand awareness among tweens. VERB is perceived as multicultural, inspirational, motivational and a source of great ideas for activities that get tweens' bodies moving.[49]

The following is a transcript of a 30 second radio spot named "Back in the Day" created for parents of the "African American" market:

Background: Mellow retro-vibe music and appropriate nostalgic sound effects.

> **Voice-over:** Remember how much simpler things were when we were kids? All we needed to play was some chalk or rope for double-dutch... Fact is, kids today are gonna watch TV and play video games. But, we've got to keep our kids active. Because an active kid is a healthy kid. Encourage creativity and activity. Hey, remember how creative we were? Check out verbparents.com for ideas and suggestions on how to get your children active every day. VERB. It's what you do.[50] Made Possible by the US Department of Health and Human Services and the Centers for Disease Control and Prevention.

Notice that the entire text is structured around the opposition between past as good and present as bad. It is from this juxtaposition that a series of

[47] Centers for Disease Control and Prevention, *Youth Media Campaign: VERB Awareness* (Atlanta, GA: February 27, accessed 7 August, 2006); available from http://www.cdc.gov/youthcampaign/advertising/index.htm

[48] Centers for Disease Control and Prevention, VERB, *Youth Media Campaign* (Atlanta, GA: February 27, accessed 7 August 2006); available from http://www.cdc.gov/youthcampaign/advertising/index.htm

[49] Ibid.

[50] Centers for Disease Control and Prevention, VERB, *Youth Media Campaign* (Atlanta, GA: February 27, accessed 7 August 2006); available from http://www.cdc.gov/youthcampaign/african_american/radio/back_in_day.htm

other oppositions are mapped. The voice-over, for example, reflects on the past, describing time when youth were healthier, more active, and, consistent with images of hop-scotching, jump-roping children, more innocent. The present, however, reveals a very different situation. Watching TV and playing video games are presented as societal ills, negative consequences of modernity. There is, therefore, a discreet "moralistic view of the present and nostalgic view of the past. The result is a steady flow of generalizations about how people live today and how things have changed."[51] There is also an implicit assumption that contemporary caregivers do not currently take the time to engage in creative family activities; subsequently kids are in front of the TV, sedentary, and inactive.

What is striking about this narrative (apart from the problematic nature of claims themselves) is the tenor of *absolute* certainty that pervades the text.[52] Consider the following four statements: life was simpler; kids are gonna watch TV and play video games; an active kid is a healthy kid; and it's what you do. There is no ambiguity present in the text; there is no footnote regarding the universality of the claims. The cataclysmic sequence of events is presented as absolute fact. A critical listener, however, might wonder: was life really simpler ten to twenty years ago for new parents of African American children? Are all kids destined to watch TV and play video games? Are active kids really healthier kids? And is encouraging physical activity something that all parents should do? Further, there are clear "intertexual moves to certainty in the form of moral imperatives" to limit access to unhealthy foods, limit television watching, and encourage exercise. Parents are incited to pursue this agenda for the health of their children and as a reflection of their parenting.

VERB offers an example of how a healthy body, defined as a physically active body, is marketed to youth and their families in the media and in schools. Through moralistic claims to social and biological betterment, health is no longer a discreet form of physicality, but a commodity, something to be bought, sold, and traded in the marketplace. A healthy, lean, active body is something that all youth are told to aspire. Such claims are based on the idea that youth require external regulation either because they are innately ungovernable or because they have not yet learned how to self-govern.[53] In either

---

[51] Gard and Wright, *The Obesity Epidemic*, 23.

[52] Ibid.

[53] Inés Dussel, "Fashioning the Schooled Self through Uniforms: A Foucauldian Approach to Contemporary School Policies," in *Dangerous Coagulations: The Uses of Foucault in the Study of*

case, health is depicted as something that can be achieved through modes of adult-endorsed discipline and training. In this way the narrative positions adults as protective agents capable of governing youthful lives. Moreover, health is presented as something that all youth must *have* and, perhaps even more disturbing, comes to embody something that all youth must *be*. Appeals are made based on guilt, desire, shame, and universality, appeals not much different than tactics used by corporate marketers.

Eating to Win: Marketing Nutrition and Competition

Eating to Win, a nutrition-based lesson plan created and disseminated by California's Project LEAN (Leaders Encouraging Activity and Nutrition), represents another example of how consumer logic is used to convince students to embrace nutrition.[54] This time the values surround the production of a specific kind of self: a lean (as implied by the project title's acronym), individualistic competitor and, most importantly, a winner. The document triggers positive (e.g., "win," "healthy") and negative ("poor performance") evaluations as well as a number of assumed values which are not triggered textually.[55] For example, winning is not only presented as desirable, but represents an indication that one has internalized and acquiesced to healthy eating patterns. A lean body is presented as an inherently healthy one which, by extension, is also a winning body. Again, one is left to ponder, why is one only eating to *win*? Why not eating to experience personal satisfaction, fulfillment, nourishment, etc.? *Eating to Win* supports the claim that youth can achieve victory and success in games and life simply by "applying technical rules and instrumental reasons to their everyday lives... abilities, habits, and relationships all become commodities to be cultivated and accumulated for the calculate purpose of personal gain."[56] Moreover, in committing to specific healthy values, winners are also able to identify themselves as "moral character[s] (e.g., action being informed by values)."[57]

Education, ed. Bernadette Baker and Katherina E. Heyning (New York: Peter Lang, 2004): 85-105, 103.

[54] California Department of Health Services and the Public Health Institute, *Jump Start Teens: Eating to Win* (Sacramento, CA: accessed 15 August 2006); available from http://www.californiaprojectlean.org/Assets/1019/files/JumpStartTeensLesson7.pdf

[55] Fairclough, *Analyzing Discourse*, 177.

[56] Grant Banfield, "Ideological Work: Health at Hillside High," *Journal of Contemporary Ethnography* 28, no. 2 (1999): 138-161, 160.

[57] Fairclough, *Analyzing Discourse*, 177.

SHAPE: Marketing Bodies

Williams writes:

> From cars to chocolate, alcohol to cigarettes, cosmetics to clothes, we are continually bombarded with idealized images and sexualized invitations to indulge our desires and endlessly consume... The trick of consumer culture, it seems, rests precisely on the perpetuation of an 'unbridgeable' gap between idealized images and the real as the guarantee of ever renewed consumption.[58]

Nowhere in my search of health-related curricula did Williams's words appear more poignant than in the case of California's SHAPE curricula. Funded through the California Department of Education, the SHAPE program consists of a website and curricular resources available to health education teachers. On the website, teachers can download lesson plans on a variety of health-related topics, everything from the pleasures of gardening to the benefits of fiber. The following lesson plan was listed under SHAPE's "Fitness" category.

The stated goal of this particular curricular activity is for students to "recognize the connections between a balanced, nutritious diet and having a physically fit body."[59] Teachers are instructed to tell students they are going to have a fitness "race." Using the activity sheet, students are asked to navigate through a maze of foods. If students follow the path of butter, chocolate, cookies, and cake, they will inevitably come up against a dead end. On the other hand, following items such as fruit, meats, and broccoli leads students to the maze's exit. The activity contains the following instructions for students:

> We would all love to have a fit body. But, it takes more than just exercise to make a fit body. It takes a fit diet that is balanced and full of the nutrients that help the body function properly and grow strong. The following is a maze of foods. Some of the foods are nutritious and would help build a fit body, they lead down the right path toward a fit body. Other foods are lacking in the nutrients that help a body function or grow strong, these foods do not lead directly toward a fit body. When the teacher

---

[58] Simon Williams, "Health as Moral Performance: Ritual, Transgression, and Taboo," *Health* 2, no.4 (1998): 435-457, 442.

[59] California Department of Education, Child Nutrition and Food Distribution Division, *Diet and Fitness* (CA: accessed 15 August 2006); available from http://www.ausd.k12.ca.us/shape/lessons/fitness/

says to go, take your pencil and trace a path of nutritious foods toward a healthy and fit body. May the best diet win![60]

At the top of the activity sheet is the following graphic:

 Without any explanation of what the graphic does or does not represent, students are left to assume that the bodybuilder image depicted on the activity sheet symbolizes the fit body that, according to the instructions, "we would all love to have." The image is not unlike those portrayed in popular magazines like *Men's Fitness* or *Muscle & Fitness* - "magazines that are founded on the premise of providing exercise and diet advice for... [those] who struggle to achieve this unobtainable body."[61]   Not only does the curriculum presuppose that everyone desires a fit body, but the picture provides a template as to what a fit body should look like. It is, however, an ideal that is not consistent with reality for the majority of students. This kind of depiction and assumption about health and bodies and, by extension, student desires is not only socially irresponsible but medically erroneous.

Discussion

I argue that reviewed curriculum works to create specific knowledges and truths concerning the ideal body which in turn come to form and shape student subjectivities. Tinning and Glasby refer to this process as part of the pedagogical work that occurs in schools. "Pedagogical work is done by such diverse things as an instructional video, a lifestyle magazine, a film, a mobile phone text message, a billboard poster, a Nike ad, or even a label on the back of a cereal box."[62] Thus, while the school constitutes only one site, it remains a significant one for most children and adolescents. In the case of health education, pedagogical work and subjectivity formation involve how students learn about what their bodies are or should be. Specifically, I contend that health education formulates a powerful discursive framework in which youth learn about their bodies through discourses of consumption, capitalism, and morality.

---

[60] Ibid.

[61] Pirkko Markula, "Beyond the Perfect Body: Women's Body Image Distortion and Fitness Magazine Discourse," *Journal of Sport and Social Issues* 25, no. 2 (2001): 158-179, 158.

[62] Tinning and Glasby, "Pedagogical Work and the Cult of the Body," 111.

Discourses of Consumption, Capitalism, and Morality

In contemporary capitalist society, the manifestation of health, as evidenced by a lean, fit body, is something of a visual indicator of self-control, restraint, and regulation. However, as Banfield argues, "in a consumer culture where there is a demand for ever increasing economic growth and consumption of goods and services, sobriety is opposed by a hedonism of competitive consumption."[63]   Despite the contradictory nature of self-control and self-indulgence both are concurrently endorsed within consumer culture. Copious consumption is therefore not negated, but reformulated in order to comply with certain health dictums. Thus while individuals are "encouraged to engage in the consumption of commodities deemed 'healthy' such as low-fat or low-salt foods, nicotine patches, sports shoes and gym memberships," they are to concurrently exercise restraint when the consumption of "unhealthy" items infringes on their health.[64] And, in the case of *Making It Happen*, students are incited to consume healthy foods not only for the sake of their health but, one could argue, ultimately, for the purposes of supplementing (and exceeding) profits "lost" on unhealthy foods.

For these kinds of reasons, Petersen and Lupton write that health education represents a means to examine the dual objectives of Western capitalist schooling: "the production of 'good' workers and the socialization of a 'healthy' moral citizenry attuned to the needs of a fully functioning market economy."[65]   Health therefore, as a symbolic category, offers a glance at the moral organization of capitalism, revealing its harsh contradictions.[66]   This paradox is particularly evident in the SHAPE curriculum and its depiction of the "fit" prototype. On one hand, the "fit" caricature has obviously embraced the necessary self-control and self-denial to achieve the muscular physique that he has. On the other hand, there is also something individualistic and decadent associated with such an achievement. Both messages serve a capitalist agenda: "excessive consumption is essential to capitalist growth, but so is the self-discipline and application of work ethic. Healthism is the space between the two."[67]

In their article, "Healthism and Physical Education," Kirk and Colquhoun ask a poignant question: who benefits from these constructions of health?

[63] Banfield, "Ideological Work," 141.

[64] Petersen and Lupton, *The New Public Health*, 67.

[65] Petersen and Lupton, *The New Public Health* as cited in Banfield, "Ideological Work," 138.

[66] Kirk and Colquhoun, "Healthism and Physical Education," 426.

[67] Ibid., 432.

The fitness industry, drug companies, and manufacturers of diet supplements and health foods, for example, all profit by selling their services, which are dependent on the values inscribed in healthism.[68] The healthy school has the potential to benefit as well. Consider the CDC's claim that schools can make *more* money through selling healthy foods to students. Finally, government and industries also benefit by constructing health as an individual achievement (or failure) and subsequently shifting the blame directly to the health "consumer." In the case of diet and fitness imperatives, overweight and obesity come to serve as an attestation of carelessness and recklessness: a life out of control.[69] Such visibility provides tangible ways to "police the boundaries" between the responsible and healthy and the irresponsible and unhealthy.[70]

Schools reinforce the ideology of personal responsibility through the identification of the overweight student as pathological, abnormal, and in need of intervention.[71] It is an ideology that holds dire consequences for individuals who find themselves deemed unhealthy, both in and outside the school.[72] If, for example, health is ultimately a personal enterprise, government and industry are exonerated from any responsibility to care for the ill.[73] Because the problem of ill health is assumed a matter of individual deficiency, then its solution must also be an individual one.

The SHAPE document posits the achievement of health as a linear, straightforward task. "[Nutritious foods] lead right down the path toward a fit body," the instructions say. The ease in which a fit body is purportedly realized leads one to conjecture that everyone can (and should) achieve a body congruent with the muscle man depicted. Documents such as this sustain the notion that health and fitness are simplistically achieved as a matter of individual agency. In this sense, health messages easily converge with victim-blaming tendencies that attribute poor health as a matter of individual pathology and inadequacy. Little attention is given "to the social, economic or political contexts of people's lives, nor to the complexities" that are inherent in the accessibility and availability of healthy foods and exercise regimes.[74]

---

[68] Ibid., 431.

[69] Evans, Evans, and Rich, "The Only Problem Is, Children Will Like Their Chips," 225.

[70] Petersen and Lupton, *The New Public Health*, 25.

[71] Markula, "Beyond the Perfect Body," 170.

[72] Wright and Burrows, "Being Healthy," 214.

[73] Kirk and Colquhoun, "Healthism and Physical Education," 431.

[74] Wright and Burrows, "Being Healthy," 226.

In what way are discourses of morality mobilized within the reviewed curriculum? The SHAPE curriculum conflates health dictums and moral imperatives by presenting the "fit" body as something all students *should* desire and achieve. It is a discourse kind of morality that is embedded in the achievement of the perfect self. The VERB radio spot also draws on moralistic appeals by amalgamating good parenting practices with the promotion of physical activity. Finally, by eliciting the "concerned" and "responsible" citizen the CDC attempts to construct the health advocate as the health apostle.

A number of scholars contend that health has become a moral construction and crucial means of personal and social evaluation.[75] Conrad, for example, describes how health and wellness are increasingly linked to notions of morality and goodness. He describes how certain issues, such as youth deviance, have been culturally reinterpreted. Youth deviance, as a seemingly moral problem, became a medical problem that could be remedied via biomedical intervention.[76] While the medicalization of youth deviance may not necessarily alter society's moral evaluation of the behavior, it shifts the definition of problem and its solution into the hands of biomedical experts. Health promotion works in the opposite way. Where medicalization turns moral deficiencies into medical problems, health promotion proposes "behavioral or lifestyle changes for previously biomedically defined events (e.g., heart disease). One turns the moral into the medical; the other turns the medical into the moral."[77] The result is that maintaining a healthy body is increasingly understood as a moral enterprise. The problem of ill health and the solution to this problem is therefore not seen to be solely under the purview of biomedical experts; rather, it is a physical state under one's own discretion and control. The idea that lifestyle risks are under personal control further moralizes the discourse. It is, as Lupton writes, "part of the 'pathologizing of life,' the obsession with making every part of one's life 'healthy,' the assumption that one's life is not healthy to begin with, that there is a lack."[78]

---

[75] See, for example, Petersen and Lupton, *The New Public Health*; Kirk and Colquhoun, "Healthism and Physical Education"; Banfield, "Ideological Work."

[76] Peter Conrad, "Wellness as a Virtue: Morality and the Pursuit of Health," *Culture, Medicine, and Psychiatry* no. 18 (1994): 385-401, 387.

[77] Ibid.

[78] Lupton, *The Imperative of Health*, 90.

Consequences

In her book *The Imperative of Health: Public Health and the Regulated Body*, Lupton asks an important question: "to what extent are official discourses on health maintenance and personal responsibility accepted and taken up by individuals in their construction of subjectivity and in the practice of everyday life?"[79] I will only suggest possibilities by reporting some of the findings from the CDC's 2005 *Youth Risk Behavior Surveillance System* (YRBSS). The following estimates were generated from a national sample of 12th graders.

> 10.2% of females and 4.4% of males took diet pills, powders or liquids without a doctor's advice to lose weight or to keep them from gaining weight during the past 30 days.
>
> 5.9% of females and 2.6% of males vomited or took laxatives to lose weight or keep from gaining weight during the past 30 days.
>
> 64.0% of females and 28.7% of males are currently trying to lose weight.
>
> 16.0% of females and 7.8% of males went without eating for 24 hours or more to lose weight or to keep from gaining weight during the past 30 days.
>
> 41.8% of females and 25.1% of males describe themselves as slightly or very overweight.[80]

Assuming these findings represent even a vague reflection of the ways in which youth have responded to discourses of healthism, I suggest a number of possibilities.[81] Through the YRBSS data it becomes apparent that some youth have indeed internalized certain health messages constructed via popular educational and medical discourses. By attempting to alter their outward appearance through using potentially harmful methods to lose weight rapidly, youth display that they have scrutinized their body and have found themselves unsatisfactory. By comparing themselves to some culturally formed ideal, students are able to make comparisons between what their body is and what it *should* be, or at least what the school and other media say it should be.

At schools in which curricular documents provide a ready-made template for what it means to be fit or thin, the cultural ideal comes in a tangible form. An ideal body is no longer something idealized from afar, a media representation, something external to the self. Rather, students are provided a tangible

---

[79] Lupton, *The Imperative of Health*, 138.

[80] Centers for Disease Control and Prevention, "Youth Risk Behavior Surveillance: United States, 2005," *Morbidity and Morality Weekly Reports* 55, no. SS5 (2006).

[81] The school is certainly not the only place where students come in contact with health-related discourses. Many of these discourses derive from a constellation of societal forces of which school health initiatives are but one manifestation.

reference: this is what a healthy body should look like and this is where you fall in relation to this ideal (i.e., consider the bodybuilder).

In a number of the documents examined, it was clear that body shape had become "a corporeal metaphor for health."[82] Overweight and obesity, on the other hand, became the primary curricular concern and served to justify whatever particular intervention is deemed appropriate. These curricular examples show how health education embodies an individualistic project of the self. Success, health, and happiness are presented as realizable through individual "lifestyle" interventions. We see how attitudes, desires, body size, and appearance have all become "objects of health education work to be fashioned in appropriately healthy ways and nurtured as individual qualities." These characteristics are presented as nothing more than individual possessions: "personal investments in an individual's own success and well being."[83] Health curriculum is able to exercise a hegemonic authority because its subtle "coercive character is often disguised [by its] normative involvement in the troubles and problems of individuals. [It is] coercive, normative, and also voluntary."[84]

While I contend that curricular discourse of healthism holds potentially powerful and negative ways for individual students, I do not wish to suggest that youth lack agency or that they are cultural dupes who simply reproduce socially constructed definitions of idealized body types or prescribed notions of health. As Foucault suggested, "the exercise of power is not a naked fact ... it is elaborated, transformed, organized; it endows itself with processes which are more or less adjusted to the situation."[85] Therefore, to propose that as subjects and subjective beings students are necessarily *produced* as a consequence of a discourse or practice does not suggest that they are consummated, essentialized, or finalized by them. Importantly, as with all curricula, health curricula and the messages that it substantiates are "negotiated, contested and resisted" in multiple ways.[86] It is a curricular space of "contest and struggle where control is always possible, but never assured."[87] Further, students come

---

[82] Kirk and Colquhoun, "Healthism and Physical Education," 430.

[83] Banfield, "Ideological Work,"160.

[84] Bryon S. Turner, "From Governmentality to Risk: Some Reflections on Foucault's Contribution to Medical Sociology," in *Foucault, Health and Medicine*, ed. Alan Peterson and Robin Bunton (New York: Routledge, 1997): ix-xxi, xiv.

[85] Michel Foucault, "Afterword: The Subject and Power," in *Michel Foucault: Beyond Structuralism and Hermeneutics*, ed. Hubert Dreyfus and Paul Rabinow (Chicago: University of Chicago Press, 1983), 224.

[86] Banfield, "Ideological Work," 140.

[87] Banfield, "Ideological Work," 140.

in contact with multiple, complex, and contradictory discourses, practices, and expert knowledges that "cross and constitute [them], that act as resource and constraint in terms of...capacities to know and do, establish the shifting grounds of [their] existences."[88] The issue of agency in the context of health messages needs to be further examined on multiple levels, examinations that consider the complex and multifarious relationships between culture and society, experts and students, and ideology and discourse.[89]

Conclusion

Of what consequence is it for students when curricular documents depict matters of health, nutrition, fitness, and the body in these ways? Health messages matter because the knowledges and practices bound up with health-related discourses wield technologies of surveillance and power which categorize students as healthy or unhealthy, virtuous or deviant, or at-risk and therefore subject to particular kinds of educational interventions.[90] Health education has become a curricular discourse that allows health experts to bestow a sense of normality and morality on those who conform to the imperative of health while at the same time "construct those who are overweight as lazy and morally wanting giving permission" for intervention, harassment, and the right to publicly monitor their bodily composition.[91] Contemporary health messages advocated in the curriculum also thwart a more eclectic approach to understanding notions of health and the body. Critical thinking, social responsibility, and gender equity, for example, had no significant place within the reviewed curriculum. Clearly, as Gard and Wright point out, themes of social equity and justice "carry less weight in a context in which healthism, underscored by the moral panic about obesity, holds sway."[92]

It remains important therefore to consider how health-related imagery "finds its way into the social-cultural fabric of schools."[93] Whether this im-

---

[88] Christine Ceci, "Gender, Power, and Nursing: A Case Analysis," *Nursing Inquiry* 11, no. 2 (2004): 72-81, 80.

[89] Evans, Evans, and Rich, "The Only Problem Is, Children Will Like Their Chips," 219.

[90] Michael Gard and Jan Wright, "Managing Uncertainty: Obesity Discourses in an Age of Uncertainty," *Studies in Philosophy and Education* 20 (2001): 535-549, 546.

[91] Evans, Evans, and Rich, "The Only Problem Is, Children Will Like Their Chips," 225.

[92] Gard and Wright, "Managing Uncertainty," 546.

[93] John Evans, Emma Rich and Rachel Holroyd, "Disordered Eating and Disordered Schooling: What Schools do to Middle Class Girls," *British Journal of Sociology of Education* 25, no.2 (2004): 123-142, 125.

agery involves the construction of a slothful, TV watching, youth; a concerned, responsible, physically active parent; a bodybuilder; or a fit, athletic "winner," these curricular documents work to construct and legitimize particular ways of seeing, experiencing, and being in the world. It is therefore incumbent on researchers to examine documents such as this for their discursive constructions of youthful lives. The ways in which matters of health are singularly and simplistically portrayed in schools contributes to the hegemony of consumerism and healthism.

Bibliography

American Heart Association. *Overweight in Children*. Dallas, TX: American Heart Association. Available from [http://www.americanheart.org/presenter.jhtml?identifier=4670]: Internet; accessed 15 June 2005.

Arnst, Catherine and David Kiley. 2004. The Kids Are Not All Right: Child Obesity a Fast-growing Problem. *Business Week* 3903, 56.

Bacchi, Carol. 2000. Policy as Discourse: What Does It Mean? Where Does It Get Us? *Discourse: Studies in the Cultural Politics of Education* 21, no. 1: 45-57.

Banfield, Grant. 1999. Ideological Work: Health at Hillside High. *Journal of Contemporary Ethnography* 28, no. 2: 138-161.

California Department of Health Services and the Public Health Institute. Jump Start Teens: Eating to Win. Sacramento, CA: California Department of Health Services and the Public Health Institute. Available from [http://www.californiaprojectlean.org/Asscts/1019/files/JumpStartTeensLesson7.pdf]: Internet; accessed 15 August, 2006.

California Department of Education, Child Nutrition and Food Distribution Division. *Diet and Fitness*. California: Department of Education, Child Nutrition and Food Distribution Division. Available from [http://www.ausd.k12.ca.us/shape/lessons/fitness/]: Internet; accessed 15 August, 2006.

Ceci, Christine. 2004. Gender, Power, and Nursing: A Case Analysis. *Nursing Inquiry* 11, no. 2: 72-81.

Centers for Disease Control and Prevention. 2006. Youth Media Campaign: VERB Awareness. Atlanta, GA: Centers for Disease Control and Prevention, Department of Health and Human Services. Available from [http://www.cdc.gov/youthcampaign/advertising/index.htm]: Internet; accessed 7 August, 2006.

Centers for Disease Control and Prevention. 2006. Youth Risk Behavior Surveillance: United States, 2005. *Morbidity and Morality Weekly Reports* 55, no. SS5.

Conrad, Peter. 1994. Wellness as a Virtue: Morality and the Pursuit of Health. *Culture, Medicine, and Psychiatry*, no. 18: 385-401.

Crawford, Robert. 1980. Healthism and the Medicalization of Everyday Life. *International Journal of Health Service* 10: 365-388.

Dean, Mitchell. 2002. Powers of Life and Death Beyond Governmentality. *Cultural Values* 6, no. 1 & 2: 119-138.

Dussel, Inés. 2004. Fashioning the Schooled Self through Uniforms: A Foucauldian Approach to Contemporary School Policies. In *Dangerous Coagulations: The Uses of Foucault in the Study of Education*, ed. Bernadette Baker and Katherina E. Heying, 85-116. New York: Peter Lang.

Dutton, Kenneth R. 1995. *The Perfectible Body: The Western Ideal of Physical Development*. London: Cassel.

Evans, John, Bethan Evans, and Emma Rich. 2003. 'The Only Problem Is, Children Will Like Their Chips': Education and the Discursive Production of Ill-health. *Pedagogy, Culture & Society* 11, no. 2: 215-240.

Evans, John, Emma Rich, and Rachel Holroyd. 2004. Disordered Eating and Disordered Schooling: What Schools Do to Middle Class Girls. *British Journal of Sociology of Education* 25, no. 2: 123-142.

Fairclough, Norman. 2003. *Analyzing Discourse: Textual Analysis for Social Research*. New York: Routledge.

Food and Nutrition Service, U.S. Department of Agriculture; Centers for Disease Control and Prevention, U.S. Department of Health and Human Services. 2005. *Making It Happen! School Nutrition Success Stories*. Alexandria, VA: United States Departments of Agriculture and Health and Human Services. Available from [http://www.cdc.gov/healthyyouth/nutrition/Making-It-Happen/pdf/background.pdf]: Internet; accessed 10 June 2005.

Foucault, Michel. 1972. *The Archaeology of Knowledge and the Discourse on Language*. Translated by A.M. Sheridan Smith. New York: Harper Colophon Books.

Foucault, Michel. 1983. Afterword. In *Michel Foucault: Beyond Structuralism and Hermeneutics*, ed. Hubert Dreyfus and Paul Rabinow, 208-226. Chicago: University of Chicago Press.

Foucault, Michel. 2003. Governmentality. In *The Foucault Effect: Studies in Governmentality*, ed. Graham Burchell, Colin Gordon, and Peter Miller, 87-104. Chicago: University of Chicago Press.

Foucault, Michel. 2003. The Subject and Power. In *The Essential Foucault: Selections from Essential Works of Foucault, 1954-1984*, ed. Paul Rabinow and Nikolas Rose, 126-144. New York: The New Press.

Foucault, Michel. 2003. The Birth of Social Medicine. In *The Essential Foucault: Selections from Essential Works of Foucault, 1954-1984*, ed. Paul Rabinow and Nikolas Rose, 319-337. New York: The New Press.

Galvin, Rose. 2002. Disturbing Notions of Chronic Illness and Individual Responsibility: Toward a Genealogy of Morals. *Health: An Interdisciplinary Journal for the Social Study of Health, Illness and Medicine* 6, no. 2: 107-137.

Gard, Michael and Jan Wright. 2001. Managing Uncertainty: Obesity Discourses in an Age of Uncertainty. *Studies in Philosophy and Education* 20: 535-549.

Goss, David. 1997. Healthy Discipline? Health Promotion at Work. *The Electronic Journal of Radical Organizational Behavior* 3, no. 2: 1-8.

Johns, David P. 2005. Recontextualizing and Delivering the Biomedical Model as a Physical Education Curriculum. *Sport, Education and Society* 10, no. 1: 69-84.

Kelly, Peter and Derek Colquhoun. 2003. Governing the Stressed Self: Teacher 'Health' and 'Well-being' and Effective Schools. *Discourse: Studies in the Cultural Politics of Education* 24, no. 2: 191-204.

Kickbusch, Ilona and Lea Payne. 2003. Twenty-first Century Health Promotion: The Public Health Revolution Meets the Wellness Revolution. *Public Health International* 18, no. 4: 275-278.

King, Samantha J. 2003. Doing Well by Running Well. In *Foucault, Cultural Studies and Governmentality*, ed. Jack Z. Bratich, Jeremy Packer, and Cameron McCarthy, 295-316. Albany: State University of New York Press.

Kirk, David and Derek Colquhoun. 1989. Healthism and Physical Education. *British Journal of Sociology of Education* 10, no. 4: 417-434.

Leahy, Deana and Lyn Harrison. 2002. Risky Business: The Limits of Risk Discourse. *Education Links* 64: 17-19.

Ling, Jack C., Barbara A. K. Franklin, Janis F. Lindsteadt, and Susan A. N. Gearon. 1992. Social Marketing: Its Place in Public Health. *Annual Review of Public Health* 13: 341-362.

Lupton, Deborah. 1995. *The Imperative of Health: Public Health and the Regulated Body*. Thousand Oaks, CA: Sage Publications.

Lupton, Deborah. 1999. Developing the 'Whole Me': Citizenship, Neoliberalism and the Contemporary Health and Physical Education Curriculum. *Critical Public Health* 9, no. 4: 287-300.

Markula, Pirkko. 2001. Beyond the Perfect Body: Women's Body Image Distortion and Fitness Magazine Discourse. *Journal of Sport and Social Issues* 25, no. 2: 158-179.

Packer, Jeremy. 2003. Disciplining Mobility: Governing and Safety. In *Foucault, Cultural Studies and Governmentality*, ed. Jack Z. Bratich, Jeremy Packer, and Cameron McCarthy, 135-161. Albany: State University of New York Press.

Petersen, Alan and Deborah Lupton. 1996. *The New Public Health: Health and Self in the Age of Risk*. Thousand Oaks, CA: Sage.

Satcher, David. U.S. Department of Health and Human Services. 2001. *The Surgeon General's Call to Action to Prevent and Decrease Overweight and Obesity*. Rockville, MD: U.S. Department of Health and Human Services, Public Health Service, Office of the Surgeon General. Available from [http://www.surgeongeneral.gov/topics/obesity/calltoaction/CalltoAction.pdf.]: Internet; accessed 1 June 2005.

Spake, Amanda. 2004. The Future of Fatness. *U.S News and World Report* 136, no. 5: 56.

Time Magazine Incorporated. 2004. Critical Condition: America's Obesity Problem. *Time Magazine* (7 June Issue).

Tyre, Peg and Julie Scelfo. 2003. Helping Kids Get Fit. *Newsweek* (22 January); 60-64.

Tinning, Richard and Trish Glasby. 2002. Pedagogical Work and the 'Cult of the Body': Considering the Role of HPE in the Context of the 'New Public Health.' *Sport, Education and Society* 7, no. 2: 109-119.

Turner, Bryon S. 1997. From Governmentality to Risk: Some Reflections on Foucault's Contribution to Medical Sociology. In *Foucault, Health and Medicine*, ed. Alan Petersen and Robin Bunton, ix-xxi. New York: Routledge.

Williams, Simon. 1998. Health as Moral Performance: Ritual, Transgression, and Taboo. *Health* 2, no.4: 435-457.

Wright, Jan and Lisette Burrows. 2004. 'Being Healthy': The Discursive Construction of Health in New Zealand Children's Responses to the National Education Monitoring Project. *Discourse: Studies in the Cultural Politics of Education* 25, no. 2: 211-230.

CHAPTER TWO

More Than a Video Ho
Hip Hop as a Site of Sex Education about Girls' Sexual Desires

Jennifer Esposito and Bettina Love, Georgia State University

"I'd rather play a maid than be one."
-Hattie McDaniel, 1939 (First African American to win an Academy Award)

In the song "Ill Na Na," female rapper Foxy Brown asks, "Who's got the illest pussy on the planet?" It is a rhetorical question because she proceeds to rap about how her womanhood is such that men crave her and want to please her. Her stance can be read multiple ways. Some may argue that Brown's freedom to assert herself sexually can be interpreted as empowering; by expressing her sexual desires, she claims sexual agency, positioning herself as a woman with desires, as a woman men would want to please, as a sexual subject. However, others may read Brown's lyrics as illustrative of male control over female sexuality and desire. This type of dualistic argument is reminiscent of the good girl/bad girl binary that all women must negotiate. The discussion of women's agency occurs in multiple sites, including cultural studies, feminism, and Hip Hop. Problematizing whether the lyrics of female rappers are representative of sexual liberation or male control over women's sexuality becomes more complex when deconstructed in a capitalist, patriarchal, racist, heteronormative society. For example, do female rappers have agency within the confines of Hip Hop, a male-dominated genre of music and entertainment? Can African American women gain power through sexual liberation even in a historically racist context that has already positioned them as oversexed?

We contend that female rappers who take a sexually explicit stance in their music are interrupting society's expectation of women as passive objects of men's desire. However, as these female rappers interrupt male domination by creating a sound that is countercultural, they also create a new form of sex education for our young females that conflicts with the "wait until you are married" sex education curriculum that is pervasive in contemporary sex education classes. We argue, much like Catherine Ashcraft, that formal sex education that stresses "abstinence only" does not prepare our youth for the sexual messages that are disseminated through popular culture.[1]

Hip Hop is a site of sex education and it may be more instructive than formal sex education programs. The tension that exists between the two occurs because formal sex education typically stresses abstinence even as youth consume music that is sexually provocative and explicit. The formal sex education curriculum becomes unrealistic to the daily realities of youth who are bombarded with sexual messages through Hip Hop. Ashcraft states, "Making matters worse, teens often decry existing programs as irrelevant to their real needs, questions, and lived experiences. In contrast, adolescents frequently rank entertainment media as one of their top sources of information on sex and sexuality."[2]

We explore the tensions girls may have to negotiate (abstinence in the formal curriculum/sexual agency in Hip Hop) through an examination of the lyrics of some popular female rappers. Although we argue that the young girls may learn to be sexual subjects instead of sexual objects through their consumption of Hip Hop, we do so with recognition of the physical dangers of irresponsible heterosexual sex: sexually transmitted diseases, including HIV/AIDS and/or unwanted pregnancies.

We begin with a discussion of formal sex education to illustrate the disconnect between these abstinence-only programs and the overtly sexual messages youth may receive through Hip Hop. We move to a discussion of the ways schools neglect female sexual desire even though many female rappers celebrate their own sexual desires. The next section of this chapter explores how popular culture (including Hip Hop) is a powerful site of learning. In order to contextualize our argument, we provide a brief history of Hip Hop

---

[1] Catherine Ashcraft, "'Girl, You Better Go Get You a Condom': Popular Culture and Teen Sexuality as Resources for Critical Multicultural Curriculum," *Teachers College Record* 108, no. 1 (2006): 2145-2186.

[2] Catherine Ashcraft, "Adolescent Ambiguities in American Pie: Popular Culture as a Resource for Sex Education," *Youth & Society* 35, no. 1 (2003): 37-70.

and then illustrate how female rappers are situated within this male-dominated site. Next, we examine the debate occurring in cultural studies and feminism regarding whether or not oppressed peoples have the power to be agents of their own lives. We move from a discussion of the possibilities of agency to an examination of rap lyrics that, we argue, assert women as sexual subjects not sexual objects. In our conclusion, we discuss the implications of this on youth.

True Love Waits

As we explore female agency within Hip Hop, we begin by examining the formal sex education curriculum in schools. Currently, abstinence-only sex education is the only form of sex education that the federal government will fund. Abstinence-only sex education is endorsed by many conservatives, the most prominent being George W. Bush. This conservative construction of sex education conflicts with Hip Hop, an often sexually explicit site of education.

Conservative views on sex, personal responsibility, and marriage shape the government's financial commitment to the well-being of young Americans. Abstinence-only education and virginity pledges serve as a hidden agenda for the Religious Right. In 1996, Congress signed into law the Personal Responsibility and Work Reconciliation Act, commonly referred to as "welfare reform." The Act included a provision allocating money to "state initiatives promoting sexual abstinence outside of marriage as the only acceptable standard of behavior for young people."[3] The federal government's definition of abstinence-only education follows these guidelines:

A) has as its exclusive purpose, teaching the social, physiological, and health gains to be realized by abstaining from sexual activity;
B) teaches abstinence from sexual activity outside marriage as the expected standard for all school age children;
C) teaches that abstinence from sexual activity is the only certain way to avoid out-of-wedlock pregnancy, sexually transmitted diseases, and other associated health problems;
D) teaches that a mutually faithful monogamous relationship in context of marriage is the expected standard of human sexual activity;

---

[3] Debra Hauser, "Five Years of Abstinence-Only-Until-Marriage Education: Assessing the Impact," *Advocates for Youth*. (2004). < http://www.advocatesforyouth.org/publictions/ stateevaluations.pdf>

E) teaches that sexual activity outside of the context of marriage is likely to have harmful psychological and physical effects;

F) teaches that bearing children out-of-wedlock is likely to have harmful consequences for the child, the child's parents, and society;

G) teaches young people how to reject sexual advances and how alcohol and drug use increases vulnerability to sexual advances; and

H) teaches the importance of attaining self-sufficiency before engaging in sexual activity.[4]

The government's eight-point explanation of sex education ignores the world outside of students' 45-minute health class. Programs like "True Love Waits" and "Choosing the Best" encourage teens to pledge to abstain from sex outside of marriage; therefore, these programs do not mention or teach students how to put on a condom, the different types of birth control, the symptoms of an STD, or even a mention of sexual desire. Also, they are based on a heterosexual model (i.e., marriage is a right available only to heterosexual couples). Furthermore, numerous studies have found that these programs are ineffective in preventing STDs, unwanted pregnancies, and the spread of HIV/AIDS. In 2005, the *Journal of Adolescent Health* released a study which found that youth who took a virginity pledge contracted an STD at the same rate as a non-pledge.[5] Cynthia Dailard contends that "Research is beginning to show that abstinence-only messages are not only unproven in their effectiveness but also may have harmful health consequences by deterring use of contraceptives when teens become sexually active."[6] The sex education that youth receive at school conflicts with the world of commercial Hip Hop, where there are no apologies for promoting sex outside the confines of marriage and where being a virgin is "uncool." In the next section, we examine how formal sex education curriculum neglects the idea of female desire, assuming that "good girls" do not experience desire or pleasure.

---

[4] Cynthia Dailard, "Abstinence Promotion and Teen Family Planning: The Misguided Drive for Equal Funding," *The Guttmacher Report on Public Policy* (February 2002): 1-3.

[5] Hannah Brucker and Peter Bearman, "After the Promise: The STD Consequences of Adolescent Virginity Pledges," *Journal of Adolescent Health*, no. 5 (2005): 271-278.

[6] Dailard, "Abstinence Promotion and Teen Family Planning: The Misguided Drive for Equal Funding," 3.

Discourses of Desire

Because society constructs women as passive recipients of male sexual desire, girls are taught to be submissive objects while boys are taught to be active
agents of their own sexuality. Girls are constituted as having less sexual desire
than boys have.[7] The ramifications of this are such that girls have less confidence in articulating their sexual desires and are less likely to understand the
consequences of being positioned as passive. As Fine argues, "young women
continue to be taught to fear and defend in isolation from exploring desire,
and in this context there is little possibility of their developing a critique of
gender or sexual arrangements."[8] In many contexts, girls are taught to mask
their desires, to avoid sexual pleasure, and to remain the chaste "good girl."
The female rappers we examine here represent a new culture of sexual empowerment and agency. Their message is one that positions sexual desire in
the forefront of their images. When female Hip Hop artists rap about pleasure, desire, and sex, girls may learn that the "good girl" is but one identity to
live out.

Current discourses about sex are often silent about female sexual desire.
Fine argues that sex education in schools is missing what she terms a "discourse of desire."[9] Female sexual pleasure is absent from sex education in
schools because the undercurrent of much formal sex education is abstinence.
Students are taught to wait to engage in sex, and therefore, there are few discussions about experiencing actual pleasure. Sex education is reflective of society's stance on female sexual desire. Fine examines a variety of discourses
around female sexuality, including sexuality as victimization and sexuality as
individual morality. The discourse of sexuality as victimization positions young
girls as potential victims of being used and abused by male predators. They
learn to be always on their guard in order to protect themselves from potential
abuse. The discourse of sexuality as individual morality positions girls to be
modest and chaste as a way of achieving self-control and self-respect. This discourse makes invisible girls' desire for sexual pleasure and teaches them that to
be moral means to ignore one's desire. Fine believes this does a disservice to

---

[7] Michelle Fine, "Sexuality, Schooling, and Adolescent Females: The Missing Discourse of Desire," in *Beyond Silenced Voices: Class, Race, and Gender in United States Schools*, ed. Lois Weis
and Michelle Fine (Albany, NY: State University of New York Press, 1993).

[8] Ibid., 76.

[9] Ibid.

girls and recommends that schools should begin to include a discourse of desire:

> The naming of desire, pleasure, or sexual entitlement, particularly for females, barely
> exists in the formal agenda of public schooling on sexuality...A genuine discourse of
> desire would invite adolescents to explore what feels good and bad, desirable and un-
> desirable, grounded in experiences, needs, limits. Such a discourse would release fe-
> males from a position of receptivity, enable an analysis of the dialectics of
> victimization and pleasure, and would pose female adolescents as subjects of sexuality,
> initiators as well as negotiators.[10]

Once schools create a discourse of desire, young girls may be able to position themselves as active subjects with the agency to define for themselves what they want.

Allen argues that not only should desire be implemented into sex education but so should what she terms a "discourse of erotics."[11] Such a discourse would posit young people as active sexual subjects with rights to experience desire and pleasure. We are positioned by discourses, and thus, discourses help create and maintain identities. For this reason, a discourse of erotics allows young women the chance to assert themselves as sexual agents and sexual beings. A discourse of erotics opens up a space for girls and young women to take on the identity of a desiring sexual being without feeling shame for it. It allows girls to position themselves in ways that are more empowering and allows a space for them to claim agency as subjects of sexuality, not just objects. The next section examines the ways popular culture is a site of education and how educators should utilize it as a pedagogical tool because students are consuming it, often uncritically, anyway.

Learning from Popular Culture

Learning occurs in spaces inside and outside of the classroom; thus popular culture texts are important sites for education.[12] Students learn about themselves and others through the consumption of popular culture texts such

---

[10] Ibid.

[11] Louisa Allen, "Girls Want Sex, Boys Want Love: Young People Negotiating (Hetero)Sex," *Sexualities* 6 (2003).

[12] See Peter McLaren, "Border Anxiety and Sexual Politics," in *Sexuality and the Curriculum: The Politics and Practices of Sexuality Education*, ed. James Sears (New York: Teachers College Press, 1992); Henry Giroux and Roger I. Simon, "Schooling, Popular Culture, and a Pedagogy of Possibility," *Journal of Education* 170 (1998): 9-29.

as music, television, and film. These texts take up issues with which students may or may not be familiar. For example, if you do not know a gay person, you can turn to popular culture for a representation of a gay person. The representation may be ideological but it is, nevertheless, an example of a gay person. Kellner has argued that popular culture teaches us lessons about race, class, gender, and sexuality.[13] We come to know what it means to be heterosexual or homosexual, black or white, through representations. We come to understand ourselves and our positions in the world through these same representations. Popular culture texts often represent identities in narrow ways. Representations must be more complex to represent identities in all of their diversity.

Popular culture is a contested terrain and a site of struggle over meanings. It is a space where our identities are produced, where we learn about ourselves and others. Many cultural theorists have argued popular culture is also a pedagogical site and as such has a deeper impact than does schooling. Given that popular culture texts both represent and inform reality, it becomes a site of messy contradictions. For example, texts may inform us about matters of sexuality in stereotypical ways. The text, however, is not consumed in isolation. Consumption of a text requires interaction between the text and the reader. As a text is being consumed, the reader engages in active meaning making or "articulation."[14] Articulation recognizes that texts are not inscribed with a singular meaning. Instead, the consumer must produce meaning and this production occurs in a specific context and for particular interests. While some cultural critics believe that popular culture exerts too great an ideological force upon consumers, that it is dangerous and must be mediated, others argue that consumers have the agency to resist ideological messages and engage with popular culture in their own interests.

Popular culture is an important source of knowledge about sex and desire, especially for young people. We learn through multiple popular culture texts who has the right to desire, who is an object of desire, and who gets to be the subject. Many theorists have argued that because popular culture is such an important part of the production of cultural meanings for young people, it should be incorporated into formal education.[15] Students have the right to

---

[13] Douglas Kellner, *Media Culture: Cultural Studies, Identity and Politics Between the Modern and the Postmodern* (New York: Routledge, 1995).

[14] Stuart Hall, "On Postmodernism and Articulation," in *Stuart Hall: Critical Dialogues in Cultural Studies*, D. Morley and K.-H Chen, eds. (London: Routledge, 1996), 141.

[15] See Peter McLaren, "Border Anxiety and Sexual Politics," in *Sexuality and the Curriculum: The Politics and Practices of Sexuality Education*, ed. James Sears (New York: Teachers College Press,

make personal connections to the material they are expected to come to understand.

Students consume popular culture and enjoy it as a site of pleasure. Educators can use this site of pleasure as a pedagogical tool. It is important that schools utilize popular culture as a tool to empower youth. Dimitriadis contends that "contemporary youth construct notions of self and their community outside of school walls and that the education system has greatly ignored youth culture that is situated within popular culture."[16] When school officials ignore learning that is taking place outside of school walls, simply because it is popular culture, they subsequently disregard countless teaching tools that could promote critical thinking skills about issues within popular culture such as sex education. It is time that students learn how to read critically the representations they consume.

Through popular culture, youth learn about race, class, sexuality, and gender roles. As stated earlier, popular culture is a contested space, filled with contradictions and narrow representations. There are multiple types of popular culture, including music, videos, sitcoms, Internet, and movies. Often these texts depict individuals and groups in the most stereotypical manner. Therefore, it is crucial that teachers interrupt some of these messages by teaching students how to critically consume popular culture texts. For example, rap videos that glorify violence and sexual promiscuity can be used as pedagogical tools that "raise important questions regarding such issues as the relevance of everyday life, the importance of student voice, the significance of both meaning and pleasure in the learning process, and the relationship between knowledge and power in the curriculum."[17] Corrigan calls for learning institutions to "widen their understanding of how we are taught, how we learn, and how we know what we know from the text of popular culture."[18] While educators focus on the formal curriculum, youth learn from the nonformal curriculum of popular culture. It is important that educators, parents, and community leaders understand how youth comprehend formal and nonformal sex education.

1992); Henry Giroux and Roger I. Simon, "Schooling, Popular Culture, and a Pedagogy of Possibility," *Journal of Education* 170 (1998): 9-29.

[16] Greg Dimitriadis, *Performing Identity/Performing Culture: Hip Hop as Text Pedagogy, and Lived Practice* (New York: Peter Lang Publishing, 2001), 31.

[17] Henry A. Giroux and Roger I. Simon, "Schooling, Popular Culture, and a Pedagogy of Possibility," *Journal of Education* 170, no. 1 (1988): 9-26.

[18] Paul Corrigan, *Schooling the Smash Street Kids* (London: Macmillan, 1979), 79.

Without the ability to critically analyze and challenge the ideology inherent in popular culture texts, youth can turn on the television or flip through a magazine and internalize the countless examples of black culture and their community represented as uneducated, over-sexed criminals. Thus, by condemning Hip Hop's usefulness as a pedagogical tool, schools fail to equip students with the knowledge to detach themselves from popular culture as fans and, instead, engage with the text of Hip Hop as an intellectual capable of separating emotions from analysis and interpretation. Utilizing formal and nonformal sex education as a site of learning allows youth to listen to Hip Hop with a discerning and conscious ear. The following section discusses a brief history of Hip Hop and situates female rappers within the larger male-dominated site.

Hip Hop and Female Rappers—Who Is in Control?

Transcending race, class, and gender consumption borders, Hip Hop music has definitely outlived the "fad" phase and is rapidly moving toward being a permanent stitch in our global society. Its influence, whether positive or negative, is one that is real and globally contagious. The contemporary sound of Hip Hop originated in the streets of New York City in the early 1970s as an outlet for youth to express the ills of their community and the pleasures of being young. Rose writes, "From the outset, rap music has articulated the pleasures and problems of black urban life in contemporary America."[19] Black urban youth in the 1970s experienced unemployment, drug abuse, poor schooling, gang violence, and teen pregnancy. These problems are still experienced by youth today. As a result of these nationwide social ills, Hip Hop became the sound and culture of inner-city youth in America with traditions, customs, and a language that is countercultural and speaks to the oppressive, impoverished urban environment where Hip Hop music and culture originated and thrives.

Over the past 30 years since Hip Hop's conception, it has grown into a billion dollar a year commodity with mass appeal to all races, genders, and socioeconomic classes. Hip Hop's mass appeal and economic successes position Hip Hop within the complex site of black popular culture, which Hall argues is a

---

[19] Tricia Rose, *Black Noise: Rap Music and Black Culture in Contemporary America* (Middletown, CT: Wesleyan University Press, 1994), 2.

"contradictory space of strategic contestation."[20] For example, the majority of black popular music, especially Hip Hop music, is created and disseminated by major record labels (Sony, Universal, Arista Records) that are owned by Caucasians.[21] Due to corporate control of Hip Hop music, a large percentage of Hip Hop's profits go directly to record companies' CEOs and executives. For example, Def Jam, one of the first "independent" Hip Hop record labels, which was founded by Russell Simmons and Rick Rubin in 1983, signed a 50/50 production deal with Columbia/Sony in 1985.[22] This partnership may seem lucrative for all parties involved; however, Basu explains that:

> In essence, hip-hop labels such as Def Jam, Roc-a-fella, and Bad Boy are not "independent." They cannot distribute without being part of a major label's network, which means that they are beholden to large corporations whose interest is spurred by the attraction of hip-hop cool to major advertisers who want to attract a mostly white demographic.[23]

To attract a white demographic, record companies sign rappers that conform to whites' stereotypes of blacks as oversexed, promiscuous, criminal-minded individuals. Hip Hop music and culture, therefore, creates a complex duality. It embodies the voice of urban youth; however, its position within the political economy maintains the dominant group's ideologies and misconceptions about black culture.

Hip Hop scholar Derrick Alridge contends that "For many youth, Hip Hop reflects the social, economic, political, and cultural realities and conditions of their lives; speaking to them in a language and matter they understand."[24] This implies that Hip Hop is a powerful force in shaping the lives of youth; for Hip Hop not only reflects reality, it helps create it. Watkins (2005) contends that:

> Whatever social or political impact hip hop has had on young people has come primarily in the world of popular culture. Hip hop's evolution launched a revolution in

---

[20] Stuart Hall, "What Is this 'Black' in Black Popular Culture?," in *Black Popular Culture*, ed. Michelle Wallace (New York: Oxford University Press, 1983), 22.

[21] Dipannita Basu, "A Critical Examination of the Political Economy of the Hip-hop Industry," in *African Americans in the U.S. Economy*, ed. Cecilia A. Conrad, John Whitehead, Patrick Mason, and James Stewart (Oxford: Rowman & Littlefield Publishers, 2005): 258-270.

[22] Ibid., 264.

[23] Ibid., 265.

[24] Derrick Alridge, "From Civil Right to Hip Hop: Toward a Nexus of Ideas," *The Journal of African American History* 90 (2005): 226-252.

youth culture. All the things that traditionally matter to young people—style, music, fashion, and a sense of generational purpose—have come under the spell of hip hop.[25]

Therefore, the image, sound, and moves of Hip Hop cannot be contained. Hip Hop style has evolved, from Run-D.M.C's shell-toe Adidas, to M.C. Lyte's asymmetric hairstyles, to how young women expressing their sexual desires through the music and culture of Hip Hop. Female rappers such as Lil' Kim, Foxy Brown, Khia, Remy Martin, and Jackie-O are part of a genre of Hip Hop music that uses sex to sell not only their music, but their overt and unapologetic sexuality. These female rappers' look and sound is one that expresses explicit sexual lyrics with an unapologetic sexual expression of self. This is part of a larger story at play in society. The use of sex as a mechanism to sell records is not new; however, this particular stance of women as sexual subjects is new. Typically women in Hip Hop are known as "video hos." They exist in the background of videos, validating male rappers' masculinity. Often missing are strong women who want to exist in their own right. This assertion of sexual agency may have a pervasive effect on youth. For female rappers, leaving the background and stepping into center stage come at a high price. As we stated earlier, whites orchestrate the sound and image of Hip Hop; however, males, regardless of race, dominate Hip Hop.

The overwhelming majority of female rappers are African American. Even though there are more African American women represented in popular culture today than ever before, especially in Hip Hop, many scholars challenge the notion of progress when men control the representations of women. Throughout history, African American women have been depicted as wild, sexually promiscuous, and amoral individuals.[26] Stephens and Phillips state that "Although there are more representations of African American females available for consumption in the mass media than ever before, the substance of these images has changed little over the past century."[27] The belief that the representations of African American women has not in the past century changed is evident in Hip Hop music. Years ago, African American women were represented as Jezebels, Mammies, Welfare Mothers, and Matriarchs.

---

[25] S. Craig Watkins, *Hip Hop Matters: Politics, Pop Culture, and the Struggle for the Soul of a Movement* (Boston, MA: Beacon Press, 2005), 148.

[26] Dionne P. Stephens and Layli D. Phillips, "'Freaks, Gold diggers, Divas, and Dykes: The Socio-historical Development of Adolescent African-American Women's Sexual Scripts," *Sexuality and Culture* 7, no. 1 (2003): 3-49.

[27] Ibid., 3-4.

Stephens and Phillips contend that Hip Hop culture has created new labels for African-American women just as demeaning as the ones above. Diva, Gold Digger, Freak, Dyke, Gangster, Bitch, Sister Savior, Earth Mother, and Baby Mama have become the new sexual scripts for African American women in the world of Hip Hop.[28] According to Stephens and Phillips, a sexual script is the interaction between representations and a person's interpretation and development of selfhood based on these representations. With this limited availability of sexual scripts for young African American women, their constructions of sexuality are mediated by the social context in which these scripts arise. Because Hip Hop is such a powerful site of meaning making, it influences the sexual scripts available to young women.

Based on the sexual scripts provided by Stephens and Phillips, the female rappers we examine here would be considered "Freaks." A Freak is "sexually aggressive and wild, a woman we all know and yet supposedly do not want to. She is seen as a woman who simply loves to have sex without any emotional attachment."[29] The Freak is a well-known phenomenon in Hip Hop and is also a site of academic contention. Discussions about the Freak center on her sexual agency versus her victimization. In other words, can the Freak be sexually empowered in a patriarchal society? We take up this issue next by examining the debates about agency and resistance occurring in cultural studies and feminism.

Is Agency Possible within a Racist, Heteronormative Structure?

Philosophical debates about the experience of agency span many disciplines. We will trace those debates within cultural studies and feminist theory, as those are the sites our work is situated within. The connection between popular culture and agency was made explicit in the work coming out of the Centre for Contemporary Cultural Studies at the University of Birmingham in Britain in the 1960s. Ethnographies detailed youth's consumption of popular culture. Many of the researchers focused on the resistive aspects of consumption of popular culture. They refused to believe youth were cultural dupes and instead read them as agents of their own lives capable of resisting ideology. Youth were understood as engaging in a dynamic relationship with popular culture texts and practices instead of being passive consumers. *Resis-*

---

[28] Ibid., 6.

[29] Ibid., 20.

tance through Rituals: Youth Subcultures in Post-war Britain was originally published in 1975. This work originated from the Birmingham School and focused on youth subculture resistance. It was argued by Clarke, Hall, Jefferson, and Roberts that youth subcultures "through dress, activities, leisure pursuits and lifestyle . . . may project a different cultural response or 'solution' to the problems posed for them by their material and social class position and experience."[30] Their resistance was conceptualized as a way of youth subcultures constructing their own means of responding to the conditions of their lives, specifically the class structure that often determined their futures.

In the late 1970s, researchers moved beyond analyzing only subculture resistance to studying the everyday practices and production of youth culture. Most notable of this early work is Willis's ethnography of working-class English "lads."[31] Willis examined the lads' lived culture as a means of investigating how they created a culture through personal social interactions with peers as well as interactions with larger social structures. Willis found that the lads helped perpetuate their own working-class statuses by rejecting the middle-class ideology of the school. This rejection was a form of resistance and manifested itself through the lads' lack of investment with school. Because many barely graduated, their next options were working-class jobs. In a similar vein, McRobbie examined how girls embraced traditional femininity as a means of rejecting the ideology of school.[32] While they utilized their consumption of the feminine as a means of resisting official school culture, the girls in McRobbie's study perpetuated the existing gender hierarchy. Cultural production theory evident in both studies posits students as agents of their own lives capable of creating their own cultures even as these cultures sometimes mirror preexisting structures of inequality. Thus, the resistant acts of youth did not necessarily liberate them from structures of domination. Agency had to be contextualized and understood as existing and manifesting itself within these structures of domination.

Feminism and cultural studies were, at one point, mutually exclusive. It was not until feminists like McRobbie forced cultural theorists to account for

---

[30] John Clarke, Stuart Hall, Tony Jefferson, and Brain Roberts, "Subcultures, Cultures and Class" in *Resistance Through Rituals: Youth Subcultures in Post-war Britain*, ed. Stuart Hall and Tony Jefferson (London: Hutchinson, 1976), 15.

[31] Paul Willis, *Learning to Labour: How Working Class Kids Get Working Class Jobs* (Farnborough, England: Saxon House, 1977).

[32] Angela McRobbie, *Feminism and Youth Culture: From Jackie to Just Seventeen* (London: Macmillan, 1991).

gender in their analyses that Stuart Hall made the comment that feminism "crapped on the table of cultural studies."[33] Agency debates occurred within cultural studies as outlined above. These debates also occurred within feminism.

Feminism has always been a site of problematization of the gender hierarchy. Feminists theorize about how best to counteract the social forces acting upon women. Some feminists have problematized structures of domination alongside women's free will to respond and counteract such structures. In 1983 Marilyn Frye troubled the issue:

> The oppression of women is something consisting of and accomplished by a network of institutions and material and ideological forces which press women into the service of men. Women are not simply free to walk away from this servitude at will. But also, it is clear that there has always been resistance to female servitude, taking different shapes in different places and times. The question of responsibility, or rather, one important question, is this: Can we hold ourselves, and is it proper to hold each other, responsible for resistance?[34]

The issue then is not whether resistance and agency are possible within patriarchy, but rather is it possible to expect women to act as agents within patriarchy? Feminists have long recognized women as victims of sexism. While some feminists believe it is inherently impossible for women to exert free will because their choices are coerced, others recognize that women have choices, but these choices are constrained.[35] Part of understanding women's agency is understanding how they navigate through the constraints placed upon their choices while also recognizing that the constraints are a consequence of race, class, and gender oppression.

Within studies of gender and sexuality, there is recognition of heteronormativity—beliefs, values, structures, and institutions that help construct heterosexuality as normal. In 1986, Adrienne Rich wrote about compulsory heterosexuality, the institutionalization of heterosexual relations. Although few feminists would dispute that heterosexuality is compulsory in this society, many reject the deterministic aspects of radical feminists such as Rich and

---

[33] Stuart Hall, "Cultural Studies and Its Theoretical Legacies," in *Cultural Studies*, ed. Lawrence Grossberg, Cary Nelson, and Paula A. Treichler (New York: Routledge, 1992), 282.

[34] Marilyn Frye, *The Politics of Reality: Essay in Feminist Theory* (Freedom, CA: Crossing Press, 1983), 215.

[35] See Catherine A. MacKinnon, *Toward a Feminist Theory of the State* (Cambridge, MA: Harvard University Press, 1989).

MacKinnon because they do not account for the possibilities of women's agency.[36] Miriam believes this rejection is problematic and argues that in order to understand heteronormativity, we must investigate the ways compulsory heterosexuality "is at once more hidden and more entrenched in our culture."[37]

The rap lyrics we examine must be understood within a heteronormative and racialized context. When we claim that Lil' Kim and Foxy Brown are asserting sexual agency when they rap about men meeting their physical needs, there are many other theorists who make the valid point that this can easily be read as fulfilling male sexual desires and being complicit in their own manipulation.[38] Agency must be contextualized. Structures like racism and heterosexism constrain women's freedom. That these structures exist, however, does not preclude women's right to resist them. Next, we complete a textual analysis of lyrics from popular female rappers.

Exploring and Exposing Lyrics of Sexual Agency

Wanna lick, get a taste of the dip in my kitty box?[39]

Lil' Kim's 2005 album entitled "The Naked Truth" debuted at number six on the Billboard charts and is filled with lyrical content about sexual agency. The lyrics above from the album illustrate Lil' Kim's confidence in her right to assert herself as a sexual being. She goes on to say, "I'm in heat like a cat... If you want it then you better come and get it."[40] She is claiming her desire aloud and telling men, if they want her, then they need to pursue her. A young girl listening to Lil' Kim may begin to understand her own sexual identity from a position of power even though society and school culture may contradict this idea. "I'm in heat like a cat" asserts Lil' Kim's sexual desire, while the formal sex education curriculum in schools never mentions how girls might desire sex. This neglect on the part of schools does a disservice to girls because it teaches them that what they feel is wrong. It is clear by the popular-

---

[36] Ibid., 9.

[37] Kathy Miriam, "Toward a Phenomenology of Sex-Right: Reviving Radical Feminist Theory of Compulsory Heterosexuality," *Hypatia* 22, no. 1 (Winter 2007): 210-228.

[38] For a discussion of the limits to African American women's sexual liberation, see bell hooks, *Sisters of the Yam: Black Women and Self-Recovery* (Boston, MA: South End Press, 1993).

[39] Lil' Kim, "The Naked Truth," *The Naked Truth* (Atlantic Records, 2005).

[40] Ibid.

ity of Lil' Kim (record sales, endorsements, TV shows) that girls consume music about female sexual desire, so it would be more relevant to their lives if schools incorporated this knowledge they gain from popular culture and perhaps teach ways about dealing with desire.

The word that Lil' Kim echoes throughout the song "Kitty Box" is "picture." The use of the word "picture" implies confidence; she is boldly ordering men to picture her in erotic positions. She orders them to submit to her sexual desires and pleasures instead of making herself available to be objectified. On the flip side, however, the command "picture" may also symbolize a representation of Lil' Kim, a representation which might be influenced and/or shaped by the men who "control" Hip Hop music. Lil' Kim's image and her sexuality might be scripted and packaged in order to make the most money for the men behind the scenes—the owners of her record label. The representation of Lil' Kim we see might very well be to suit male desires.

What we think is important, however, is that Lil' Kim is initiating her desires with sexual language, a key element of Hip Hop for male artists. Overtly sexual lyrical content, like this example from Lil' Kim, is pervasive in Hip Hop though it is typically males who rap about sexual pleasure and desire. Countless male rappers rap about their sexual desires in a sexist, misogynistic, and degrading way towards women.[41] Rap music is bombarded by males explaining their sexual superiority, teaching young men and women that females exist to be objectified. Female rappers, such as Lil' Kim, therefore create a subgenre of rap music that embraces and exposes the desires of women. Both young men and women learn from this subgenre that girls have a right to pleasure instead of learning that their sexual desires are promiscuous in nature.

In the same song, Lil' Kim boldly announces she masturbates, a source of pleasure for many women; but, because of the missing discourse of desire around female sexuality, many women do not openly admit to it. Not only does Lil' Kim talk about masturbation, but she incorporates it as part of a sexual fantasy. She wants men to gain pleasure from the image of her touching herself. She can touch it, but they can only imagine it without touching. Using visual imagery, Lil' Kim has now switched roles with her male counterpart and become the initiator of pleasure. She no longer needs a man for pleasure and has become sexually independent. Lil' Kim not only expresses a freedom about her sexual desires, but an independence of self. Lil' Kim's "in your face" sexual

---

[41] See rap artists such as NWA, 2 Live Crew, 50 cent, and the Ying Yang Twins as examples of this.

confidence illustrates her self-assurance outside the bedroom with her body, beauty, and sexual ability. Masturbation, thus, becomes more than pleasure; it is confidence in one's self and embracing being a woman. Since masturbation is being discussed within Hip Hop already, it might be a topic included in the formal sex education curriculum. This curriculum could address the issue of masturbation and teach it as a healthy alternative to sex with another person.

In the same song Lil' Kim raps about pleasuring a man through oral sex. She clearly states, however, her own enjoyment of the act by calling his manhood "candy." The word "candy" conjures up something sweet, something enjoyable.

Lil' Kim asserts her right to gain pleasure through performing oral sex on a man. The act gives her sexual agency as she refuses to be merely an object of male desire. Of course, this interpretation is open to contestation as it might also be argued that given patriarchal, heteronormative structures Lil' Kim is colluding in her own oppression by giving in to male desires. We choose to read this as an example of sexual subjectivity. Lil' Kim is able to assert that she desires sex, wants to please as well as be pleased.

The next song we have chosen to examine is one by Foxy Brown called "Candy," which also features another female artist, Kelis. The term "candy" is used in ways similar to the metaphor used earlier by Lil' Kim in her song "Kitty Box"; candy represents something that is sweet and satisfying. She also echoes the command "picture" used by Lil' Kim. Brown, however, furthers her sexual confidence by quantifying her womanhood as "priceless."

> I'm real sweet like a candy corn...
> Picture me, t-shirt, no panties on
> ... I'm priceless boy.[42]

Foxy Brown alludes to her own sexual womanhood flavor as a metaphor for candy. She explains that she is sweet like candy and then dares men to taste her. She is confident in her assessment of herself: she may taste sweet, but she is not your typical good girl. She warns men that she "talks shit," especially when she is the one on top during sex. She is taking on the dominant role. Here, Foxy Brown interrupts the notion of wanting to be a good girl. Of course, some may argue that bad girl status hurts women more, that bad girls are used sexually by men, while good girls are the ones men want to marry.

---

[42] Foxy Brown, "Broken Silence," *Broken Silence* (Def Jam, 2001).

Her unapologetic line "let me know when you're ready to eat" clearly illustrates her desire and expectation about oral sex. Foxy Brown's language is not
the language of a woman that is passive, a victim, or a woman who is unsure
about what she wants sexually. This stance, in fact, contradicts Fine's notion
of sexuality as victimization.[43] However, mainstream society places social constraints on the sexual aggression of young females. They are taught that they
are victims, while males are described as predators. Young women are taught
to say "no" to sex without considering their own sexual desires and answering
"yes." Conversely, when the female takes on the role as the predator she is
looked down upon and is viewed as a slut, ho, or tramp. Brown's lyrics interrupt this very notion and make it clear that women can desire sex and can ask
for pleasure.

Foxy Brown in her song "Ill Na Na" raps about how it is her turn, as a
woman, to enjoy herself:

This is ladies night... When I'm coming home? Maybe tonight.[44]

She affects a traditionally masculine role by going out to hang with her
girlfriends. She instructs the man in her life to leave her dinner and kiss her
baby goodnight. She continues to assume a more masculine role with the following:

I left some money on the dresser, find you a cab.[45]

She asserts her economic independence by providing money for the man
to leave once she is done with him. Her agency as a woman is unmistakable as
she makes it clear she does not need a man for anything except for sexual pleasure.

In 2007, Kelly Rowland's song "Like This," featuring female rapper Eve,
illustrates the duality female rappers assert as they negotiate agency as sexual
beings while living in a male-dominated world. Throughout the song, both
women celebrate themselves as powerful women who are economically independent and, therefore, do not need a man. They can choose which men they

---

[43] Michelle Fine, "Sexuality, Schooling, and Adolescent Females: The Missing Discourse of
Desire," in *Beyond Silenced Voices: Class, Race, and Gender in United States Schools*, ed. Lois Weis
and Michelle Fine (Albany, NY: State University of New York Press, 1993), 79.

[44] Foxy Brown, "Ill Na Na," *Ill Na Na* (Def Jam, 1996).

[45] Ibid.

want to have a sexual relationship with. In Eve's verse, she explores the notion of being sexually confident. She raps:

> Dudes get excited, seeing what they likin
> Hopin they the one u choose, hope they get invited[46]

Eve shows through her lyrical word play that being a woman and having confidence is possible. Eve raps about how females can be assertive and choose their mates. The idea of choice is important here—females are capable of choosing a mate and being responsible for their actions. The current formal sex education curriculum lacks knowledge of how girls might be sexual agents and be responsible for themselves. Instead, girls are taught to be passive and, therefore, they cannot assert themselves sexually. It is obvious that girls hear contradictory messages through popular culture. In the above stanza, they learn how to be assertive sexually and economically. Schools must stop ignoring popular culture that disseminates sexual messages to youth and, instead, recognize their world is filled with sexual temptations that are real and, sometimes, deadly.

As educators, we cannot dismiss the words of Lil' Kim, Foxy Brown, and other female rappers because they are heard by countless youth. We cannot pretend that these sexually explicit lyrics are not educational and we must find ways of dialoguing with youth about these lyrics. We are neither endorsing nor condemning Lil' Kim and other female rappers like her, but we cannot ignore the impact they have on youth. Youth receive contradictory messages from popular culture and the formal sex education curriculum. Educators should, therefore, bridge the gap between what students hear in the classroom and what they hear in the world of popular culture and especially Hip Hop.

We have chosen to complete our own textual analysis of Hip Hop lyrics. Of course, there are limitations to this method. David Buckingham, for example, argues:

> Ultimately, textual analysis has distinct limitations: while it may provide a useful means of generating hypotheses, it is clearly incapable of accounting for the ways in which real audiences actually make sense of television. Viewers are not 'positioned' by

---

[46] Kelly Rowland, "Like This," *Ms. Kelly: Kelly Rowland* (Music Group/Sony, 2007).

television: they are also positioned in society and history, and will therefore bring different kinds of prior knowledge to the text.[47]

The interpretations we have made of these lyrics stem from our own histories as adult women of color who regularly consume Hip Hop. Our readings, because they are based on our positions within society, might be different from the girls for whom we are advocating. This does not mean, of course, that our textual analysis is invalid. It means, however, that as cultural studies theorists we recognize that texts have multiple meanings and it is the consumer's relationship with the text that matters most. An ethnographic study on girls' consumption of sexually explicit lyrics might shed further light on the issues raised in this chapter.

Implications for Youth

This is not the first time a popular culture icon has spawned academic debate. In fact, analysis of Madonna occurred regularly at the time she was most popular. Questions were posed as to how sexually liberating Madonna really was. On the one hand she was viewed in terms of resistance. As Fiske claimed, "Madonna's popularity is a complexity of power and resistance, of meaning and counter meaning, of pleasure and struggle for control."[48] Some theorists viewed Madonna as a feminist icon, as a woman who helped redefine female sexuality. Others regarded her as a corrupter of youth. Part of this criticism stemmed from the fact that critics believed Madonna, much like prostitutes, used sexuality for economic gain. Some feminists believed it was impossible for Madonna to trump the good girl/bad girl binary. As Wolff stated, "There are problems with using the female body for feminist ends. Its pre-existing meanings, as sex object, as object of the male gaze, can always prevail and re-appropriate the body, despite the intentions of the woman herself."[49] Wolff's argument presumes that structures not only constrain agency but make it impossible for women ever to resist oppression. This is a deterministic view of the choices, or lack thereof, we have as women. This argument contradicts the cultural production argument which posits that "making culture is complex and contradictory, and cannot be explained by simple notions of determination, false consciousness (whether capitalist, imperialist or patriarchal), co-

---

[47] David Buckingham, *Public Secrets: EastEnders and Its Audience* (London: British Film Institute, 1988), 115.

[48] John Fiske, *Understanding Popular Culture* (Boston: Unwin Hyman, 1989), 113.

[49] Janet Wolff, *Feminine Sentences: Essays on Women and Culture* (Oxford: Polity Press, 1990), 121.

option and manipulation. Meanings are never definitive but always provisional, always dependent on context"[50] In other words, consumption of popular culture can be viewed as a type of agency. Of course, this agency must be contextualized. Consumption occurs within the larger political economy. Thus, as Kellner argues, "the production and distribution of culture takes place within a specific economic system, constituted by relations between the state, the economy, social institutions and practices, culture, and organizations like the media."[51] Thus, consumption is mediated by factors such as race, class, and gender. These factors obviously shape and constrain agency. As girls negotiate the binary of good girl/bad girl, they are never one or the other. Their relationship with popular culture enables them to construct contradictory identities as they negotiate between hearing about desire in Hip Hop and not hearing about it in school.

When many girls are asked how and why they had sexual intercourse, they respond, "It just happened."[52] This response allows girls to position themselves as passive non-actors. It denies their agency or the possibility to make choices that suit their best interests. Many girls utilize this passivity because they have been taught along the way that their desire should not exist. In fact, having desire often precludes the label "bad girl" that so many girls want to avoid. Deborah Tolman argues that educators "have to engage in the subversive work of making it possible for girls to get beyond 'it just happened' by fighting for girls' right to feel and act upon their own sexual feelings without having to be encumbered by the dilemma of desire."[53] Girls who consume Hip Hop hear female rappers rap about their own sexual desires. These girls also most likely experience desire in some way. By pretending their desire is non-existent, schools do not provide girls the tools necessary to successfully negotiate the good girl/bad girl binary. Instead, schools collude in the positioning of girls as passive beings who do not take responsibility for their sexual selves.

Because Hip Hop is a site of education and is regularly consumed by youth regardless of race, class, or gender, we continually must critique it. The

---

[50] John Storey, *Cultural Consumption and Everyday Life* (London: Oxford University Press, 1999), 168.

[51] Douglas Kellner, *Media Culture: Cultural Studies, Identity and Politics Between the Modern and the Postmodern* (New York: Routledge, 1995), 104.

[52] Deborah L. Tolman, "Getting Beyond 'It Just Happened': Adolescent Girls' Experience of Sexual Desire," paper presented at the Annual Convention of the American Psychological Association (Boston, MA: August 20-24, 1999), 3.

[53] Ibid., 10.

sexually explicit lyrics we have included in this chapter are listened to by children of all ages. Youth come to school with knowledge about sex that they have learned from popular culture. The lyrics we have examined here teach girls and boys about something often unspoken in schools—female sexual desire. We should not pretend girls do not have a right to sexual pleasure when they are taught the opposite by many female rappers. Educators must take up the issue of female sexual desire and pleasure in ways that empower young girls to make the healthiest choices. We are not arguing that young women should be taught to use young men for sexual pleasure. We do, however, urge educators to teach young women that it is normal for them to feel desire and that they, like their male counterparts, have a right to feel pleasure. The more we teach young women to understand their sexual selves, the more empowered they will be to make wise decisions about taking care of themselves.

The confidence exuded by these female rappers is sexually liberating and fosters the idea of claiming agency over one's sexuality. The lyrics of Foxy Brown, Lil' Kim, and others can lead to an increase in girls' self-esteem and may empower them to confront their sexual desires in healthy ways. Educators cannot be afraid of discussing the sexual desires of young females since the desires of their male counterparts are discussed and oftentimes celebrated. We need to equally celebrate the sexual desires of young females as they learn about who they are, what they are capable of, and how to interrupt what society has deemed appropriate for them. As evidenced by the female rappers we have examined here, Hip Hop teaches girls about sexual pleasure and gender roles. It is time schools utilize this as a teaching tool.

Bibliography

Alridge, Derrick. 2005. From Civil Right to Hip Hop: Toward a Nexus of Ideas. *The Journal of African American History* 90: 226-252.

Allen, Louisa. 2003. Girls want sex, boys want love: Young people negotiating (hetero)sex. *Sexualities*, 6: 215-236.

Allen, Louisa. 2004. Beyond the Birds and the Bees: Constituting a Discourse of Erotics in Sexuality Education. *Gender and Education* 16: 151-167.

Ashcraft, Catherine. 2006. 'Girl, You Better Go Get You a Condom': Popular Culture and Teen Sexuality as Resources for Critical Multicultural Curriculum. *Teachers College Record* 108 (1): 2145-2186.

Ashcraft, Catherine. 2003. Adolescent Ambiguities in American Pie: Popular Culture as a Resource for Sex Education," *Youth & Society* 35 (1): 37-70.

Basu, Dipannita. 2005. "A Critical Examination of the Political Economy of the Hip-hop Industry." In *African Americans in US Economy*. Cecilia A. Conrad, John Whitehead, Patrick Mason, and James Stewart, eds. Oxford: Rowman & Littlefield Publishers.

Brown, Foxy. 2005. Broken Silence. *Def Jam*.

Brown, Foxy. 1996. Ill Na Na. *Def Jam*.

Brucker, Hannah and Bearman, Peter. 2005. After the Promise: The STD Consequences of Adolescent Virginity Pledges. *Journal of Adolescent Health* (5): 271-278.

Buckingham, David. 1987. *Public Secrets: EastEnders and Its Audience*. London: British Film Institute.

Clarke, John, Hall, Stuart, Jefferson, Tony, and Roberts, Brian. 1976. Subcultures, Cultures and Class. In *Resistance Through Rituals: Youth Subcultures in Post-war Britain*, Stuart Hall and Tony Jefferson, eds. London: Hutchinson.

Corrigan, Paul. 1979. *Schooling the Smash Street Kids*. London: Macmillan.

Dailard, Cynthia. 2002. Abstinence Promotion and Teen Family Planning: The Misguided Drive for Equal Funding. *The Guttmacher Report on Public Policy*, 1-3.

Dimitriadis, Greg. 2001. *Performing Identity/Performing Culture: Hip Hop as Text Pedagogy, and Lived Practice*. New York: Peter Lang Publishing.

Fine, Michelle. 1993. Sexuality, Schooling, and Adolescent Females: The Missing Discourse of Desire. In *Beyond Silenced Voices: Class, Race, and Gender in United States Schools*, Lois Weis and Michelle Fine, eds. Albany: State University of New York Press.

Fiske, John. 1989. *Understanding Popular Culture*. Boston: Unwin Hyman.

Frye, Marilyn. 1983. *The Politics of Reality: Essay in Feminist Theory*. Berkeley: Crossing Press.

Giroux, Henry and Simon, Roger I. 1998. Schooling, Popular Culture, and a Pedagogy of Possibility. *Journal of Education* 170: 9-29.

Hall, Stuart 1983. "What is this "Black" in Black Popular Culture." In *Black Popular Culture*, Michelle Wallace, ed. New York: Oxford University Press.

Hall, Stuart. 1992. Cultural Studies and its Theoretical Legacies. In *Cultural Studies*, L. Grossberg, C. Nelson, and P. Treichler, eds. New York: Routledge.

Hall, Stuart. 1996. On Postmodernism and Articulation. In *Stuart Hall: Critical Dialogues in Cultural Studies*, D. Morley and K.-H Chen, eds. London: Routledge.

Hauser, Debra. 2004. Five Years of Abstinence-Only-Until-Marriage Education: Assessing the Impact. *Advocates for Youth*. < http://www.advocatesforyouth.org/publications/stateevaluations.pdf>.

hooks, bell. 1993. *Sisters of the Yam: Black Women and Self-Recovery*. Toronto, ON: Between the Lines.

Kellner, Douglas. 1995. *Media Culture: Cultural Studies, Identity and Politics Between the Modern and the Postmodern*. New York: Routledge.

Lil' Kim. 2005. The Naked Truth. *Atlantic Records*.

MacKinnon, Catherine A. 1989. *Toward a Feminist Theory of the State*. Cambridge, MA: Harvard University Press.

McLaren, Peter. 1992. Border Anxiety and Sexual Politics. In *Sexuality and the Curriculum: The Politics and Practices of Sexuality Education*, James Sears, ed. New York: Teachers College Press.

McRobbie, Angela. 1991. *Feminism and Youth Culture: From Jackie to Just Seventeen*. London: Macmillan.

Miriam, Kathy. 2007. Toward a Phenomenology of Sex-Right: Reviving Radical Feminist Theory of Compulsory Heterosexuality. *Hypatia 22*, no. 1 (Winter): 210-228.

Rich, Adrienne. 1986. Compulsory heterosexuality and lesbian existence. *Blood, Bread, and Poetry: Selected Prose*. New York: Norton.

Rose, Tricia. 1994. Black Noise: Rap Music and Black Culture in Contemporary America. Middletown, CT: Wesleyan University Press.

Rowland, Kelly. 2007. Ms. Kelly World. *Music Group/Sony*.

Stephens, Dionne P and Phillips, Layli D. 2003. Freaks, Gold diggers, Divas, and Dykes: The Socio-historical Development of Adolescent African-American Women's Sexual Scripts," *Sexuality and Culture* (7): 3-49.

Storey, John. 1999. *Cultural Consumption and Everyday Life*. London: Oxford University Press.

Tolman. Deborah L. 1999. "Getting Beyond "It Just Happened": Adolescent Girls' Experience of Sexual Desire," paper presented at the Annual Convention of the American Psychological Association, Boston, MA, August 20-24, 1999.

Watkins, S. Craig. 2005. *Hip Hop Matters: Politics, Pop Culture, and the Struggle for the Soul of a Movement*. Boston: Beacon Press.

Willis, Paul. 1977. *Learning to Labour: How Working Class Kids Get Working Class Jobs*. Farnborough, England: Saxon House.

Wolff, Janet. 1990. *Feminine Sentences: Essays on Women and Culture*. Oxford: Polity Press.

CHAPTER THREE

Consumption Is the Message
Television Advertising and Adolescents

Dennis Attick, Georgia State University

A recent study by the Kaiser Family Foundation revealed that more than 80 percent of young people between the ages of eight and eighteen watch more than three hours of television programming each day.[1] The same study revealed that 68 percent of those young people have televisions in their bedrooms. Further, a television industry report from 2006 indicates that TV viewership was at an all-time high during the 2005-2006 television season.[2] This report also revealed that the highest increase in television viewing was amongst teenage girls. Douglas Kellner has argued that most adolescents will have spent more time watching television before starting elementary school than they will in a classroom during their entire school career.[3] Young people continue to consume television programming at alarming rates despite the rise of other media platforms such as computers, video games, and cell phones.

---

[1] *Generation M: Media in the lives of 8-18 Year Olds*, Kaiser Family Foundation Report (March 2005). This report is based on a random survey of 2,032 young people between the ages of eight and eighteen. The report indicates that despite an increase in computer usage and other portable media, this age demographic continues to use television as their primary source of media entertainment. Further, 99% of young people interviewed for this survey said their family owned a TV and 65% of the families owned more than three televisions. The report can be found at http://www.kff.org/entmedia/upload/Executive-Summary-Generation-M-Media-in-the-Lives-of-8-18-Year-olds.pdf. Accessed 7/21/06.

[2] Andrew Wallenstein, "TV Viewership Hits Record High," *Reuters* (9/22/06).

[3] Douglas Kellner, *Television and the Crisis of Democracy* (Boulder, CO: Westview Press, 1990), 126. Kellner argues that TV is an isolating force that erodes both our sense of community, as well as our potential to see democracy realized in action. For further discussion on adolescent usage of TV see Victor Strasburger, *Adolescents and the Media: Medical and Psychological Impact* (Thousand Oaks, CA: Sage, 1995).

Due to this ongoing early exposure to television, most children have received an almost immeasurable number of advertising images and sounds via television before beginning school. Further, much of the content of television advertising to children and adolescents encourages young people to consume specific items or ideals if they wish to be considered normal.[4] The main goal of this advertising is to get young people to think of consumption as a worthwhile activity and possession of "things" as an indicator of one's worth in society.

In this chapter, I examine the relationship between television advertising, youth, and the promotion of a consumer culture. I argue that television advertising serves to promote the idea of consumerism in adolescents. In a culture of consumption, it is beneficial to advertisers, and the multinational corporations that own the television networks, for young people to grow up without understanding the consequences of consumerist behavior. As Alex Molnar argues, "Commercialism has already helped make the term *citizen* virtually synonymous with the term *consumer* and the possession of objects synonymous with happiness."[5] I argue that the cultivation of young consumers who desire things they may not actually need is a central goal of the advertising that permeates television programming geared toward children and adolescents. I contend that television advertising is a central contributor to the development of the consumer-citizen of which Molnar speaks. Further, in this chapter, I argue for public schools to be arenas where television's role in promoting consumerism can be countered and critiqued.

Throughout the last 50 years, television has provided an effective vehicle by which children can be exposed to the idea that consumption is desirable and that possessions lead to happiness. While one could argue that adults possess the knowledge and awareness needed to discriminate about the information forwarded by television advertising, the same argument does not hold true in regard to children and adolescents. Maxine Greene has offered that many young people are unable to interpret their own reality in relation to vis-

---

[4] Sam Stack, "Reclaiming Our Children: The Aesthetic as Transforming and Emancipating," *Journal of Philosophy and History of Education* 49 (1999): 1-11. Stack argues that advertising directed at children promotes a "socialization of desire that attempts to convert them into indiscriminate consumers with little understanding of the consequences of choice."

[5] Alex Molnar, *Giving Kids the Business: The Commercialization of America's Schools* (Boulder, CO: Westview Press, 1996), 68. Molnar asserts that advertising has defined our pervasive consumer ethos that has "helped create and sustain a disposable culture that is choking on its own waste." Molnar sees this consumerism as contributing to both the decline of civic life as well as the destruction of the natural world.

ual media and cannot separate themselves from the reality presented by television.[6] Further, research has shown that adolescents as old as 16 cannot cognitively or psychologically defend themselves against television advertising.[7] In this sense, advertising is a pseudo-reality that is homogenized and packaged for consumption and exists apart from each young person's experiences and conditions.

Historical Perspective

Television's popularity exploded in the late 1940s, forever changing the American landscape. Initially, television, and therefore television advertising, was geared toward adults, with minor attention paid to young viewers.[8] This was largely due to the fact that children were not seen as a valuable market at that time and the television networks were mostly concerned with selling televisions to American adults. As adolescents were not yet seen as a valuable market, television programming and advertising catered to the interests of adult viewers.[9] In fact, not until the mid-1950s did television executives begin to explore the possibility of luring in young viewers with programs specifically targeting the youth audience. It is not surprising that one of the pioneers in the field of children's television programming was the Disney Corporation, which aired the "Mickey Mouse Club" in 1955.[10] It was also during this time

---

[6] Maxine Greene, *The Dialectic of Freedom* (New York: Teachers College Press, 1988). Greene argues that this inability to interpret television imagery contributes to young people becoming immersed in a fabricated reality that privileges a "preoccupation with *having* more rather than *being* more" (p. 7). Greene sees this as a central factor in the maintenance of a culture based in unreflective consumerism.

[7] Roy Fox, *Harvesting Minds: How TV Commercials Control Kids* (Westport, CT: Praeger, 2000). Fox examines the ability of adolescent students to comprehend television advertising presented on Channel One programming in schools in Missouri. Fox found that adolescents do not have the ability to critically analyze advertisements and instead embrace the materialism presented in the advertisements viewed.

[8] Melissa D. Johnson and Brian M. Young, "Advertising History of Televisual Media," in Edward L. Palmer and Brian M. Young, eds., *The Faces of Televisual Media: Teaching, Violence, Selling to Children* (Mahwah, NJ: Lawrence Erlbaum Associates, 2003), 265-285. Johnson and Young argue that television was initially conceived as a transmitter of relevant factual information for the general public. However, once the power of television advertising was realized, television became primarily a vehicle for corporate advertisers.

[9] Edward L. Palmer, *Children in the Cradle of Television* (Lexington, MA: Lexington Books, 1987), 2. Palmer offers a thorough analysis of the development of children's television programming while also tracing the history of televisual media in the United States.

[10] Ibid.

that networks discovered that youth programming could fill the dead space of Saturday morning television. It was then that the "Mickey Mouse Club" joined "Howdy Doody" and "Captain Kangaroo" as regular fixtures of Saturday morning kids' television.[11]

Television programming options for youth continued to grow and thrive throughout the 1960s, but the 1970s represents a golden era for children's television. According to television critic Edward Palmer, to look at the 1970s is to "Look at the history of television itself."[12] It was during the 1970s that television became entrenched in the American landscape, and it was during the 1970s that critics of the medium began to speak out against the dangers represented by television's scope and popularity. It was during the 1970s that Action for Children's Television (ACT) first began to call upon the Federal Communications Commission (FCC) to adopt regulations restricting the content of children's programming and the coinciding advertisements.[13] Throughout the 1970s, ACT, which began as a grassroots organization founded by concerned parents, focused on calling attention to the dangers of exposing young children to television advertising. By the mid-1970s ACT, as well as the Center for Science in the Public Interest (CSPI), frequently petitioned both the FCC and the Federal Trade Commission (FTC) to encourage limits for advertising on children's television. While the ongoing petitions by ACT and CSPI generated debate throughout the decade, the FCC's position was that children's television and advertising practices would be left to industry self-regulation.[14] I would argue that self-regulation is an odd concept to attempt to instill in corporations who are in business to generate profits and not police their own efficacy at doing so. Self-regulation could lead to fewer profits and can be understood as antithetical to business.

In the 1980s, youth television viewing options expanded in a newly deregulated marketplace and this led to the creation of sub-categories of programming for children of all ages—from infants to teenagers.[15] No longer did

---

[11] Ibid.

[12] Ibid., 3.

[13] Ibid.

[14] James U. McNeal, Kids as Customers: A Handbook of Marketing to Children (New York: Lexington, 1992). McNeal is a leading authority in the field of marketing and specializes in helping corporations profit off of the child and youth market.

[15] Valerie Crane and Milton Chen, "Content Development of Children's Media," in Edward L. Palmer and Brian M. Young, eds., The Faces of Televisual Media: Teaching, Violence, Selling to

marketers have to sell their products to all young people through the same few television channels. More television channels opened the door for age-specific children's programming and this meant that products such as toys, fast food, and clothing could be marketed to children within specific age demographics. Further, the 1980s saw the onset of cable television and, while there were still fewer than 20 television channels available at that time, by the year 2000, the growth of cable and satellite television had expanded the number of channels available to more than 80.[16]

With the increasing number of television channels available on cable television came the proliferation of channels devoted to 24-hour programming for youth between the ages of 6 and 16. The creation of 24-hour kids' networks put an end to the primary network's battles for the coveted Saturday morning cartoon times.[17] Today, there are more than ten channels devoted to around-the-clock programming for young people with the most popular channels being *Nickelodeon, Fox Kids,* and *Disney Channel.*[18] I argue that any reasonable person should question the existence of twenty-four hour television programming for school-aged children and adolescents. It would seem that offering youth programming in the middle of the night is contrary to creating a healthy environment for young people who should probably be asleep at one or two o'clock in the morning, but that argument is reserved for another time.

The Rise of Advertising

In his 1961 book, *The Image: A Guide to Pseudo-Events in America,* Daniel Boorstin examines the rise of advertising in the twentieth century. Boorstin coined the term "pseudo-event" to describe the encroachment of synthetic experiences upon reality.[19] Boorstin argued that television and television advertising were creating a non-reality that was pre-scripted and packaged for

---

Children (Mahwah, NJ: Lawrence Erlbaum Associates, 2003), 55-81. It is important to note that the number of channels available varies based on cable or satellite television provider.

[16] Daisy Whitney, "Defining Distinct Niches: Building the Brand Is the Name of the Game in Kids TV," *Television Week.* Trade publication originally published on 3/10/2003.

[17] Valerie Crane and Milton Chen, "Content Development of Children's Media," in Edward L. Palmer and Brian M. Young (Eds.), *The Faces of Televisual Media: Teaching, Violence, Selling to Children* (Mahwah, NJ: Lawrence Erlbaum Associates, 2003), 55-81.

[18] Ibid.

[19] Daniel Boorstin, *The Image: A Guide to Pseudo-Events in America* (New York: Vintage, 1961/1992).

public consumption. Boorstin extended his concept of the pseudo-event to advertising with the "pseudo-ideal":

> An advertisement conjured up an image in order to persuade people that something was worth buying. It combined a pseudo-event with a pseudo-ideal. The pseudo-event must be vividly newsworthy, the pseudo-ideal must be vividly desirable.[20]

In this sense, advertisements represented a pseudo-ideal by promoting items which were not necessarily needed, but rather, desirable. Further, advertisements as pseudo-ideals did not just promote certain items, they promoted certain items as good and worthy of public consumption. Once the advertising-consumption model was established, advertisers had only to convince the public that the next hot trend had arrived to assure that consumption continued. With the arrival of television in the mid-twentieth century, advertisers found the perfect tool by which to present new items to the consuming public.

Joel Spring extends Boorstin's argument in offering that the professionalization of advertising in the twentieth-century was essential to the creation of the consumer-citizen in the United States.[21] Advertising promoted the idea that new products were better than existing products and that trends and fashions could and should change. Professional advertising shifted the model of consumers making rational choices in the marketplace to consumers making buying decisions based on emotional attachments to branded products.[22] Further, advertising contributed to the idea that consuming was an incessant activity by always providing the consumer with the next best thing. By leading the television viewing audience to believe that the items advertised could lead to the positive attitudes featured in the advertisements, the advertisers had only to create new ways to elicit the viewers' emotional response to confer a new item's importance to the public.

Adolescents and Advertising's Sway

Victor Strasburger has argued that adolescents are especially vulnerable to the influence of television advertising, as young people are developing their

---

[20] Ibid., 41.

[21] Joel Spring, *Educating the Consumer-Citizen* (Mahwah, NJ: Erlbaum Associates, 2003). Spring argues that "Advertising prompted desires for new products; it convinced consumers that existing products were unfashionable and, therefore, obsolete; it made brand names into playthings in personal fantasies," 3.

[22] Ibid.

own identities and are highly susceptible to external messages.[23] Similarly, Roy Fox has argued that television advertising plays an important role in developing adolescents' self-image during a time when young people are searching to make meaning of themselves and their world.[24] In this sense, adolescents may easily internalize the messages they receive from advertising and these messages greatly influence their self-identity and consumerist behavior.

In his study conducted in the mid-1990s, Roy Fox examined the ability of one group of adolescents to comprehend and evaluate television advertising. Fox conducted his study using advertisements presented on Channel One, the television network that beams programming and advertisements to over 40 percent of American classrooms each day.[25] Fox's study was the first study to examine the impact that the advertisements featured on Channel One have on the captive teen audience that views them. Fox conducted study groups and interviews with 200 high school students who had been exposed to Channel One, and his study reaveled several important consequences of Channel One's influence. Fox examined how well students understood the commercials and the degree to which the commercials influenced the students' consumerist behavior. Fox's results indicate that even adolescents as old as 16 are vulnerable to the sway of television advertising. Fox's study revealed that the advertisements featured on Channel One became a part of the cultural landscape of the adolescents as the students reported talking about the commercials throughout the day as well as consuming the products featured in the ads.[26] The study showed that most students were unable to interpret the television advertising viewed. According to Fox:

---

[23] Victor Strasburger, *Adolescents and the Media: Medical and Psychological Impact*, p. 12. Strasburger argues that young people are likely to be influenced by TV, as they don't often understand that TV represents fantasy. Further, Strasburger argues that television acts as a "super peer group" where adolescents receive messages about group norms that influence their behaviors and attitudes. (13).

[24] Roy Fox, *Harvesting Minds: How TV Commercials Control Kids*, 6.

[25] Ibid. Channel One is the brainchild of Chris Whittle, who designed Channel One as a way for advertisers to capitalize on the captive audience of school children. Channel One is beamed into classrooms where students watch Channel One's "educational" programming (without interruption) in class each day in exchange for television sets and other technology equipment. Coupled with Channel One's programming are advertisements that the students are also forced to watch. For an in-depth analysis of the creation of Channel One and its impact on schools, see Ann DeVaney, *Watching Channel One: The Convergence of Students, Technology & Private Business* (Albany, NY: State University of New York Press, 1994).

[26] Ibid., 3.

Of the 150 students who discussed the commercials with me, only five said it had
been fashioned by an external force such as the Pepsi Corporation, its marketer, or its
commercial producers and directors. The students never acknowledged any *external*
people involved in making or telling the ad's story. They seldom viewed commercials
for what they are; highly contrived constructions that have been filtered through
countless other people and processes, each with its own purposes.[27]

Fox argues that the adolescents in his study had an overall inability to
comprehend that advertisements exist to persuade them to do or buy certain
items. Further, Fox found that the adolescents embraced the ads and considered them as givens in their world. In his conclusion, Fox offers that

They (the adolescents in the study) rarely questioned the dominant presence of ads in
their lives. Today's kids have grown up with commercials...but what surprised me
most was the kids' positive, often warm regard for ads.[28]

The students in Fox's study demonstrated little concern for the impact
that the advertisements had on their lives and offered no critical evaluation of
the consumerist notions embedded within. Their primary focus was on consuming that which was presented as desirable according to the advertisements.

Television Advertising and Consumerist Behavior

Researchers have offered that 15 to 20 percent of television content is
composed of commercial advertisements.[29] If up to 20 percent of television
programming is dedicated to advertising, then young people who watch television will most likely be exposed to numerous advertisements. It might seem
that dutiful parenting is enough to combat the effects of television as prudent
parents should be able to ensure that their children watch only programs
which are considered "family-friendly." However, television programming directed specifically at children and adolescents is often presented in conjunction with advertising that attempts to promote the latest fads and trends and is
therefore not without consequence. Further, items advertised on kids' television rarely feature factual product information such as price and availability.[30]

---

[27] Ibid.

[28] Ibid.,127.

[29] Dale Kunkel and Mary McIlrath, "Message Content in Advertising to Children," in Edward
L. Palmer and Brian M. Young, eds., *The Faces of Televisual Media: Teaching, Violence, Selling to
Children* (Mahwah, NJ: Lawrence Erlbaum Associates, 2003): 287-300.

[30] Ibid.

I argue that the lack of factual information in advertisements further promotes uncritical consumerism in adolescents.

In recent years, psychologists and medical researchers have offered that television viewing by children contributes to such things as poor health, consumerism, and strains the parent-child relationship.[31] Further, scholars have offered that the overarching goal of kids' television is not to provide quality programming, but rather to expose young people to the maximum number of advertisements possible.[32] Therefore, it should not be surprising to learn that the average American adolescent views between 35,000 and 40,000 advertisements on television each year.[33] The number of advertisements viewed becomes especially problematic when considering the items most heavily advertised on kids' television. In 2005, the most advertised products were sugar-laden candy and fastfood, as corporations spent $480 million on television advertisements for those items alone.[34]

While the Federal Communication Commission (FCC) has established limits to the number of advertisements networks can include in kids' programming, it should not be surprising to learn that some networks violate the FCC limits. In 2004, Nickelodeon, a children's network owned by the Disney Corporation, was fined $1 million for violating FCC limits on advertising during programs directed at children and adolescents.[35] It would appear that what

---

[31] See, for example, Rebecca A. Clay, "Advertising to Children: Is It Ethical?" *Monitor on Psychology, 31* (8). The report can be retrieved at http://www.apa.org/monitor/ sep00/ advertising.html. Accessed on 5/10/05. Also, see Richard Linnett, "Psychologists Protest Kids' Ads," *Advertising Age, 71,* 4, 69. For a thorough discussion of the impact of television viewing on children see George Gerbner, "Cultivation Analysis: An Overview," *Mass Communication & Society,* 1 (3/4) (1998), 175-194. Gerbner's cultivation theory holds that heavy television viewers have their conception of the world shaped by what they see on television.

[32] Stacy L. Smith and Charles Atkins, "Television Advertising and Children: Examining the Intended and Unintended Effects," in Edward L. Palmer and Brian M. Young (Eds.), *The Faces of Televisual Media: Teaching, Violence, Selling to Children* (Mahwah, NJ: Lawrence Erlbaum Associates, 2003), 305-325. Smith and Atkins argue that younger children are uniquely susceptible to advertising given their inability to differentiate between commercials and television programs.

[33] American Academy of Pediatrics, "Television and the Family" fact sheet. The fact sheet can be found at www.aap.org/family/tv1.htm. Accessed 5/1/05.

[34] Kevin Downey, "The Messenger Changes Tactics," *Broadcasting & Cable* (11/14/2005).

[35] Todd Wasserman, "Curbing Their Appetite," *Brandweek* 45 (2004): 24-28. In 2005, the FCC limited advertising during children's television programming to ten minutes per hour during weekends and twelve minutes per hour during the week. Doug Halonen, "Kids Regs Draw Big 3 Fire," *Television Week* (10/23/2005). It is not surprising that the owners of the three

is important to the advertisers, and therefore the networks, is not necessarily the content of television programs, but rather exposing children to products.

Many of the advertisements presented during youth programming promote the idea that specific products define one's ability to be accepted in social settings by establishing norms regarding what is considered cool.[36] In fact, advertisers spend more than $10 billion per year informing young people about the hottest trends.[37] I argue that the relationship between television, identity, and materialism can be understood as circuitous in that teenagers who want to be accepted socially may find themselves trying to remain abreast of that which is the latest version of "cool." Deron Boyles has offered that corporations often manipulate the societal norms that young people respond to and those norms are usually rooted in consumption of the latest trends and fads.[38] Further, the advertisements that are featured on youth television programming are not designed to encourage children to question or generate debate about consumerism. Instead, the advertisements provide corporations with a vehicle to promote the consumption of things without consideration of the consequences involved.

The majority of the advertising that accompanies youth television programming features advertisements that promote specific behaviors. Often, those behaviors can be understood as anti-adult and anti-intellectual, as well as

---

biggest networks—The Walt Disney Co., Viacom, and NBC—threatened to sue the FCC if the limits were not loosened in 2006.

[36] Juliet B. Schor, *Born to Buy: The Commercialized Child and the New Consumer Culture* (New York: Scribner, 2004), 47-51. Schor argues that the "marketing of cool" is a relentless aspect of modern advertising that is directed at children and adolescents and consistently seeks to redefine the hottest trends. This, in turn, creates a never-ending cycle of consumption, as children seek that which is defined as most desirable at any given moment in time.

[37] Katy Kelly and Linda Kulman, "Kid Power," *U.S. News & World Report* (2004), 46-52. Recent figures for advertising dollars spent specifically on children's television programming indicate that corporations spent $2.1 billion for ads on kid's TV in 2004. See also Kevin Downey, "What Children Teach Their Parents," *Broadcasting & Cable* (3/13/2006). It would appear corporations are aware that advertising on kids' television will lead to huge profits. How else could they justify spending more than $2.1 billion to be sure kids see their advertisements?

[38] Deron Boyles, "Uncovering the Coverings: The Use of Corporate-Sponsored Textbook Covers in Furthering Uncritical Consumerism," *Educational Studies* 37, no. 3 (2005): 255-266. In his examination of textbook covers Boyles argues that corporations often "sell" established (often sexist) norms back to young girls through various social institutions. Where schools provide textbook covers to students for "free," the cost of the commodified imagery on the covers is actually "paid" by the students whose consumerist tendencies are reinforced by the covers. See Chapter Eight.

promoting consumption of products over human interaction.[39] Many products are promoted in advertising campaigns that portray adults as bungling and out-of-touch. Fruit-To-Go fruit chews are advertised with a promotion that tells kids, "When it comes to fashion class, your principal is a flunkie."[40] Starburst candy and Nickelodeon's popular "Slime Time Live" show are marketed in advertisements that specifically mock teachers and school administrators by portraying them as unfit to be considered professionals.[41] This type of advertising attempts to empower young people through the negation of adults in authority roles. I argue that this empowerment is an attempt by advertisers to usher adolescents into adulthood in order to "liberate" them to be more efficient consumers.

While the empowerment of young people is a positive concept, the advertisements cited here seek to empower children only to serve the interests of the advertisers who are selling the latest fads and trends. The advertisements do not promote an empowerment rooted in personal development or ethical responsibility, but rather, it is an empowerment that marketing guru Elissa Moses refers to as "self-navigation," which leads teens to work harder than ever to gain control of their financial lives so that they can participate in the consumer culture.[42]

---

[39] Schor, 51-54. Schor argues that the goal of this type of advertising is the "adultification" of children so that they may challenge adult authority and become free to consume without restriction. See also Neil Postman, *The Disappearance of Childhood* (New York: Vintage, 1994). Postman offers a deft analysis of the role of television and advertising in the "adultification" of children. Postman also contends that television promotes role reversal where children on television are "adultified" and adults on television are "infantilized".

[40] Ibid. Inherent in this advertisement is not just the idea that fashion is important, but that school principals are subject to ridicule over how they look or dress, not based on their qualifications or limitations as scholars or school leaders. In this sense, everyone and everything is subject to the privileging of image over substance, which, I argue, is the primary goal of television advertising.

[41] Ibid. Writes Schor, "Consider a well-known Starburst classroom commercial. A nerdy teacher writes on the board, kids open the candy, and the scene erupts into a riotous party. When the teacher faces the class again, all is quiet, controlled and dull." (53). The underlying point in this advertisement is that school is boring, teachers are nerds, but with Starburst candy, life is a party.

[42] Elissa Moses, *The $100 Billion Allowance: Accessing the Global Teen Market* (New York: John Wiley & Sons, 2000), 6.

Television and the Youth Market

It is becoming increasingly clear that television plays an important role in developing adolescents into consuming subjects. This is essential to the global youth industry that thrives on the consumption-oriented thinking that exists among young people. As Elissa Moses argues in her handbook on marketing to adolescents, "Teens who speak different languages all speak the same language of global brand consumption."[43] To maintain the global youth market, corporations know that teens must learn to embrace consumerism at a young age and television is a primary vehicle by which this is accomplished. Moses advises her corporate clients to focus on American teens and American television to spread global consumerism:

> Youth want to own the brand that is the hottest, the most cool, and of the moment, right now. It is part of the youthful pack mentality. The desire leads to the yearning for products from the United States, because the zenith of teen aspiration is to be as much like American teens as possible. How did America get to be so cool? I believe the first answer is television.[44]

Moses believes that American teens define "cool," and that their television-driven desire to consume is at the epicenter of the expanding global youth market.

Another contributing factor to the development of adolescents into customers is branding, which is a prominent feature in television advertising to youth. For the purpose of this chapter, branding is the practice of using an image or logo as a label to identify a product or service.[45] Branding first emerged as a marketing tool in the late nineteenth century as the industrial revolution led companies to seek ways to single out their products in an increasingly crowded marketplace. It was during this time that Aunt Jemima maple syrup and Quaker Oats oatmeal became some of the first widely recognized brands.[46] By placing an easily identifiable logo or image on their prod-

---

[43] Ibid., 13.

[44] Ibid., 39.

[45] Naomi Klein, *No Logo* (New York: Picador, 2000), 5-7. Klein traces branding to the dawn of the industrial revolution when the American marketplace was awash with new products that were not easily distinguishable. See also Deron R. Boyles, "Marketing Sameness: Consumerism, Commercialism, and the Status Quo," in J.C. Smart, ed., *Higher Education: Handbook of Theory and Research* XXII (Dordrecht: Springer, 2007): 537-582.

[46] Ibid.

ucts, companies hoped to lead customers to attach value to the products based on an attraction to the image and not necessarily the quality of the product.

Branding became a popular marketing tool in the twentieth century, but it was not until the last 25 years that branding mania flourished.[47] An individual needs only to participate in modern life to see that branded products are ubiquitous in modern society. What is most troubling is that a connection to brands begins at an early age, as children as young as two years old have demonstrated brand recognition.[48] How does this happen, one must ask? I argue that those messages are effective at creating brand-conscious consumers who learn to desire what is presented to them via the visual imagery of television.

While television is a means by which advertisers can sell their brand to adolescents, many of the networks that cater to youth are also branded.[49] Nickelodeon, one of the most popular television networks amongst adolescents, begins aggressively marketing its branded name and image to young children before they are preschoolers through television.[50] Nickelodeon, Disney Channel and Cartoon Network are able to establish a brand name with young people because they emerged as leaders in children-specific network programming. One result of this is that children learn first to internalize the brand of the network to which they will later turn to so as to receive more branded products as they enter school age and adolescence. In this sense, the television networks devoted to children and youth programming can be seen as an important early component to the training of young people to accept that brands exist *a priori* in the modern world.

Branding and marketing to youth has become such a lucrative business that entire national conferences are now dedicated to developing youth con-

---

[47] Naomi Klein, "The Tyranny of The Brands," *New Statesman* 13 (1/24/2000), 25-28. Klein writes, "Branding seems like a fairly innocuous idea. It is slapping a logo on a product and saying it's the best. And when brands first emerged, that was all it was. At the start of the industrial revolution, the market was flooded with nearly identical mass-produced products. Along came Aunt Jemima and Quaker Oats with their happy comforting logos to say: our mass-produced product is of the highest quality." In this sense, branding offered corporations a competitive edge over other unbranded products in a crowded marketplace.

[48] See Schor, Klein, *No Logo*, and McNeal, *Kids as Consumers*, for discussions of brand-recognition in young children.

[49] Daisy Whitney, "Defining Distinct Niches." In her article, Whitney quotes John Wagner, media director at Starcom Worldwide who offers, "Nickelodeon goes out and aggressively seeds the brand at a very young age and it's not because there's a huge advertiser demand for 2-to-5-year-old eyes, but it educates kids about where they [Nickelodeon] are on the dial."

[50] Ibid.

sumers. One such conference is the "Connecting with Youth: Fresh Approaches to Youth Marketing" conference which was held in Chicago in June 2005.[51] At this conference, conducted by the MFM Group, companies such as Disney Entertainment, Lion's Gate Films, and Atlantic Records shared branding strategies to assist each other as well as emergent corporations in developing "new strategies and tools to help them achieve their youth marketing goals."[52] These companies appear to be aware of the money that can be made from selling their products to children and therefore are willing to expend the resources needed to participate in a three-day conference on the subject. The conference agenda includes the following exciting highlights that attendees can look forward to:

- Assessing the Guidelines of What is Viewed as Right and Wrong in Kids Advertising
- Preventing ethical problems when marketing to minors
- Assessing 'The Blame Game' in Kids and Youth Marketing: How Corporate Responsibility and Ethics Fit into Today's Marketing Puzzle
- Re-evaluating effective strategies for in-school marketing: what still works and why[53]

What appears to be important for the corporations and conference attendees, many of whom advertise on television, is finding ways to expose young people to their products. The conference agenda makes no mention of how human energy can be used to positively impact children's lives; instead, reading the published agenda one could garner that the goal of the conference is the reduction of youth into pure consumers. In order to accomplish this, corporations must find ways to get children and adolescents to accept the mythology of each company's brand. Television continues to offer a vehicle through which this can be accomplished.

---

[51] MFM Group, "Connecting with Youth: Fresh Approaches to Youth Marketing." Conference information can be found at www.trademeetings.com/ssmeeting/Details.asp Accessed 7/21/06. There are undoubtedly numerous such conferences that deal with the youth market. For the purpose of this chapter I have chosen to focus on one that is indicative of corporate efforts to profit from youth. This conference is devoted to the youth market and is therefore useful to examine the means by which advertisers and corporations attempt to generate greater profits from youth spending.

[52] Ibid.

[53] Ibid.

The Role of Schools?

In his 2004 book, *Educating the Consumer-Citizen*, Joel Spring argues that schools have been complicit in the twentieth-century rise of consumerism in youth.[54] Spring argues that schools have reinforced the consumerist ideal promoted by television by not offering students an opportunity to evaluate critically television's messages. For Spring, schools have reinforced the consumerist culture by promoting competition and consumption while refusing to create spaces where corporate media's influence over schools and students can be critiqued.

If adolescents are to learn to counter the messages that television advertising delivers to them, then public schools must become sites where television and media are contested and debated. Henry Giroux poses challenges to schools in his critique of the Disney Corporation's media empire and its impact on young people:

> How do we link public pedagogy to a critical democratic view of citizenship? How do we develop forms of critical education that enable young people and adults to become aware of and interrogate the media as a major political, pedagogical, and social force? At the very least, such a project suggests developing educational programs, both within and outside of schools, that offer students the opportunity to learn how to use and critically read media technologies and their cultural productions.[55]

While Giroux articulates a notion of schools as arenas where students engage in dialogue about the forces that shape the world, he also contends that schools must allow adolescents to be constructors, not just consumers of media. However, there is little room for critical dialogue regarding media to emerge in schools where teachers hand students a pre-scripted curriculum replete with isolated and uncontested bits of information.

A question that remains is what public schools can do to counter television advertising and the impact it has on adolescents. As Giroux has offered, schools can counter the corporate media if they do so in a manner that offers students the ability to construct their own media. Giroux argues:

> Educators and other progressives must not only provide students with the knowledge and skills to read the media critically, they must also equip them with the skills to de-

---

[54] Joel Spring, *Educating the Consumer-Citizen.*

[55] Henry Giroux, *The Mouse that Roared: Disney and the End of Innocence* (Lanham, MD: Rowman & Littlefield, 2001), 11.

velop counter-media spheres in which students can produce their own radio and television programs, newspapers, magazines, films, and other forms of public art.[56]

Giroux does not argue for the elimination of media, but rather he calls for schools to be open to student-directed media that can confront and debate corporate-sponsored media. Roy Fox has similarly argued that students can learn to analyze and decipher televisual messages by becoming producers of their own media.[57] Both scholars call for the opening of new arenas in schools where students can reclaim their voices from the omnipresent media conglomerates that confine students to narrowly defined roles within the consumerist culture.

Looking Ahead

Television plays a central role in the development of consumers by offering corporations a vehicle through which to expose their products to large numbers of young people simultaneously. As young people can be impressionable and subject to market-driven notions of norms, it is not difficult to imagine adolescents accepting the representative images of products advertised on television. Therefore, advertisers are at an advantage in that they can rely on the naiveté of youth to help sell products. In this sense, children and adolescents can be particularly vulnerable to the sway of products that are tied to manufactured notions of what is considered hip or cool within peer groups.

It is clear that television is positioned as a major force in modern society. While one could argue for the beneficial aspects of television (there may be some), that is not my intention here. It is my contention that there are more pressing issues regarding the part television plays in shaping and supporting a consumer culture amongst young people in the United States. While parents own the most responsibility over the choices their children make regarding consumerism, schools have the opportunity to affect the issue as well. Currently, schools are complicit in the development of adolescent consumers, as

---

[56] Henry Giroux, *Channel Surfing: Racism, Media, and the Destruction of Today's Youth* (New York: St. Martin's Press, 1998), 33. Giroux sees schools as places where students should learn to critically evaluate television's messages as part of their developing into critical citizens. However, this is not currently the case, as Giroux writes that "In the new world order, citizenship has little to do with social responsibility and everything to do with creating consuming subjects. Such a constrained notion of citizenship finds a home in an equally narrow definition of education that abstracts equity from excellence and substitutes a hyperindividualism for a concerted respect for the collective good" (15).

[57] Roy Fox, *Harvesting Minds: How TV Commercials Control Kids*, 195.

most schools do little to counter the consumerism embedded in American culture. As Joel Spring argues, schools are "training grounds for consumer-citizens."[58] Schools have become partners in the promotion of everything from fashion trends, to fast food, and new media technologies. Until schools become contested arenas where television's role in the promotion of consumerism can be critiqued and debated, they will continue to promote the corporate-sponsored culture of consumerism among youth in this country.

Bibliography

American Academy of Pediatrics, "Television and the Family" fact sheet. The fact sheet can be found at www.aap.org/family/tv1.htm.

Boorstin, Daniel. 1961/1992. *The Image: A Guide to Pseudo-Events in America.* New York: Vintage.

Boyles, Deron. 2005. "Uncovering the Coverings: The Use of Corporate-Sponsored Textbook Covers in Furthering Uncritical Consumerism," *Educational Studies,* Spring, pp. 255-266.

Crane, Valerie and Milton Chen. 2003. "Content Development of Children's Media," in Edward L. Palmer and Brian M. Young (Eds.), *The Faces of Televisual Media: Teaching, Violence, Selling to Children.* Mahwah, NJ: Lawrence Erlbaum Associates, pp. 55-81.

DeVaney, Ann. 1994. *Watching Channel One: The Convergence of Students, Technology & Private Business.* Albany, NY: State University of New York Press.

Downey, Kevin. 2005. "The Messenger Changes Tactics," *Broadcasting & Cable,* November.

Fox, Roy. 2000. *Harvesting Minds: How TV Commercials Control Kids.* Westport, CT: Praeger.

Gerbner, George. 1998. "Cultivation Analysis: An Overview," *Mass Communication & Society* 1 (Spring), pp. 175-194.

Giroux, Henry. 2001. *The Mouse that Roared: Disney and the End of Innocence.* Lanham, MD: Rowman & Littlefield.

Giroux, Henry. 1998. *Channel Surfing: Racism, Media, and the Destruction of Today's Youth.* New York: St. Martin's Press.

Halonen, Doug. 2005. "Kids Regs Draw Big 3 Fire," *Television Week,* Fall.

Johnson, Melissa D., and Brian M. Young. 2003. "Advertising History of Televisual Media," in Edward L. Palmer and Brian M. Young (Eds.), *The Faces of Televisual Media: Teaching, Violence, Selling to Children.* Mahwah, NJ: Lawrence Erlbaum Associates, pp. 265-285.

Kaiser Family Foundation Report. 2005. "Generation M: Media in the Lives of 8-18 Year Olds," March. The report can be accessed at http://www.kff.org/entmedia/upload/Executive-Summary-Generation-M-Media-in-the-Lives-of-8-18-Year-olds.pdf.

Kellner, Douglas. 1990. *Television and the Crisis of Democracy.* Boulder, CO: Westview.

Kelly, Katy and Linda Kulman. 2004. "Kid Power," *U.S. News & World Report,* October 12, pp. 46-52.

Klein, Naomi. 2000. *No Logo.* New York: Picador.

Klein, Naomi. 2000. "The Tyranny of the Brands," *New Statesman* 13, January, pp. 25-28.

---

[58] Spring, *Educating the Consumer-Citizen,* 2003, 208.

Kunkel, Dale and Mary McIlrath. 2003. "Message Content in Advertising to Children," in Edward L. Palmer and Brian M. Young (Eds.), *The Faces of Televisual Media: Teaching, Violence, Selling to Children.* Mahwah, NJ: Lawrence Erlbaum Associates, 287-300.

McNeal, James U. 1992. *Kids as Customer: A Handbook for Marketing to Children.* New York: Lexington.

MFM Group. "Connecting with Youth: Fresh Approaches to Youth Marketing." Conference information can be found at www.trademeetings.com/ssmeeting/Details.asp

Molnar, Alex. 1996. *Giving Kids the Business: The Commercialization of America's Schools.* Boulder, CO: Westview.

Moses, Elissa. 2000. *The $100 Billion Allowance: Accessing the Global Teen Market.* New York: John Wiley & Sons.

Palmer, Edward L. 1987. *Children in the Cradle of Television.* Lexington, MA: Lexington Books.

Postman, Neil. 1994. *The Disappearance of Childhood.* New York: Vintage.

Schor, Juliet B. 2004. *Born to Buy: The Commercialized Child and the New Consumer Culture.* New York: Scribner.

Smith, Stacy L. and Charles Atkins, 2003. "Television Advertising and Children: Examining the Intended and Unintended Effects," in Edward L. Palmer and Brian M. Young (Eds.), *The Faces of Televisual Media: Teaching, Violence, Selling to Children.* Mahwah, NJ: Lawrence Erlbaum Associates, 305-325.

Spring, Joel. 2003. *Educating the Consumer-Citizen.* Mahwah, NJ: Erlbaum Associates.

Stack, Sam. 1999. "Reclaiming Our Children: The Aesthetic as Transforming and Emancipating," *Journal of Philosophy and History of Education* (Spring), *49*, 1-11.

Strasburger, Victor. 1995. *Adolescents and the Media: Medical and Psychological Impact.* Thousand Oaks, CA: Sage.

Wallenstein, Andrew. 2006. "TV Viewership Hits Record High," *Reuters*, September 22.

Wasserman, Todd. 2004. "Curbing Their Appetite," *Brandweek*, 45, pp. 24-28.

Whitney, Daisy. 2003. "Defining Distinct Niches: Building the Brand Is the Name of the Game in Kids' TV," *Television Week*, March 10.

CHAPTER FOUR

The Automobile Industry's Influence on Adolescents' Choice of Transportation
How Marketing Techniques Are Used to Cultivate Consumers of Automobiles

Permeil Dass, Georgia State University

Introduction

At most high schools, you will find a parking lot filled with cars. Some of the cars are obviously old and in need of repair, but you will also see brand new cars, even high-end luxury models. At first you might assume these cars belong to the faculty and administrators, but they do not. They belong to students. The number of students who have their own cars has doubled in the last 20 years to just under 50 percent.[1] Some students are driving more expensive cars than their teachers. Since most 16-17-year-olds generally cannot buy themselves a $25,000 car, from where do they come? What is the motivating factor behind adolescents' urge to own and use a car? What role do schools have in maintaining adolescents' infatuation with cars? How does the automobile industry use marketing techniques to perpetuate adolescents' consumption and use of cars? This chapter investigates consumerism, marketing strategies, the historical context of the automobile, school culture, curriculum, and the activities of the automobile industry, both in and out of schools.

---

[1] John Higgins, "Carmakers See Teenage Market as Lucrative Arena," *Akron Beacon Journal* (2 February 2003).

Background

Consumerism, defined as the accumulation and use of products regardless of their necessity, has a long history in the United States.[2] As information technology has advanced, marketers have had greater influence on society. Newspapers were among the first distributors of information, influencing people across the nation by providing readers with uniform stories. For the first time, readers came across the same articles and saw the same ads. This universal exposure resulted in the foundation of our mass consumer culture.[3] The significance of large numbers of people being exposed to the same information is extremely powerful as people's values, interpretations of information, and reactions to events became homogenized.[4] Consumer behavior is in part motivated by the social environment that influences a buyer's purchasing decision.[5] Exposure to common experiences provided in the media generates a society where the social environment becomes increasingly similar.[6]

Once a mass consumer culture has been established, marketers can evoke a desired action,[7] specifically, the purchasing of their product. "Advertising is a symbolic artifact constructed from the conventions of a particular culture. The sender crafts the message in anticipation of the audience's probable response, using shared knowledge of various conventions. Receivers of the message use the same body of cultural knowledge to read the message, infer the sender's intention, evaluate the argument, and formulate a response. Cultural knowledge provides the basis for interaction."[8] The end goal of marketers is to capitalize on commonalities and patterns of a group by creating an advertisement that evokes purchasing a product based on consumers' standardized values and experiences, even if the consumption of a product is completely irrational. This form of power is well known to corporations, as evidenced by the massive

---

[2] Deron Boyles, *Schools or Markets? Commercialism, Privatization, and School-Business Partnerships* (Mahwah, NJ: Lawrence Erlbaum Associates, 2005), 61.

[3] Joel Spring, *Educating the Consumer-Citizen* (Mahwah, NJ: Lawrence Erlbaum Associates, Inc., 2003), 18.

[4] Ibid., 140; Marieke de Mooij, *Consumer Behavior and Culture: Consequences for Global Marketing and Advertising* (London: Sage Publications, Inc., 2004), 225.

[5] Mooij, 138.

[6] Spring, 152; Mooij, 57.

[7] Susan Linn, *Consuming Kids* (New York: The New Press, 2004), 51.

[8] Mooij, 211.

amounts of money spent on advertising.[9] Any available medium for advertising that is projected to large numbers of people is fiercely sought after. Prime time television is, therefore, prime time for commercials. Since marketers have studied and researched consumers' values and what their reactions will be to their advertisements, it is only a matter of how often they can expose consumers to their logos, products, and messages in order for more products to be consumed brashly.

Creating Frames through Marketing

People in the United States are not a homogeneous group; we have a large variety of cultures and subcultures within our society. In order for marketers to encourage the consumption of their products, they must customize ads to a specific target group in order to make the product appealing and desirable. It seems advertisements actually serve two purposes: (1) stimulating the desire in a targeted market to purchase a product, and (2) attempting to homogenize the public in order for marketers to more effectively and easily target and manipulate potential customers. These ideas are best explained by applying George Lakoff's ideas on framing to the field of marketing.[10] Lakoff states that people think in frames, which are socially constructed subconscious ideas or a collection of ideas in our brain that predetermines how we view the world.[11] Frames can be evoked when keywords or images are used. People from similar backgrounds tend to have comparable frames. Marketers capitalize on a group's framing structure by using specific language and images to induce a desired emotion or thought that is associated with that frame.[12]

From a marketer's perspective, the more frames there are in the population, the harder it is to find common images and words that are linked to a desired frame. In this case, advertisements are only effective for a limited number of people. It is therefore advantageous for corporations to attempt to create or at least influence the frames of people in the general public. One method used to force items into consumers' frames is through word choice. For example, the Patriot Act sounds like something positive, but one could argue that it has negatively affected basic civil rights. Using the bill's name

---

[9] Robin Andersen and Lance Strate, eds., *Critical Studies in Media Commercialism* (New York: Oxford University Press, 2000), 28.

[10] George Lakoff, *Don't Think of an Elephant: Know Your Values and Frame the Debate* (White River Junction, VT: Chelsea Green, 2004), xv.

[11] Ibid.

[12] Ibid., 22.

along with other key words is effective in getting people to support something they really do not support, simply because of the symbols and associations those words represent—a tactic Lakoff refers to as "Orwellian Language."[13]

In addition to the basic concept of frames, Lakoff also mentions that repetition of an idea over many years can create a new frame.[14] The basis for this theory is tied to how our brains are wired and which neurons have created synapses with other neurons.[15] The critical question regarding marketing techniques and advertising is: How are adolescents and even young toddlers affected by ads? Research in neuroscience has found the brains of adolescents are more malleable than an adult's brain.[16] Marketers have also figured out that the brains of young children and adolescents are loosely wired or configured and are still in the process of being shaped. Advertisements can therefore greatly influence what frames are created in children. The American Psychological Association's Task Force on Advertising to Children warns that children under the age of eight do not have the ability to recognize they are being advertised to.[17] It is frightening to realize the impact that marketing has on a developing child's perception of the world around him, and what powerful influence corporations have in creating the foundation in which future experiences will be processed. According to Lakoff, any information that contradicts this frame later on in life is baffling and most often dismissed, even if the information is logical and makes sense. Once these frames are created they are not easily dismantled.[18]

Lakoff's frames might then better enable us to understand the emotional attachment we have to our cars; we love them. "Transportation" rarely means mass transit; it more often means "cars."[19] When and how did this automobile frame develop? How has consumption of cars affected our society? And even more concerning, how are cars positively framed by and for young people and perpetuated with each generation? This chapter addresses these issues by

---

[13] Ibid., 23.

[14] Ibid., 25.

[15] Ibid., 17.

[16] Cornelia Pechmann, et al., "Impulsive and Self-Conscious: Adolescents' Vulnerability to Advertising and Promotion," *Journal of Public Policy & Marketing* 24, no. 2 (2005): 202.

[17] Tiffany Meyers, "Marketing to Kids Comes Under Fresh Attack," *Advertising Age* 76, no. 8 (2005): 2.

[18] Lakoff, 17.

[19] Mary MacDonald, "Parents Urged to Embrace Big Yellow for Safety, Earth," *Atlanta Journal-Constitution.* August 13, 2006.

examining the influence of the automobile industry both in and out of the school environment.

How Our Love Affair Began

"I'm more of a Hybrid Civic type of a person than a BMW SUV type." It would not be strange to hear a statement like this on the streets today. When people describe themselves by a car brand and everyone knows what they mean, it is clear the marketing of cars has become so pervasive that we actually perceive cars to have personalities.[20] How did this happen, and has the United States always had a love affair with cars?

A film by Jim Klein and Martha Olson entitled *Taken for a Ride* answers the question "why does America have the worst public transit in the industrialized world, and the most freeways?"[21] In the early 1900s only 10 percent of the U.S. population owned an automobile; most used the vast streetcar system. During this time period, our public transportation system was one of the best in the world. The automobile industry began an aggressive campaign to make owning a car the norm. The president of General Motors (GM), using a subsidiary company, started to purchase streetcar systems around the nation. Streetcars were taken off the line, tracks were torn out, and service purposefully declined.[22] GM was aware of the amount of money it would take to reconstruct what they destroyed. After dismantling the streetcars, buses were used and intentionally underfunded so service would decline and riders would get increasingly frustrated, pushing them to invest in their own automobile. Only those who could afford this option chose it, leaving poorer riders with an inefficient system with infrequent service.[23] The buses from then on became associated with the poor and cars with the wealthy. GM repeated this same strategy in many cities, effectively ending the United States' quality public transportation system.[24]

With the end of World War II, an influx of young men with disposable incomes came back home, got married, left the city, and bought homes in the suburbs. The layout of suburbs created sprawl and were designed for automo-

---

[20] "Exclusive: Teens' Take on Brands," *Advertising Age* (Midwest edition) 76, no. 8 (2005): S4.

[21] New Day Films, *Taken for a Ride*, available at http://www.newday.com/films/ Taken_for_a_Ride.html (accessed August 6, 2006).

[22] *Taken for a Ride*. VHS. Directed by Jim Klein and Martha Olson (New Jersey: New Day Films and Independent Television Series, 1996).

[23] Ibid.

[24] Ibid.

bile use, leaving suburbanites with few options for transportation besides the car.[25] Unlike an urban setting, residential and business properties were physically separated, so people could no longer walk out of their homes to shop, work, and dine. Concurrently, the lobbyists representing road builders became a strong influence on Congress and interstates were being built right through the hearts of cities. Despite protests from local community groups, a national highway system was created.[26] With mass marketing that is still continued today, the automobile industry asked citizens to request additional government funds to make more roads and associated owning a car, particularly specific models, with wealth, popularity, and success.[27] Cars were framed as a status symbol and Americans reacted to advertisements the way the automobile industry wanted; they bought cars. Despite car accidents, pollution, and traffic jams, a love affair with the automobile began as advertisements reassured people that owning a car would make all their desires come true.[28] Currently automobiles are standard in middle-class and upper-class households. The emphasis on car ownership and driving is passed on to the next generation through various means, including schools. Driving and owning a car is encouraged via school culture, social context, and curriculum.

Back to School

In preparation for the first day of school, "back-to-school" advertisements flood the media and reinforce the idea that school is not just a place for learning. Massive amounts of money are spent by families in consuming products that have nothing to do with learning, in order to fulfill the misconception that material goods prepare children to be successful students. Specifically, back-to-school spending in 2003 totaled $14.1 billion, which is around $450 per family.[29] The office supply store Staples stated back-to-school sales attributed to a 47 percent increase in net income.[30] Only 16 percent of sales were related to school supplies, 65 percent were spent on clothes and shoes, and the

---

[25] Ibid.

[26] Ibid.

[27] Ibid.

[28] Frank S. Washington, "Aim Young; No, Younger," *Advertising Age* (Midwest edition) 72, no. 15 (2001): S16. Mooij, 112.

[29] Diane Brady and Wendy Zellner, "Back-to-School Is Getting High Marks," *Business Week* (1 September 2003).

[30] Ibid.

remaining 19 percent on electronics.[31] OfficeMax's website stated "new year, new you,"[32] and Target's website read, "head back to college in style."[33] Both encourage and equate consumerism with starting the school year. Advertisements have done a great job at associating purchasing materials with academic success. The underlying message sent to parents insinuates they must provide their child with new clothes and school supplies if they are good parents. Nurturance, care, consumption, materialism, and academic achievement have successfully been framed together by marketers.

The pressure to consume in preparation for the upcoming school year is not only encouraged by businesses but also by local governments. For example, in an election year the governor of Georgia, Sonny Perdue, gave every teacher in the state one hundred dollars and declared the weekend before school as "tax free" so families and teachers could prepare for school.[34] Although this gesture seems altruistic, the governor simply diverted the public's tax money into the hands of corporations, while perpetuating the idea that the beginning of school starts with material consumption.

Due to competition, corporations have to increase sales through many creative methods. Associating companies with trends is one example.[35] Office Depot, for instance, recently sponsored a school competition to win technology and classroom supplies. To win, schools had to have the most points, which are earned when customers give their school's identification number during checkout. The more expensive the purchase, the more credits are given to the school. To make the awards even more desirable, Office Depot teamed up with NASCAR to have a popular driver deliver gifts to the school.[36] Not only does this competition promote cars, but the company is presented to the public as a charitable corporation, despite the increase in profits the competi-

---

[31] Ibid.

[32] OfficeMax. available at http://www.officemax.com (accessed August 12, 2006).

[33] Target. available at http://www.target.com (accessed August 12, 2006).

[34] Perdue for a New Georgia, "State Tax-Free Holiday Set for August 3-6: School Teachers Able to Use $100 Gift Cards to Purchase Classroom Supplies," press release, July 10, 2006, available at http://www.votesonny.com/ (accessed September 23, 2006).

[35] Peter Zollo, *Getting Wiser to Teens: More Insight into Marketing to Teenagers* (New York: New Strategist Publications, Inc., 2004), 389.

[36] Auto Channel, "Office Depot Sends NASCAR Star Carl Edwards 'Back to School,'" July 13, 2006, available at http://www.theautochannel.com/news/2006/07/13/014671.html (accessed October 3, 2006).

tion provides the company.[37] Even more blatantly, General Motors in 1999 teamed up with a popular clothing brand for its marketing strategy called "Ride the Wave Back to School." This program was a sweepstakes competition, and the winners received a car decorated with the clothing brand's logo on the sides, back, and floor mats of the car.[38] In another example, a high school in Arizona promoted automobiles by having a back-to-school charity event around stylish "muscle cars." The event was a car parade so people could show off their cars in a festive atmosphere complete with music and food.[39]

Corporations' back-to-school sales are a significant amount of their annual revenue. Items such as paper, books, rulers, and pencils are a small part of the growing school supply list, as corporations are pushing families to now include items such as clothes, technology products, and even cars. For example, the school/automobile relationship is demonstrated by automobile companies that have coined the phrases "starter car," "college car," and "back-to-school car" that are now used in society. An article on an auto repair website stated: "Well, it's almost that time of year again. School will be open in about six weeks and there will be a lot of brand new drivers out there. With parents working and busy schedules, it's not really practical to let students drive the family car to school. If they are off to college they will need a car of their own. The obvious answer is to get another car."[40] Edmunds.com, a popular website to educate automobile buyers about car ratings and prices, states, "Whether it's college freshmen heading away from home for the first time or newly licensed drivers hoping to wow their friends this fall, one thing is certain: back-to-school just got a bit more enjoyable with the Top 10 Cars for Drivers Under 25."[41] Advertisements such as these have changed how schools are viewed from a place of learning to a place to show off your material goods, and for

---

[37] Alex Molnar, *School Commercialism: From Democratic Ideal to Market Commodity* (New York: Routledge, 2005), 36.

[38] Jeff Green, "Coveting Hang Ten's Teen Demo, Chevy Ties in for Tracker Sweeps," *Brandweek* 40, no. 28 (1999): 12.

[39] Mike Walbert, "Classic, Muscle Cars Heading Back to School," *The Arizona Republic* (February 4, 2005). available at http://www.azcentral.com/community/gilbert/articles/0204gr-mesquiteZ12.html (accessed September 3, 2006).

[40] Vincent T. Ciulla, "Buying a Back to School Car," *About.com* (2000). Available at http://autorepair.about.com/library/ weekly/aa072800a.htm (accessed October 4, 2006).

[41] Jeannine Fallon and Pam Krebs. "Laptop, Notebooks... Cool Car? Edmunds.com Makes Back-to-School Shopping More Fun with Top 10 Cars for Drivers Under 25," *Edmunds.com* (August 23, 2004). Available at http://www.edmunds.com/help/about/press/102903/article.html (accessed July 10, 2006).

some people back-to-school shopping now includes buying a car. Repetition of these ideas and values eventually will result in them becoming standard. "Back to school" has become an event that highlights one example of the intricate relationship between consumerism, automobiles, corporations, and schools. Due to pervasive advertising, many people would not notice these as strange bedfellows.

Grand Entrance

With so much attention given to the first day of school, students, especially in high school, take time to plan how they will arrive at school.[42] Seeing students come to school is a show to watch.[43] How students enter school and who they arrive with is a very important aspect of high-school culture. As promoted in ads, students use their material possessions along with their social clique to present themselves.[44] One of the most defining items is a student's car.[45] What type of car a student drives associates them with a specific social group.[46] A hybrid car places a student within an environmentally minded circle, a BMW with upper-class students, or a loud car that vibrates from excessive bass with students interested in Hip Hop. The brand and style of cars students drive associates them with a specific subculture within a school. Author Juliet Schor states that "Children's advertising equates consumption with coolness, unnecessarily linking children's identity to products. Marketers would do well to dispense with advertising that sells the 'social symbolic value of the product.'"[47] Many students will customize and alter their cars to represent their desired social clique. It is not uncommon to see cars decorated with large tires, expensive rims, spoilers, bumper stickers, paint, and most importantly an expensive sound system. Daniel Harris captures the energy behind teenagers and loud music:

> Breaking the domestic sound barrier with the ear-splitting din of car radios and boom boxes becomes a harmless way to shatter the bourgeois tranquility of bucolic neighborhoods, and is thus the ultimate anti-social assertion of the unfettered self. Panasonic even goes so far as to describe its stereo speakers as accessories in these seditious

---

[42] Erin Crawford, "When Lime Green Is Desirable," *Des Moines Business Record* 16, no. 39 (2000): 23.

[43] Higgins, "Carmakers See Teenage Market as Lucrative Arena."

[44] Zollo, 196.

[45] Spring, 56.

[46] Zollo, 138.

[47] Meyers, "Marketing to Kids Comes Under Fresh Attack."

acts of gratuitous pandemonium, next to the words "Blast it. Crank it. Blare it. Let everyone know you're there." Turning up the volume and blowing the roof off is an ersatz way of destroying property, of rattling windows without breaking them, a form of sonic vandalism that produces the effect of chaos and destruction but nevertheless leaves everything intact. Noise, like the affectation of nihilism, constitutes the perfect consumerist rebellion: an apolitical radicalism that reduces activism to acoustics and carefully preserves the world it so blusteringly sets out to destroy.[48]

Riding into school in a car packed with friends playing music that is so loud the car shakes is many students' dream. No matter how often this scene occurs, it is unusual to not have students and teachers stop and see who is making all the noise. It is clear that students in lavish cars at school attract attention.

A grand entrance for students who do not come to school in their own or their friend's car is different. Many students are dropped off by family and others take the school bus. For reasons noted above, the bus is the least desirable way for students to arrive at school. Even parents discourage children to ride buses, citing safety, extra time, and lack of amenities such as air conditioning as major concerns.[49] A student's social class becomes obvious if he or she has a car, especially one that is a popular model. Students who are dropped off by family members are also cognizant of what kind of car their family owns. The social divide is illuminated when students are given a car from their parents after turning 16. Seeing those students drive into school with a brand new car, a symbol of being from a wealthy family, is a daily reminder for other students of material possessions they currently do not have. Absence of such symbols of wealth is indirectly a symbol of being a low-income student.

The school curriculum promotes the use of cars as well. Many schools offer driver education classes that can be taken for school credit. Publishing companies such as Glencoe, McGraw Hill, and Prentice Hall sell textbooks for driver education courses for approximately $40 per student. Safety topics are promoted to help sell the textbook by covering items such as drinking and driving and how to be a safe, responsible driver.[50] General Learning, a publisher for General Motors, created a magazine that was given to high-school students in their driving class. Also, the company built goodwill with parents

---

[48] Daniel Harris, "Coolness," *American Scholar* 68, no. 4 (1999): 39.

[49] MacDonald, op. cit.

[50] Florida Department of Education, "Instructional Materials and Library Media," available at http://www.firn.edu/doe/instmat/pdf/drive9.pdf (accessed October 19, 2006).

with its parent-teen partnership program called Partners in Safety used in driv-ing courses.[51] Getting a driver's license becomes standardized and accepted as the norm when schools take the time and money to accommodate teenage driving.

Added pressure at school to drive comes from hearing students sharing stories of their driving instructor and driving experiences. At school, students jingle their car keys to make it known to others that they drive as they talk about where they will be driving to and who is coming with them. Students without a license or car are not able to share in these experiences and most likely feel left out. Riding the school bus or having your parents drop you off becomes an embarrassing sore spot and leaves the student feeling like a child rather than an independent young adult. It is currently unknown how many teenagers have a real need to drive since being able to drive is just as or more important than actually reaching a specific destination.[52] Teenagers under the age of 16 who are not able to drive still have travel needs but use other modes of transportation. As these teenagers turn 16 and driving a car is allowed, most students will cease using alternative modes and become increasingly depend-ent on cars.[53]

In this country, turning 16 and getting a driver's license is treated as a rite of passage into adulthood.[54] A "Sweet Sixteen" birthday party celebrates this milestone and also marks the age a teenager can start to drive. The enjoyment of activities without parental involvement that comes with the driver's license is thrilling for students since they can begin to create their own schedule and plan their own activities, asserting their newly found independence. Students see many social advantages to having a license and car. In fact, 25 to 30 per-cent of teenagers stated "driving around" as the most frequent activity they do with friends,[55] meaning their group socializes around driving aimlessly around town. This activity is enjoyed so much that 17 percent of teenagers listed driv-ing as the best privilege of being an adolescent.[56] Moreover, the number one event for teens between the ages of 12 and 15 were excited about was getting

---

[51] Zollo, 29.

[52] Leo Tasca, "Mobility Needs of Novice Drivers," *Transportation Research Circular* E-C024, Janu-ary (2001): 6.

[53] K. J. Clifton, "Independent Mobility among Teenagers," *Transportation Research Record*, 1854 (2003): 74.

[54] Tasca, "Mobility Needs of Novice Drivers."

[55] Zollo, 237.

[56] Ibid., 71.

their driver's license.[57] All of the new experiences that a driver's license and car provide to a teenager are very exciting. Those students who do not get a driver's license or a car are held back from this transition into adulthood. High schools become the backdrop where enthusiasm and the desire for cars run high.

Power of the Adolescent Market

Corporations are well aware of the buying power that adolescents have. Even pre-adolescents are collectively spending $10 billion a year,[58] while adolescents are spending $94 billion a year[59] and influencing family purchases that top $600 billion annually.[60] Pre-adolescents are spending more every year, since the family unit, which increasingly consists of single parents, requires them to do more of their own and the family's shopping and cooking. Young people, out of necessity, have to be more independent and make buying decisions on their own.[61] As large as spending is for pre-adolescents, it is shocking to realize that adolescents, in comparison, are spending a tremendous amount more.[62] The total buying power of people aged 5 to 20 has not been overlooked by corporations.

Currently 9,000 driver's licenses are issued every day in the U.S.,[63] and over the next decade, 65 million people will be of driving age.[64] The number of new and used cars sold to people under 20 years old has increased to over half a million cars per year. Motivated by large numbers of cars being sold, corporations are working hard to ensure they get their share of this market, by working with consultants who specialize in marketing to adolescents, pre-adolescents, and even toddlers.[65] Focusing advertising on future consumers earlier and earlier in life leaves an imprint of the corporation's brand on the child. An employee of a consultant group that targets to young people ex-

---

[57] Ibid., 74.

[58] George R. Kaplan, "Profits R Us," *Phi Delta Kappan* 78, no. 3 (1996): K1.

[59] Murray Milner, *Freaks, Geeks, and Cool Kids: American Teenagers, Schools, and the Culture of Consumption* (New York: Routledge, 2004), 158.

[60] Linn, 1.

[61] Ken Gronbach, "Generation Y ~ Not Just 'Kids'," *Direct Marketing* 63, no. 4 (2000): 36.

[62] Kaplan, "Profits R Us."

[63] Rafael Lemaitre, Rosanna Maietta, and Fleishman-Hillard, "Driving High: Teens Cite Cars As a Top Place To Use Marijuana," *Office of National Drug Control Policy*, November 28, 2005, available at http://www.ondcp.gov/news/press05/112805.html (accessed June 28, 2006).

[64] Drew Winter, "Think Outside the Box," *Ward's Auto World* 40, no. 12 (2004): 5.

[65] Kaplan, "Profits R Us."

plains, "It's early branding. You are branding your product at a relevant time to the person. You're establishing that brand presence and positive associa-tion, since important buying decisions are forthcoming. But the key to reach-ing younger consumers is to capture them before they have any opinions on brands."[66] Babies, even before they start to walk, are looked at by corporations in terms of revenue, profits, and customer loyalty. An example of advertising to babies is Jeep's strollers and rockers that have their logo and names of their car models for babies to focus on. These new items are called: Baby's First Jeep Rocker, Jeep Cherokee Stroller, Jeep Wagoneer Tandem Double Stroller, and Jeep Liberty Urban Terrain 3-Wheel Stroller. The result of such tactics is the ability of five year olds to identify car brands[67] and six year olds who can name cars.[68] Former president of Kids-R-Us, Mike Searles, adds, "If you own this child at any early age, you can own this child for years to come. Companies are saying, 'Hey, I want to own this kid younger and younger.'"[69]

Young kids are not the only ones being courted by car companies; luxury car makers tap into the teen and young adult market by providing cars that are affordable in order to provide them an experience with their brand in hopes those consumers will purchase pricier cars later on in life. Competition be-tween automakers to attract the largest number of future customers has re-sulted in new marketing strategies that focus on younger and younger people. Both BMW and Mercedes-Benz have created cars that are priced between $16,000 and $20,000. Now young adults can possess a car that associates them with wealth without having to be wealthy.[70]

Advertising to the young requires a major shift in marketing tactics. Nao-mi Klein, a critic of marketing, describes how companies have shifted from producing goods to producing "ideas and images for their brand."[71] She states that a logo and brand name used to be a symbol of quality for a product, but now the product is the logo and brand name. Brands are strategically associ-ated with ideas, images, attitudes, and lifestyles that are fashionable and desir-

---

[66] Julie Bosman, "Hey, Kid, You Want to Buy a Toyota Scion?" *New York Times (Late Edition East Coast)* (14 June 2006): C2.

[67] Higgins, "Carmakers See Teenage Market as Lucrative Arena."

[68] Jean Halliday, "Automakers Agree, Winning Youth Early Key to Future," *Advertising Age* 73, no. 13 (2002): S16.

[69] Kaplan, "Profits R Us."

[70] Higgins, "Carmakers See Teenage Market as Lucrative Arena."

[71] Naomi Klein, "The Tyranny of the Brands," *New Statesman* 13, no. 589 (2000): 25.

able.[72] The more frequently ads are shown, the stronger the association between a brand and idea becomes. Any available space to display ads and logos
is highly sought after. We now see ads online; before movies; while pumping
gasoline; in buses, trains, bathrooms, sidewalks, and airplanes; and, most concerning, in public schools. Schools are considered great places to advertise,
since consumers are already separated based on age and in some cases by race
and social class, allowing companies to easily cater their ads to a specific population.[73] "School systems remain multibillion dollar markets for a huge as-
sortment of goods and services."[74] Corporations are using football fields,
school buses, book covers, donated materials, walls inside and outside of
schools, and now even inside of textbooks to advertise to an important future
market.[75] The earlier in life a corporation can advertise to students in schools,
the more likely they can create consumers that are loyal to their brand.[76]

Characteristics of Today's Adolescents

To maximize the effectiveness of advertisements, corporations must know
what values and lifestyles are fashionable and desirable within a subgroup.
Corporations have certainly done their homework when it comes to understanding how to excite and capture the interest of the adolescent and pre-
adolescent market. This subgroup has become so lucrative that new businesses
have been created to help corporations market to young people and capitalize
on their interests. "The explosion of marketing aimed at kids today is precisely
targeted, refined by scientific method, and honed by child psychologists—in
short, it is more pervasive and intrusive than ever before."[77]

Items that are important to teenagers seem to be fashion, sports, entertainment, phones, and cars. Advice given to advertisers states, "How can marketers use the information about teens' top activities to reach this on-the-go
audience? Consider these facts: in a given week, teens spend more than one
full day using traditional media (Internet, radio, TV, magazines, and newspapers). They spend another 32 hours per week participating in activities that
expose them to other marketing messages—whether at concerts, sports events,
fast-food restaurants, or simply driving around. So the opportunities to (ap-

---

[72] Ibid.

[73] Molnar, 6.

[74] Kaplan, "Profits R Us."

[75] Molnar, 22.

[76] Ibid., 55.

[77] Linn, 5.

propriately) pervade teens' lives with your messages are abundant, and the payoff is rich—the change is to become part of their lifestyle."[78] By focusing on the teenage lifestyle and values, a youth marketing strategist explains how advertising has experienced "a shift in mind-set to where we're trying to make a connection from a lifestyle perspective rather than just traditional product benefits in our advertising."[79] The product is less important than the brand with which it is associated. For luxury car makers, marketers realize advertisements may not get 16-20-year-olds to buy their cars. However, repeated exposure of the brand will have an impact on their future purchases.[80]

Marketing research has found that adolescents have special characteristics and like specific features in their products. Teens like to customize their products so they can fulfill their desire to be unique.[81] Possessions and their brand names are one way for teens to express their desired lifestyle and image.[82] Teenagers like to be seen in large groups in order to feel popular and confident. Advertisements for large cars like SUVs emphasize its large carrying capacity. Teenagers also care about the value of a product and seek out getting a good deal. Fair prices and quality products are recognized by teens.[83] They cling to items that are personalized or include them in a group, like club cards that reward them for shopping. Gifts, samples, and free items are also appreciated by this population.[84] It is not surprising to learn that adolescents are more self-conscious and impulsive than adults when it comes to shopping.[85] Products also have to be linked with technology. Based on these research findings, marketers have adjusted their advertisements to match adolescents' unique characteristics. The more information that is gathered on adolescents and their preferences, the easier it is for corporations to market their products to match their interests and to find a way to fit into their lifestyle.

---

[78] Zollo, 268.

[79] Washington, "Aim Young; No, Younger," S16.

[80] Barrie Gunter and Adrian Furnham, Children as Consumers: A Psychological Analysis of the Young People's Market (New York: Routledge, 1998), 144.

[81] "Exclusive: Teens' Take on Brands."

[82] Ibid.

[83] Zollo, 403.

[84] Gronbach, "Generation Y—Not Just 'Kids.'"

[85] Pechmann et al., "Impulsive and Self-Conscious."

Green Cars

Research has found that adolescents want to patronize companies and products that match their own values and concerns.[86] The automobile industry has capitalized on values and issues that are important to adolescents, like the environment. Portraying a company as environmentally friendly is a tactic that many automobile industries use to draw attention of adolescents to their products. Corporations are very aware that green is fashionable. A *Newsweek* cover read, "The New Greening of America: From Politics to Lifestyle, Why Saving the Environment Is Suddenly Hot."[87] Products that are environmentally friendly are estimated to generate $200 billion a year. A large number of consumers are prepared to choose eco-products over regular products even if a higher cost is involved. This new consumer group is referred to amongst marketers as LOHAS (Lifestyles of Health and Sustainability).[88] A survey of 2,000 adults by Cone/Roper revealed 78 percent are willing to purchase a product that is affiliated with a cause they support, 66 percent are willing to change products or where they shop if the change is aligned with a particular cause, and 55 percent are willing to spend more on products that relate to issues they care about.[89] As one marketer pointed out, "Emotional factors play a role in purchase decisions. If you get into a cause that's meaningful to your customers, you tap into that emotional well."[90] No single answer explains the burst of interest in the environment. Some have speculated interest was stimulated by the media's focus on global warming, recent natural disasters such as Hurricane Katrina, a rise in fuel prices, Al Gore's environmental movie *The Inconvenient Truth*, or the visible change in weather patterns.[91] Although it is not noted in current research findings, there is the possibility of adolescents' influence on family spending as a source for this profitable concern for the environment.

---

[86] Zollo, 142.

[87] Jerry Adler, "Going Green," *Newsweek* 148, no. 2 (2006): Cover.

[88] Ibid., 48.

[89] Paul T. Carring, "Not Just a Worthy Cause: Cause-Related Marketing Delivers the Goods and the Good," *Public Service Advertising Research Center*, available at http://www.psaresearch.com/bib4306.html (accessed September 23, 2006).

[90] Nancy Arnott, "Marketing with a Passion," *Sales and Marketing Management*, 146, no. 1 (1994): 64.

[91] Moises Velasquez-Manoff, "A Grass-Roots Push for a 'Low Carbon Diet'," *Christian Science Monitor* (28 December 2006).

Whatever the motivation behind this new market, car makers are redesigning their image, particularly for adolescents, with an eco-friendly message in hopes of catching this new wave. GM's website that focuses on children, education, and the environment asks, "Why GM Developed This Site?" The response is, "For many years, GM has supported a strong and diverse base of education programs for children in grades kindergarten through 12. These programs include hands-on experimental environmental education activities, mentoring programs by GM engineers and scientists, technology curriculum dissemination to schools, and a website created to educate children and their parents about environment, energy, and technology issues."[92] Contrary to this response, the content of what is actually on the website indicates other motivations. For example, their homepage has five options to click on: Games, Energy, Cars & Trucks, Our Earth, and Parents. One of these five options does not fit, the Cars & Trucks. After selecting this option the only activity is for the user to flip through images of GM's cars. Under the "Energy" section a brief description of ethanol is provided. From there you can choose a game. One game begins, "Did you know that as much as 80% of GM vehicles are recyclable? An additional 5% is recoverable, which means that the material can be burned for energy. See how much of the Silverado you can recycle."[93] Once you click to begin the game, you are placed in a recycling center with a big blue Silverado inside. The object of the game is to click and drag parts of the truck into the recycling bin and identify its material. The "Our Earth" section allows you to read about how GM and the Nature Conservancy are bringing back the rainforest. It states that GM and other groups are working to rejuvenate five square miles of the rainforest. Overall, the educational value of this site is questionable, since there is minimal information regarding the rainforest or the species that reside within this habitat. The website does allow children and their parents to see a link between GM and the environment while at the same time familiarizing them with GM and its products.

For young adults and adults, GM also has a website geared towards their age group called "Innovation and Technology." One product that is mentioned is "Ecotec engine." According to its name it would seem like the engine is a new technology that helps the environment. Yet the description does not

---

[92] Lori Wingerter, "Why GM Developed This Site," *General Motors GMability*, available at http://www.gm.com/company/gmability/edu_k-12/k-4/parents/index.html (accessed September 5, 2006).

[93] General Motors, "Games," *GM GMability*, available at http://www.gm.com/company/ gmability/edu_k-12/ 5-8/games/index.html (accessed September 5, 2006).

mention anything about the environment.[94] This is a good example of the power of word choice, as described by Lakoff, to call to mind caring for the earth and ecology. Furthermore, GM is promoting ethanol fuel through its "Live Green, Go Yellow" campaign. Ethanol, made from corn, helps fuel vehicles without using as much oil, and ethanol burns cleaner than regular fuel so it pollutes the air less. Despite what is known about GM dismantling our transit system, which resulted in our dependence on automobiles and fossil fuels, the site states, "It's [referring to ethanol capable vehicles] just the beginning of our commitment to help end our dependence on fossil fuels."[95] This statement contradicts GM's past efforts.

GM is not the only car company using environmental concerns to increase sales of their products. Looking through car companies' websites, none of the major car companies omitted stating the company's environmental values in descriptions of themselves. A great example of re-branding a company's image to match environmental concerns is BP (British Petroleum). The company has dropped the name "British Petroleum" from most of its recent ads and uses just the acronym BP. To present itself as a company that is interested in alternatives to fossil fuels, it reinvented its acronym to stand for "Beyond Petroleum." A new logo was created to match this new name and includes an image of the sun and leaves. To further disconnect from fossil fuels, BP focuses ads on eco-products like solar panels, despite the fact that nearly all of their revenue is generated from oil sales.[96] Marketers have a talent of reinventing a company and disassociating from the reality of its past in order to reach new consumers.

Safety Is Key

One of the easiest ways for the automobile industry to tap into the adolescent market is to offer schools and parents information on driving safety. Both car and car insurance companies easily get the attention of parents and school administrators when the safety of their children and students is mentioned. Automobile insurance companies benefit twofold from providing safety programs for young drivers. First, the audience in these programs is the com-

---

[94] General Motors, "Ecotec engines," available at http://www.gm.com/automotive/ gmpowertrain/engines/ ecotec/index.htm (accessed September 5, 2006).

[95] General Motors, "Only GM," available at http://www.gm.com/company/ onlygm/energy/index.html (accessed October 14, 2006).

[96] Frank Ahrens, "Oil Doesn't Want Focus on Big Profit: Companies Stepping Up Advertising," *Washington Post*, 26 October 2005: D01.

pany's target. Plus the more safety information drivers receive, the fewer accidents and claims they will have, allowing the company to increase profits.[97] Small discounts are given as incentives to teenagers who complete a safe driving program. Savings are also provided to students who maintain good grades, have few school absences, or do community service. Students who meet these criteria tend to be more responsible, leading the insurance companies to think they are less likely to get into accidents. Companies appear to be encouraging students to maintain good habits when really they are attracting less costly customers.[98] High schools, where companies can cater materials specifically for teenagers, are given free driver education programs, magazines, discount promotions, and videos that promote safe driving to benefit their auto insurance company.

Allstate Insurance Company has a nonprofit foundation that sponsors forums for teenagers to learn about driving safety skills from other teenagers. Those involved in severe accidents are given the opportunity to share their stories and what they learned from their tragic experiences with their peers.[99] As a sponsor, the merits of these forums become Allstate's merits as well. A positive brand image of Allstate is created by association. Since the website helps teenagers, then Allstate as a brand is coupled with the supportive and caring atmosphere its website has produced. Participants will most likely be advertised to directly if they complete a form to sign up and share their stories. The form requires an address, home phone number, e-mail, date of birth, and gender. It is optional to fill out your cell phone number, school name, grade, and what type of license you have, if any. You can also e-mail your friends about the site directly from the page.[100]

Ford and the Governors Highway Safety Association have a website called "Driving Skills for Life" [101] that helps new drivers learn how to be a safer driver. The opening page is filled with music, animations, and of course a sporty-

---

[97] Lynna Goch, "Gearing Up," *Best's Review* 104, no. 6 (2003): 23.

[98] InsureMe, "Teen Car Insurance," *InsureMe.com*, available at http://www.insureme.com/ content/rsrc/auto/ teen-car-insurance (accessed October 1, 2006).

[99] Peter Valdes-Dapena, "Teen Drivers: Keeping Your Kid Alive," *CNNMoney.com*. November 18, 2005, available at http://money.cnn.com/2005/11/16/Autos/tipsandadvice/ teen_drivers/index.htm (accessed July 7, 2006).

[100] Keep the Drive. "Teen-Led Movement Promoting Smart Teen Driving," *KeeptheDrive.com*, available at http://www.keepthedrive.com (accessed November 3, 2006).

[101] Ford, "Driving Skills for Life," available at http://www.drivingskillsforlife.com/ (accessed October 14, 2006).

looking car that even has video screens in the back seats. Users are asked to register so they can start earning points towards computers, Ipods, and gift certificates. Other ways to earn points are as follows:

Activity	Points
Register with Driving Skills for Life	100 points
Finish an eLearning lesson	50
Score 8 out of 10 or better on eLearning Quiz	500
Play the Concentration Game	25
Play the Driving Game	25
Login In—Once per day	1
Refer-a-Friend to Driving Skills for Life	5 points per referral
Complete the Eco Driving Module	50

Only by providing an e-mail address do you learn about more ways to earn points and when winners are announced. The learning module opens up a 25-minute, MTV-looking screen with four safety lessons and a quiz to choose from. Another link goes to two games that also help you earn points. Other options are links for educators and parents. A lesson plan is provided under the educators section and a coaching guide is found on the parents' page.[102] The lesson plan is not a lesson plan at all but a set of questions and a quiz associated with each online learning module. The overall educational quality of this website is minimal. The information is inundated with games, entertainment, and gimmicks, and the registration process is intended to gather marketing information on teenagers. Once an e-mail address is provided, the company can start a database for specific subgroups and can advertise to them electronically.

While some car insurance companies are targeting teenagers themselves, other companies are taking a different angle that focuses on parents of teenagers and their concern for their children's safety. Obtaining parents as customers increases overall sales since teenagers tend to stay with the same insurance company as their parents.[103] To attract families, State Farm offers teenagers a discount only if they complete a safety program and if every car in the family is

---

[102] Ibid.

[103] Goch, 22.

insured with them.[104] Liberty Mutual works with SADD (Students Against Destructive Decisions, formerly known as Students Against Drunk Driving) to make themselves easily available to teenagers and their concerned parents. A video on dangerous driving behaviors advises parents on how to communicate with their teenagers about drinking and driving. Although it may seem strange that parents are listening to the advice of an automobile insurance company on improving parenting skills, Liberty Mutual's association with SADD's positive reputation arguably gives them more credibility as a family-oriented and concerned corporation. When it comes to children's safety, parents will probably stop and listen without scrutinizing the source of the information since the seriousness of the issue overshadows its details.

Volvo's "Drive for Life" program is another example of how showing concern about safety can be a means to advertise. Volvo has teamed up with LEGO to attract children aged three or more to drive a pretend Volvo car made out of oversized Legos. During the ride, children learn the importance of using seat belts and obeying traffic rules. Volvo decided to become the official car of LEGOLAND, a theme park in California, as a way to promote safe driving. According to Volvo's CEO, "It's a logical addition to our 'Drive for Life' initiative that focuses on affecting driver behavior and safety. In working with LEGOLAND, it's never too early to learn about the rules of the road."[105] This is a classic example of promoting a brand name by using parents' concern for the safety of their children.

Still another example is demonstrated by the combination of popular children's television shows and safety, uniquely coupled together by Ford. In 2001, the Ford Company teamed up with Nickelodeon's magazine to create ads with a safety focus, while at the same time encouraging readers to visit their we site. *Blue's Clues*, which is a favorite television show among elementary school children, offered parents the opportunity to have their children fingerprinted at Ford dealerships. Ford's creative marketing was effective, as indicated by the 500,000 children who were fingerprinted.[106] The main objective of bringing parents into a Ford dealership is for parents to have an opportunity to view their cars and associating Ford as a company that is concerned about safety.

---

[104] Ibid., 23.

[105] Jack Nerad, "Cars for Kids," *Drivers.com* (April 7, 2004). Available at http://www.drivers.com/article/674 (accessed June 15, 2006).

[106] Halliday, "Automakers Agree, Winning Youth Early Key to Future," *Advertising Age*, 2002, Online from Proquest ID: 112710613.

Emotional appeal is a reliable way for automobile companies to attract customers. Advertisements in general have an emotional base that captures viewers' interests, but fear is one of the more striking emotions.[107] Considering the leading cause of death of adolescents, as well as those between the ages of 4 and 34, is car accidents, parents' concerns and fears regarding their teenager driving is warranted. In 2003, there were 7,570 deaths of people aged 8-20 years old caused by car accidents.[108] This emotional factor is what makes advertising to parents of teenagers easy, as the automobile industry poses itself as concerned for the safety of young drivers.

Technology

One of the main characteristics that separate current adolescents and pre-adolescents from other consumer groups is use of the Internet. Online shopping, entertainment, and information resources, primarily used by young people, have reshaped marketing strategies aimed at teenagers. The World Wide Web is a new platform that requires companies to be innovative and creative in order to capture financially strong, emerging young consumers.

Progressive Insurance Company has been particularly aggressive when it comes to piquing the interest of teenagers. They have a teen-only website that offers a slew of different information and activities: games titled "The Lame Date Escape," where you ditch your date and dash for the exit in three different levels; a forum to write and share personal stories such as relationship problems; free downloads of Instant Message icons and wallpaper; a driving quiz; word scrambles; safety tips; dealing with a flat tire and accidents; use of cell phones; and Insurance 101 discusses how to get an insurance quote and whether it is advantageous to share a policy with parents, why rates are high for teenagers, and myths about insurance policies.[109] The goal of the site is to speak to teenagers in their environment and focus on issues that are interesting to them, such as fashion, music, dating, and technology, while attempting

---

[107] Jeremy Cato, "Fear Is a Powerful Motivator," *Special Globe Auto*, October 19, 2006, available at http://www.globeauto.com/servlet/story/RTGAM.20061018.wh-safety-main19/BNStory/ (accessed April 18, 2007).

[108] Rajesh Subramanian, "Top 10 Leading Causes of Death in the U.S. for 2003, by Age Group," *National Highway Traffic Safety Administration's National Center for Statistics and Analysis*, March 2006, available at http://www-nrd.nhtsa.dot.gov/pdf/nrd-30/NCSA/RNotes/2006/810568.pdf (accessed April 6, 2007).

[109] Progressive Casualty Insurance Company, "Progressive Teens Site," *Progressive*, available at http://www.progressive.com/teens/ home.aspx (accessed October 10, 2006).

to establish their company as friendly and easy to do business with. Making decisions on auto insurance may seem daunting the first time a teenager is confronted with a policy, so making young customers feel at ease in a familiar environment is important in developing a business relationship.[110]

One of the more successful uses of the Web by a car company is Toyota's product placement of its Scion car in the educational virtual community of Whyville. In Whyville users can personalize their face, talk with other visitors, buy and customize their own Scion car (the only car allowed in Whyville), and drive around the city with their friends. Although Whyville's users are 8-15 years old, the influence this age group has on their parents' purchasing decisions is enormous and in a few years these users will be purchasing their own cars. According to Toyota, the goal is to develop brand loyalty and to have customers purchase their first Toyota. This strategy is working because 80 percent of Scion buyers had never owned a Toyota before. Moreover, Scion is purchased by the youngest age group out of all the cars in the industry.[111]

A teen site that appears more like an online dating site called bolt.com has received attention from Ford. The website hosts over 31,000 users under age 20 where homemade videos, artwork, photo albums, blogs, and profiles are shared. Ford has invested in bolt.com in order to market to people where they spend their time online. The two companies will create an offshoot of bolt.com called cars.bolt.com. Ford will solicit information from users by using surveys, chat rooms, and contests. Information gathered from these activities will be integrated with plans for future car models. An example is a contest where users create their dream car.[112] Many websites use contests to extract preferences and trends amongst users. The teenagers who are active on bolt.com are unaware that they are freely sharing ideas that may eventually become future products or features in Ford's future automobiles. If teenagers knew the potential of their creativity, they might ask to be compensated. Until then, companies like Ford will benefit from the imagination of teenagers.

Car companies also know that children who shop for cars with their parents will push them to buy those with more technology. It is not uncommon to find cars with entertainment features like TVs, DVDs, and video screens inside of them. Gadgets for teenagers are also available like the new Bluetooth-enabled music playing rearview mirror that comes with sound control buttons

---

[110] Goch, 21.

[111] Bosman, "Hey, Kid, You Want to Buy a Toyota Scion?"

[112] Michael Woodyard, "Ford Wants to Visit Teens on Their Turf," *Automotive News* 74, no. 5851 (1999): 3.

directly on the mirror. For those pre-adolescents who cannot drive, there is a miniature computer car called PC Ride. The PC Ride comes in a choice of a Dodge Magnum, Charger, or Viper. "It comes with special features so owners can customize: an adjustable chassis for interchangeable bodies, name-brand rims and rubber tires, and grumbling HEMI engine sound effects when you start up. The CD tray will extend from the car's grille, and its computer connectors fit into the rear bumper."[113] As marketers in the automobile industry have learned, technology and teenagers go hand in hand in order for a product to be desirable.

Hip Sells

Marketing companies that cater specifically to people under 20 years old know that aligning and imbedding your brand within the lifestyle of young people is key to creating brand recognition. Lifestyle marketing strategically places products where a specific target group spends its time or associates a product with its interests. The key areas that are a major part of young people's lifestyle are technology, music, fashion, and being entertained. An unusual fashion trend came out a few years ago, NASCAR-logo jackets. These jackets are priced between $225 and $650, but the items that sell the most are $400 to $500. The shocking price of the jackets is not what is unusual. What is strange is students have no concept of what NASCAR is. The jackets are popular because of their bright colors, style, and the logos of familiar corporate sponsors including M&M, Hot Wheels, Kellogg's Corn Flakes, Miller Beer Company, and McDonald's.[114] The recognition of logos that have been in these teenagers' environment is what popularized the jackets. As mentioned before by Naomi Klein, the logo is the product.

Car companies are improving their brand image amongst young adults by associating themselves with popular musicians. Honda promoted its Civic by sponsoring concert tours and giving away cars autographed by teenage music icons.[115] Similarly, Ford discreetly advertised its Focus by loaning it to DJs who were well known in a community. As they drove through the city the Fo-

---

[113] Errol Pierre-Louis, "The PC that Looks Like a Dodge," *TechnoRide.com*, August 10, 2006, available at http://www.technoride.com/article/The+PC+that+Looks+Like+a+Dodge/185092_1.aspx (accessed August 27, 2006).

[114] Mark Yost, "NASCAR-Logo Jackets Fuel Latest Craze in Urban Fashion," *Wall Street Journal (Eastern edition)* (20 December 1999).

[115] Halliday, "Automakers Agree, Winning Youth Early Key to Future."

cus went with them and their nightlife, Hip Hop lifestyle for everyone to see.[116]

Toyota has promoted its Scion by going as far as creating its own record label called Scion A/V. What is interesting is that Toyota is not concerned about how profitable the record label is, but is simply trying to find a new way to connect to consumers by supporting struggling artists.[117] Scion's manager of sales promotions states, "The goal is simply brand extension by association with underground music. If we did make money, it would not have such a positive effect. We don't want to cross that line."[118] Maintaining an underground focus for Scion is key to selling to young adults who do not like to be directly advertised to. Positioning a product in places where potential customers are creates the illusion that the product is discovered.[119] Toyota is very purposeful in how and where it advertises to young people. Toyota and other companies are using a new marketing technique, referred to as guerrilla marketing,[120] to tap into young adults by surrounding and saturating them with ads placed on frequently used objects or in areas where people walk by every day. Guerrilla marketing creates a consumer base at the grass-roots level. Traditional car commercials are avoided. A shift from traditional marketing to lifestyle marketing is acknowledged as a great marketing strategy to capture young consumers.

Inside Schools

As noted above, marketers have learned to find out where adolescents spend their time and the importance of advertising within a familiar environment. The first location to come to mind that matches these two criteria is high schools. Through philanthropic activities, corporations have found access to the adolescent market. Services and donations from businesses may seem altruistic, but a closer examination reveals public schools and students are often exploited while the corporations end up getting more from the relationship than the beneficiaries.[121] A typical school/business relationship consists

---

[116] Crawford, "When Lime Green Is Desirable."

[117] "Brand Stunt of the Month: Audio Auto Alignment," *Brand Strategy* (April 5, 2005): 8.

[118] Ben Sisario, "Toyota, a Different Sound System," *New York Times (Late Edition East Coast)* (14 March 2005). Available online at Proquest (accessed date August 9, 2006).

[119] Steve Kichen, "Scion's Smart Moves," *Forbes.com*, available at http://www.forbes.com/2004/10/12/ cz_sk_1012feat.html (accessed June 8, 2006).

[120] Linn, 6.

[121] Boyles, 23.

of schools in need of monetary resources, facilities, and equipment due to poor funding of public schools; while, on the other hand, corporations are in need of skilled labor and consumers. Businesses provide schools with some of their needs and in return are able to influence and have more control over future laborers and consumers.[122]

Businesses are transferring the responsibility of training their workers onto schools as shown in a competition Ford sponsored to encourage students to become auto mechanics. Students competed for scholarship money and were timed to see how long it took them to repair a Ford vehicle. This competition has been occurring since 1949 when large numbers of automobile repair specialists began retiring, causing a shortage of certified auto technicians.[123] There are only a few high schools that provide students with an intensive automotive curriculum: Automotive High School in Brooklyn, New York, is one example. To address the shortage in automobile technicians, Mercedes-Benz created an automobile lab for this school. The company "views education as an opportunity to ensure that as many of today's youth as possible are given the tools, guidance and support they need to reach their full potential" and, "to empower future generations, particularly those who are underserved."[124] How a high school that is focused on one specific career helps a student reach their full potential is not clear. Teenagers may be too young to be receiving a specialized education. What courses would these students have taken instead of their automotive classes? What they are not learning is just as important as what they are learning. A liberal arts education is better able to provide a wider range of skills and knowledge. Will these students be prepared to pursue new goals and emerging interests? Will limited exposure to other subjects leave students feeling disempowered to interpret and adapt to challenges they will face in their future?

Allstate, GMAC, NASCAR, and General Motors have collectively sponsored another type of automotive school called the Urban Youth Racing School, which is located in Philadelphia. The purpose of this school is to let

---

[122] Kaplan, "Profits R Us."

[123] Auto Channel, "Illinois High School Students Compete in 2003 Ford/AAA Auto Skills Competition," *AutoChannel.com*, May 9, 2003, available at http://www.theautochannel.com/news/2003/05/09/161012.html (accessed August 13, 2006).

[124] Auto Channel, "Automotive High School Opens Mercedes-Benz Lab," December 14, 2004, available at http://www.theautochannel.com/news/2004/12/14/303003.html (accessed August 13, 2006).

urban youth learn about the automotive and motor sports industries.[125] The school is able to keep students focused on academics by using racing cars to motivate them to work hard. Applications that can be applied to cars from different disciplines help keep students interested in their academic course-work. Students exposed to cars may consider a field in the automotive industry, something that car companies severely are in need of. Moreover, as sponsors of the Racing School, companies' advertisements and logos will be displayed when students compete in car races. Large crowds of people enjoy watching motor sports, and the competitions the students travel to provide opportunities for sponsors to advertise. The company's reputation is also viewed more positively since they help inner-city youth follow their dream of racing within an academic environment.

Currently 37,000 auto mechanic jobs are vacant in the U.S. In dealing with this shortage, GM created a nonprofit organization called Automotive Youth Educational Systems (AYES) in 1997. The main goal for AYES is to form a strong coalition of car dealers, students, state and federal organizations, teachers, and corporations to address this shortage. Currently 14 car companies have joined AYES to work with 410 high school vocational programs in supporting students who are interested in auto mechanics.[126] High schools must be certified by the National Institute for Automotive Service Excellence (ASE) to participate in the AYES program. The program provides these high schools with a local dealership that will sponsor vocational students as they complete a paid internship at the dealership. The dealer also mentors students, pays two-thirds of the cost for a starter tool kit, and offers graduates an entry-level job position upon completion of the program. Dealerships are encouraged to participate in the school's advisory council, career day, and other events to promote the field of auto mechanics. AYES is not satisfied with the number of students in its program and applied for the Department of Labor's (DOL) $2.2 million grant, which it received in early 2006. The grant will help AYES create its program online so any student can take advantage of this program and more skilled mechanics will be available for dealers to employ.[127] Here is another example of taxpayers' money assisting corporations with their

---

[125] Anthony Martin, "Motorsports and Beyond," *Urban Youth Racing School*, available at http://www.urbanyouthracingschool.com (accessed September 7, 2006).

[126] Automotive Youth Educational Systems, "Background Information on the Department of Labor's Grant Awarded to AYES," available at http://www.urbanyouthracingschool.com (accessed August 19, 2006).

[127] Ibid.

needs. The corporations themselves do not contribute much money for the AYES program, yet the federal government does. Students are not just trained to work on cars in general but to work on cars made by a specific manufacturer. The AYES program aims to increase the number of auto mechanics. As the supply of workers increases, so does their expendability since there are other trained people ready to take their place. An abundance of workers with highly specialized skills provides corporations with more bargaining power and dominance over its workers, something that both public schools and the federal government are indirectly assisting. AYES exemplifies how public high schools are treated as training facilities for corporations and are helping them to meet their business goals.

Another way for corporations to influence curriculum and advertise to students in schools is through free materials. Weekly Reader is a publishing company that has been producing educational materials since 1902 with the help of corporations, nonprofit organizations, and government funding. General Motors formed a joint program in 2002 with Weekly Reader to promote hydrogen-powered fuel cells. Over 24 million students have received this free curriculum on energy sources in either the English or Spanish version.[128] Elizabeth A. Lowery, GM's vice president, states, "GM is committed to promoting education in math and science among today's youth. The creation and distribution of this curriculum on hydrogen as an energy source supports our education mission...."[129] Reading about energy sources from corporate-sponsored materials will no doubt be biased in favor of the company. If GM truly examined the energy sources we use today, they would have to admit that its own automobile products have had a serious impact on our environment since it uses energy from fossil fuels. GM's image is skewed within these educational materials since its promotion of hydrogen fuel technology may be mistaken for what products GM primarily makes and sells. Creating curriculum materials about environmentally friendly fuel technology captures students' interests in and concern for the environment in order for GM to rebrand itself as a green company. These marketing tactics warrant concern as to the academic and scientific value of GM's educational material.

Another curriculum that was developed by an automobile company is Ford's Partnership for Advanced Studies (PAS). Ford notes that a skilled work-

---

[128] General Motors, "General Motors and Weekly Reader Bring the Energy of Tomorrow into Classrooms Today," *GM GMability*, available at http://www.gm.com/company/gmability/edu_k-12/news/hydrogen_091206.html (accessed August 19, 2006).

[129] Ibid.

force is critical to the company's continued success.[130] According to Ford, the PAS program "provides high school students with high quality interdisciplinary learning experiences that challenge them academically and develop their problem-solving, critical thinking, and communication skills" and prepares students for careers in business, engineering, and technology.[131] An important component to the PAS program is linking the classroom to higher learning and the workplace. The two and a half year curriculum starts in the 10th grade and contains five topics: building foundations (developing problem-solving, communication, and research skills), adapting to change (careers, communities, environment, and efficiency), managing and marketing with data (business success, quality, data, and knowledge), designing for tomorrow (new ways of engineering), and understanding a global economy (global citizen, change in economy, and globalization).[132] Despite the claims that this curriculum helps students obtain careers in business, engineering, and technology, the topics covered do not appear to be academically rigorous nor in depth. The curriculum seems more pertinent to careers in management, the type of workers Ford most likely needs. The PAS program is another example of a corporation using public school money to train its workers.

The cost of the PAS program is $10,921 for a classroom of 30 students.[133] Not mentioned are the costs of field trips that meet the goal of connecting classrooms to the community and workplace. Furthermore, videos, software, teacher and student guides, and simulations are other ancillary materials for the PAS program that also incur a cost.

Guest speakers, mentoring, and job shadow activities also are considered critical to the PAS program to apply information outside of school. Ford's description of PAS uses popular educational terminology and phrases, for example, "hands-on," "project-based," "inquiry-based," and "collaboration," so its curriculum seems up to date. Knowing schools emphasis on high-stakes tests

---

[130] Ford Motor Company, "Global Education: Expanding Access to Education," available at http://www.ford.com/en/goodWorks/community/globalEducation/default.htm (accessed September 17, 2006).

[131] Ford Partnership for Advanced Studies, "Our Mission." available at http://www.fordpas.org/mission.asp (accessed June 11, 2006).

[132] Ford Partnership for Advanced Studies, "Using the Ford PAS Curriculum Materials," available at http://www.fordpas.org/downloads_public/UsingFordPASMaterials.pdf (accessed June 11, 2006).

[133] Ford Partnership for Advanced Studies, "Curriculum Costs," available at http://www.fordpas.org/about/costs.asp (accessed June 11, 2006).

and standards, PAS mentions that its material is aligned to national standards and that extra material helps PAS relate to state standards as well. Unknowingly or not, Ford insults educators by explaining to teachers how students learn and offers professional development for those teachers who lack this knowledge.[134] How Ford has become an educational expert remains unanswered.

To make the PAS program more valuable and meaningful, some colleges provide up to 15 credits for completion of the entire PAS program.[135] Since the program takes up time in a student's schedule, what skills and courses are they not learning that they otherwise would? Not only does the PAS program cut into secondary education, but if colleges are giving credit for this program, then students will not be taking as many college classes, further limiting their exposure to other subjects.

Other Ford educational projects include Youth & Adult Training Centers placed in the communities of at-risk students to train them for entry-level service jobs in the automotive sector. The training centers are also open to adults. Ford, seeing itself as an authority on educational issues, has gone so far as to create a charter public high school on the site of Ford in Michigan. This school will presumably be for the children of its corporate employees. The Henry Ford Academy is designed as a model for educational reform. In other words, Ford wants to let educators know how they should be teaching. What problems Ford finds with current educational practices are not clearly stated. Being critical of education might be a way for corporations to garner support for their own lesson plans, curriculums, and schools in order to influence how and what is taught in public schools. Unlike the educational initiative for inner-city students that focuses on service jobs, the Academy describes itself as academically rigorous, using current educational methods to prepare students for a challenging future. There is even a Henry Ford Learning Institute that manages the Academy and works on replicating its model. Ford employees also assist teachers with creating lesson plans and tutoring students on Saturdays in its Detroit Area Pre-College Engineering Program that works to prepare minority students for science careers. Science, Technology & Engineering Preview Summer Camp (STEPS) and League of United Latin American Citizens (LULAC) are other programs to help prepare minorities, particularly

---

[134] Ford Partnership for Advanced Studies, "Frequently Asked Questions," available at http://www.fordpas.org/about/faqs.asp (accessed June 11, 2006).
[135] Ibid.

women, for science careers during the summers and after school.[136] Ford's involvement in schools is extensive as it designs programs that will help in developing future employees for its company. While implementing its programs, the Ford name, logo, and business values are embedded into the students.

The Cost of Automobile Use

At the end of 2006, after months of paying high gas prices, Exxon Mobil announced its quarterly profit was $9 billion, the highest amount of profit that any corporation has ever made in one quarter.[137] To avoid accusations of price gouging, oil companies have increased the amount of money it spends on ads to inform consumers how to conserve energy. The cause for high gas prices is attributed to the increase in demand for oil internationally.[138] Despite the 30 percent increase in fuel costs since 2003,[139] the number of people who used their cars did not change. Due to incentives to buy cars, the number of car sales did not change; however, the value of the cars had decreased significantly.[140] On average fuel is 16 percent of a household's budget.[141] According to the Bureau of Labor Statistics' Consumer Expenditure Survey, in 2000 the average household spent $1,292, or 3.4 percent, of all expenditures compared to $2,013, or 4.3 percent, in 2005.[142] This figure is significant considering 5.7 percent of all expenditures in 2005 went towards health care and 12.8 percent towards food.[143]

The amount of time and energy teenagers expend on cars is greatly underestimated. One study found that

---

[136] Ford Motor Company, "North American Educational Initiatives," available at http://www.ford.com/en/goodWorks/community/globalEducation/northAmericanEducation.htm (accessed June 11, 2006).

[137] Ahrens, "Oil Doesn't Want Focus on Big Profit."

[138] Ibid.

[139] Driven to Spend, available at http://www.transact.org/library/reports_pdfs/driven_to_spend/Driven_to_Spend_Report.pdf (accessed April 19, 2007).

[140] Walter McManus, "Economic Theory Trumps Conventional Detroit Wisdom," *University of Michigan Transportation Institute*, available at http://www.umtri.umich.edu/content/ McManusBusinessEconomics.pdf (accessed April 6,2007).

[141] Driven to Spend.

[142] "Consumer Expenditure Survey," *Bureau of Labor Statistics*, available at http://www.bls.gov/cex/csxann00.pdf   Consumer Expenditures in 2000 U>S> depart of labor bureau of labor statistics april 2002 report #958 (accessed April 6, 2007).

[143] Ibid.

teenagers want jobs and cars as means to other objectives such as avoiding boredom, socializing, and obtaining goods and services. Active teenagers appear willing to spend as much as 50 percent of their budgets on transportation that satisfies their complex requirements for off-peak, unchaperoned dating and social and part-time employment trips. Many teenagers' perception of car ownership and use benefits far outweigh their perceptions of car costs; no evidence suggests that increased public education programs dealing with true car costs or the provision of inexpensive transit service are likely to significantly affect the model preferences and travel.[144]

Students are working long hours, sometimes between 25 and 30 hours a week, to pay for the cost of driving and owning their own car. Working so many hours during the school year negatively affects students' academic performance.[145] Not only are they paying for gas, car insurance, and making car payments, but they incur more costs to decorate their cars. Students' cars have tinted windows, loud mufflers, flashing lights, spoilers, tires, oversized rims, and expensive sound systems.[146] They try to imitate the types of cars they see in movies and music videos.

If students are caught up in the materialism and symbolic value of having a car, then it would seem that their parents would be the ones to put their foot down and not allow their children to spend so much time and money on cars; parents should refocus their energy on schoolwork. Unfortunately that is not the case. In fact more children, even those in their twenties who have graduated from college, are depending on their parents to help meet the cost of their expensive lifestyle.[147] More than a fourth of the revenue auto insurance companies receive comes from parents who are paying for their child's policy. One third of young drivers aged 23 to 29 years old are not paying for their own car insurance.[148] A large amount of effort from parents and teenagers are needed to satiate teenagers' need for cars.

Rather then being practical and sensible regarding their children's transportation needs, some parents are teaching their children to dismiss public transportation and encouraging dependence on automobiles. Despite the congestion, prices of gas, and long wait times to transport kids to and from school

---

[144] D.B. Gurin, "Economics of Car Ownership and Use by Teenagers (Abridgment)," *Transportation Research Board* 583 (1976): 78.

[145] Cynthia Kopkowski, "From Legos to Logos," *NEA Today* 24, no. 8 (2006): 36.

[146] Higgins, "Carmakers See Teenage Market as Lucrative Arena."

[147] Louise Story, "More Parents Let Adult Kids Stay on Auto Policies," *Wall Street Journal (Eastern edition)* (13 July 2004): D2.

[148] Ibid.

in the family car, some parents refuse to allow their children to ride the school bus. Only 54 percent of school children use the school bus. Safety is cited as the most common reason that parents fear the bus, despite the fact that buses are 87 times safer than cars.[149]

Every year more teenagers die from car accidents than any other cause.[150] This is true even though teenagers take courses on how to be safe drivers. Moreover, studies have found that cars are the most popular place teenagers choose to use marijuana.[151] Risky behavior and driving under the influence of alcohol are also serious concerns for teenagers who drive. The cost of adolescents driving cars goes far beyond financial concerns.

Conclusion: How to Curb the Desire for Automobiles

Considering the death rate, financial cost, and dangerous behaviors associated with teenage driving, it is ironic that society places so much emphasis on encouraging teenagers to drive. Due to the clever framing of cars and their brands via advertising and marketing, our society has increased its use and desire for automobiles. The media reinforces the false concept that everyone wants and needs an automobile. Car companies have gone great lengths to associate their product and brand with every aspect of an adolescent's lifestyle—music, fashion, social causes, entertainment, and use of technology. The result of aggressive marketing provides adolescents the opportunity of "living their life inside a brand."[152]

Many attempts have been made to provide drivers with information on the costs and effects of automobile use. Education and information campaigns have been found to have little effect on driving behavior or automobile dependency.[153] As Lakoff mentions, once frames have been created, any contradictory information that challenges the frame will be ignored and scoffed at.

---

[149] MacDonald, "Parents Urged to Embrace Big Yellow for Safety, Earth."

[150] Keep the Drive.com, available at http://www.keepthedrive.com/getrowdy.aspx (accessed September 3, 2006).

[151] Pennsylvania Department of Health. Driving High: Teens Cite Cars as a Top Place to Use Marijuana, available at http://www.dsf.health.state.pa.us/health/lib/health/bdap_ driving_high_teens_cite_cars_top_place_to_use_marijuana.pdf (accessed September 3, 2006).

[152] Klein, "The Tyranny of the Brands."

[153] Beatrice Torgnyson, "Student Attitudes Toward Incentives to Reduce Automobile Use" (master's thesis, Sveriges Lantbruksuniversitet), available at http://ex-epsilon.slu.se/archive/00000762/01/exabea.pdf (accessed April 4, 2007).

"There is no longer a conscious, rational evaluation of pros and cons of different [transportation] alternatives...and rational arguments are usually inefficient. Once car dependency is established, it is very difficult to alter."[154] It then becomes challenging for other transportation modes to be considered and for attitudes towards these alternatives to be changed.[155]

If disseminating information on the pros and cons of automobile use has been found to be ineffective, then educators need to use materials, activities, lesson plans, and curriculum developed by corporations as objects to teach students how to evaluate materials for themselves. Assumptions that are made by companies through their advertisements need to be questioned and scrutinized. For example, does an automobile represent its owner? Do material goods and brands affect the importance or quality of an individual? Does consumption of products provide an intoxicating effect, allowing one to evade unfulfilled relationships and a forlorn social life? Giving students information about automobiles has not affected their attitudes, but having them evaluate and construct their own opinions may allow them to understand and identify marketing tactics. The process of deconstructing images and subtle messages in advertisements could change the way cars are framed. The reality of car accidents, fatalities, pollution, financial costs, and risky behavior juxtaposed against what is purported in automobile advertisements stimulates adolescents to continue seeking a connection to a desired lifestyle by consuming more automobiles.

Bibliography

Adler, Jerry. 2006. Going Green. *Newsweek* 148 (2): 42-52.

Ahrens, Frank. 2005. Oil Doesn't Want Focus on Big Profit: Companies Stepping Up Advertising. *Washington Post* (26 October): D01. Available at http://www.washingtonpost.com/wp-dyn/content/article/2005/10/25/AR2005102501655.html.

Andersen, Robin and Lance Strate, eds. 2000. *Critical Studies in Media Commercialism*. New York: Oxford University Press.

Arnott, Nancy. 1994. Marketing with a Passion. *Sale and Marketing Management* 146 (1): 64. Online from Proquest, ID: 791026.

AutoChannel. 2003. Illinois High School Students Compete in 2003 Ford/AAA Auto Skills Competition. *AutoChannel.com*, 9 May. Available at http://www.theautochannel.com/news/2003/05/09/161012.html.

---

[154] Ibid, 11.
[155] Ibid.

AutoChannel 2004. Automotive High School Opens Mercedes-Benz Lab Auto Technicians of Tomorrow Get High-Tech Training Today. *AutoChennel.com*, 14 December. Available at http://www.theautochannel.com/news/2004/12/14/303003.html.

AutoChannel 2006. Office Depot Sends NASCAR Star Carl Edwards 'Back to School'; New 'Great Tools for Your School Sweeps' Awards a School Over $65,000 Worth of New Technology and Classroom Supplies to Be Personally Delivered by Edwards. *AutoChannel.com*, 13 July. Available at http://www.theautochannel.com/news/2006/07/13/014671.html.

Automotive Youth Educational Systems. Background Information on the Department of Labor's Grant Awarded to AYES. Available at http://www.urbanyouthracingschool.com/.

Bosman, Julie. 2006. Hey, Kid, You Want to Buy a Toyota Scion? *New York Times (Late Edition East Coast)*. (14 June): C2. Online from Proquest, ID: 1059518711.

Boyles, Deron R. 2005. *Schools or Markets? Commercialism, Privatization, and School-Business Partnership*. New Jersey: Lawrence Erlbaum Associates.

Brady, Diane and Wendy Zellner. 2003. Back-to-School Is Getting High Marks. *Business Week* (1 September 2003): 38.

Brand Stunt of the Month: Audio Auto Alignment. *Brand Strategy* (5 April 2005): 8. Online from Proquest, ID: 818264531.

Carring, Paul T. Not Just a Worthy Cause: Cause-Related Marketing Delivers the Goods and the Good. *Public Service Advertising Research Center*. Available at http://www. psaresearch.com/bib4306.html.

Cato, Jeremy. 2006. Fear Is a Powerful Motivator. *Special Globe Auto*. Available at http://www.globeauto.com/servlet/story/RTGAM.20061018.wh-safety-main19/BNStory/.

Ciulla, Vincent. 2000. Buying a Back to School Car. *About.com*. Available at http://autorepair.about.com/ library/weekly/aa072800a.htm.

Clifton, K. J. 2003. Independent Mobility among Teenagers: Exploration of Travel to After-School Activities. *Transportation Research Record* 1854: 74-80. Available at http://pubsindex.trb.org/ document/view/default.asp?lbid=683907.

Consumer Expenditure Survey. 2000. *Bureau of Labor Statistics*. Available at http://www.bls.gov/cex/csxann00.pdf.

Consumer Expenditure Survey. 2005. *Bureau of Labor Statistics*. Available at http://www.bls.gov/cex/csxann05.pdf.

Crawford, Erin. 2000. When Lime Green Is Desirable. *Des Moines Business Record* 16 (39): 23.

Driven to Spend. June 2005. *Center for Neighborhood Technology*. Available at http://www.transact.org/library/reports_pdfs/driven_to_spend/Driven_to_Spend_Report.pdf

Exclusive: Teens' Take on Brands. *Advertising Age* (Midwest edition) 76 (8): S4. Online from Proquest, ID: 798528981.

Fallon, Jeannine and Pam Krebs. 2004. Laptop, Notebooks... Cool Car? Edmunds.com Makes Back-to-School Shopping More Fun with Top 10 Cars for Drivers Under 25, *Edmunds.com*, 23 August. Available at http://www.edmunds.com/help/about/ press/102903/ article.html.

Florida Department of Education. Instructional Materials and Library Media. Available at http://www.firn.edu/doe/instmat/pdf/drive9.pdf.

Ford Motor Company. Global Education: Expanding Access to Education. Available at http://www.ford.com/en/goodWorks/community/ globalEducation/default.htm.

Ford Motor Company. North American Educational Initiatives. Available at http://www.ford.com/en/goodWorks/community/globalEducation/northAmerican Education.htm.

Ford Motor Company and Governor's Highway Safety Association. Driving Skills for Life. Available at http:// www.drivingskillsforlife.com.

Ford Partnership for Advanced Studies. Curriculum Costs. Available at http://www.fordpas. org/about/costs.asp.

Ford Partnership for Advanced Studies. Frequently Asked Questions. Available at http://www. fordpas. org/about/faqs.asp.

Ford Partnership for Advanced Studies. Our Mission. Available at http://www. fordpas.org/mission.asp.

Ford Partnership for Advanced Studies. Using the Ford PAS Curriculum Materials. Available at http://www.fordpas.org/downloads_public/UsingFordPASMaterials.pdf.

General Motors. Ecotec engines. Available at http://www.gm.com/automotive/ gmpowertrain/engines/ ecotec/index.htm.

General Motors. Games. GM G*Mability.* Available at http://www.gm.com/company/gmability/ edu_k-12/5-8/games/index.html.

General Motors. General Motors and Weekly Reader Bring the Energy of Tomorrow into Classrooms Today. GM G*Mability.* Available at http://www.gm.com/company/gmability/ cdu_k-12/news/hydrogen_091206.html.

General Motors. Only GM. Available at http://www.gm.com/company/onlygm/energy/index. html.

Goch, Lynna. 2003. Gearing Up: Insurers Are Using Driver Safety Programs, Sharply Focused Advertising and the Internet to Court Teen Drivers. *Best's Review* 104 (6): 20.

Green, Jeff. 1999. Coveting Hang Ten's Teen Demo, Chevy Ties in for Tracker Sweeps. *Brandweek* 40 (28): 12.

Gronbach, Ken. 2000. Generation Y—Not Just 'Kids'. *Direct Marketing* 63 (4): 36. Online from Proquest, ID: 58970385.

Gunter, Barrie and Adrian Furnham. 1998. *Children as Consumers: A Psychological Analysis of the Young People's Market.* New York: Routledge.

Gurin, D.B. 1976. Economics of Car Ownership and Use by Teenagers (Abridgment). *Transportation Research Board* 583: 78-83. Available at http://pubsindex.trb.org/document/ view/default.asp?lbid=47239.

Halliday, Jean. 2002. Automakers Agree, Winning Youth Early Key to Future. *Advertising Age* 73 (13): S16. Online from Proquest, ID: 112710613.

Harris, Daniel. 1999. Coolness. *American Scholar* 68 (4): 39. Online from Proquest, ID: 46956078.

Higgins, John. 2003. Carmakers See Teenage Market as Lucrative Arena. *Akron Beacon Journal.* (2 February). Available at http://www.highbeam.com/doc/ 1G1-97160042.html.

InsureMe. Teen Car Insurance. Available at http://www.insureme.com/content/rsrc/ auto/teen-car-insurance/.

Kaplan, George R. 1996. Profits R Us: Notes on the Commercialization of America's Schools. *Phi Delta Kappan* 78 (3): K1. Online from Proquest, ID: 10401154.

Keep the Drive, Teen-Led Movement Promoting Smart Teen Driving. *KeeptheDrive.com.* Available at http://www.keepthedrive.com.

Kichen, Steve. 2004. Scion's Smart Moves. *Forbes.com.* Available at http://www.forbes.com/2004/10/12/cz_sk_1012feat.html.

Klein, Naomi. 2000. The Tyranny of the Brands. *New Statesman* 13 (589): 25. Online from Proquest, ID: 49011396.

Kopkowski, Cynthia. 2006. From Legos to Logos. *NEA Today* 24 (8): 36-37. Online from Proquest, ID: 1032625051.

Lakoff, George. 2004. *Don't Think of an Elephant! Know Your Values and Frame the Debate.* White River Junction, Vermont: Chelsea Green Publishing.

Linn, Susan. 2004. *Consuming Kids: The Hostile Takeover of Childhood.* New York: The New Press.

Lemaitre, Rafael, Rosanna Maietta, and Fleishman-Hillard. 2005. Driving High: Teens Cite Cars as a Top Place to Use Marijuana. *Office of National Drug Control Policy,* 28 November. Available at http://www.ondcp.gov/news/press05/112805.html.

MacDonald, Mary. 2006. Parents Urged to Embrace Big Yellow for Safety, Earth. *Atlanta Journal-Constitution.* (13 August). Available at http://www.ajc.com/news/content/ metro/cherokee/stories/0813metbus.html.

Martin, Anthony. Motorsports and Beyond: A Message from the UYRS Found. *Urban Youth Racing School.* Available at http://www.urbanyouthracingschool.com/.

McManus, Walter. Economic Theory Trumps Conventional Detroit Wisdom. *University of Michigan Transportation Research Institute.* Available at http://www.umtri.umich.edu/ content/McManusBusinessEconomics.pdf.

Meyers, Tiffany. 2005. Marketing to Kids Comes Under Fresh Attack. *Advertising Age* 76 (8): 2-8. Online from Proquest, ID: 798528501.

Milner, Murray. 2004. *Freaks, Geeks, and Cool Kids: American Teenagers, Schools, and the Culture of Consumption.* New York: Routledge.

Molnar, Alex. 2005. *School Commercialism: From Democratic Ideal to Market Commodity.* New York: Routledge.

Mooij, Marieke de. 2004. *Consumer Behavior and Culture: Consequences for Global Marketing and Advertising.* London: Sage Publications, Inc.

Nerad, Jack. 2004. Cars for Kids. *Drivers.com,* 7 April. Available at http://www.drivers.com/ article/674.

New Day Films. *Taken for a Ride.* Available at http://www.newday.com/films/ Taken_for_a_Ride.html.

Office Max. http://www.officemax.com (accessed August 12, 2006).

Pechmann, C., P. L. Levine, S. Loughlin, and F. Leslie. 2005. Impulsive and Self-Conscious: Adolescents' Vulnerability to Advertising and Promotion. *Journal of Public Policy & Marketing* 24 (2): 202-21. Online from Proquest, ID: 1014316391.

Pennsylvania Department of Health. Driving High: Teens Cite Cars as a Top Place to Use Marijuana. Available at http://www.dsf.health.state.pa.us/health/lib/health/bdap_driving_

high_teens_cite_cars_top_place_to_use_marijuana.pdf.

Perdue for a New Georgia. 2006. State Tax-Free Holiday Set for August 3-6: School Teachers Able to Use $100 Gift Cards to Purchase Classroom Supplies. 10 July. Available at http://www.votesonny.com/default.asp?pt=newsdescr&RI=329.

Pierre-Louis, Errol. 2006. The PC that Looks Like a Dodge. *TechnoRide.com*, 8 August. Available at http://www.technoride.com/article/The+PC+that+Looks+Like+a+Dodge/185092_1.aspx.

Progressive Casualty Insurance Company. Progressive Teens Site. Available at http://www.progressive.com/teens/home.aspx.

Sisario, Ben. 2005. Toyota, a Different Sound System. *New York Times (Late Edition East Coast)*. (14 March). Online at Proquest, ID: 807151991.

Spring, Joel. 2003. *Educating the Consumer-Citizen: A History of the Marriage of Schools, Advertising, and Media*. Mahwah, New Jersey: Lawrence Erlbaum Associates.

Story, Louise. 2004. More Parents Let Adult Kids Stay on Auto Policies. *Wall Street Journal (Eastern edition)*. (13 July): D2. Online from Proquest, ID: 662446551.

Subramanian, Rajesh. March 2006. Top 10 Leading Causes of Death in the U.S. for 2003, by Age Group. *National Highway Traffic Safety Administration's National Center for Statistics and Analysis*. Available at http://www-nrd.nhtsa.dot.gov/pdf/nrd-30/NCSA/RNotes/2006/810568.pdf.

Taken for a Ride. VHS. Directed by Jim Klein and Martha Olson. Harriman, New York: New Day Films and Independent Television Series, 1996.

Target. http://www.target.com (accessed August 12, 2006).

Tasca, Leo. 2001. Mobility Needs of Novice Drivers. *Transportation Research Circular E-C024*, January: 6-8. Available at http://gulliver.trb.org/publications/circulars/ec024.pdf.

Torgnyson, Beatrice. 2005. Student Attitudes Toward Incentives to Reduce Automobile Use. Master's thesis, Sveriges Lantbruksuniversitet. Available at http://ex-epsilon.slu.se/archive/00000762/01/exabea.pdf.

Valdes-Dapena, Peter. 2005. Teen Drivers: Keeping Your Kid Alive. *CNNMoney.com*. 18 November. Available at http://money.cnn.com/2005/11/16/Autos/tipsandadvice/teen_drivers/index.htm.

Velasquez-Manoff, Moises. 2006. A Grass-Roots Push for a 'Low Carbon Diet'. *Christian Science Monitor* 99 (23):14-16.

Walbert, Mike. 2005. Classic, Muscle Cars Heading Back to School. *The Arizona Republic*, 4 February. Available at http://www.azcentral.com/community/gilbert/articles/0204gr-mesquiteZ12.html.

Washington, Frank S. 2001. Aim Young; No, Younger. *Advertising Age* (Midwest edition) 72 (15): S16

Wingerter, Lori T. Why GM Developed This Site. *General Motors GMability*. Available at http://www.gm.com/company/gmability/edu_k-12/k-4/parents/index.html.

Winter, Drew. 2004. Think Outside the Box. *Ward's Auto World* 40 (12): 5. Online from Proquest, ID: 771851981.

Woodyard, Michael. 1999. Ford Wants to Visit Teens on Their Turf. *Automotive News* 74 (5851): 3. Online from Proquest, ID: 47240061.

Yost, Mark. 1999. NASCAR-Logo Jackets Fuel Latest Craze in Urban Fashion—Teens Don't Follow the Sport but Are Happy to Spend Their (not so) Petty Cash. *Wall Street Journal (Eastern edition)*. (20 December). Online from Proquest, ID: 47333006.

Zollo, Peter. 2004. Getting Wiser to Teens: More Insight into Marketing to Teenagers. New York: New Strategist Publications, Inc.

Would You Like Values with That?
Chick-fil-A and Character Education

Deron Boyles, Georgia State University

"Character education" represents a long-standing staple of U.S. schools. From the "Old Deluder Satan" Law of 1647 to *The New England Primer* in the eighteenth-century to McGuffey Readers from the late 1830s (and well into the 1920s), the idea of transmitting core values to the young is so deeply rooted in the history of schooling that "morals" is often assumed to be a "given."[1] Over time, various social and religious concerns melded into a taken-for-granted presupposition that schools should play a major role in transmitting "good character" and fostering character development. In contemporary schools, state curricula often include character education and a series of organizations have been established to advance the idea that character education is fundamental to schools.

National programs that currently exist include, among others, "Character Counts!" from the Josephson Institute and "A 12-Point Comprehensive Approach to Character Education" from The Center for the 4th and 5th Rs (respect and responsibility). Other national and international organizations

---

[1] See, for example, Richard Mosier, *Making the American Mind: Social and Moral Ideas in the McGuffey Readers* (New York: Russell & Russell, 1965); Carl F. Kaestle, *Pillars of the Republic: Common Schools and American Society, 1780-1860* (New York: Hill and Wang, 1983); Joel Spring, *The American School, 1642-2004* (Boston: McGraw-Hill, 2005), sixth edition; and Thomas Lickona, *Character Matters: How to Help Our Children Develop Good Judgement, Integrity, and Other Essential Virtues* (New York: Simon and Schuster, 2004); Ernest J. Zarra, "Pinning Down Character Education," *Kappa Delta Pi Record* 36, no. 4 (Summer 2000): 154-157; and Mary M. Williams, "Models of Character Education: Perspectives and Development Issues," *Journal of Humanistic Counseling, Education and Development* 39, no. 1 (September 2000): 32-40. See also Martin E. Marty and R. Scott Appleby, eds., *Fundamentalism and Society: Reclaiming the Science, the Family, and Education* (Chicago: The University of Chicago Press, 1997).

include the Character Education Partnership (CEP) and the Institute for Global Ethics.[2] These organizations proclaim themselves to be nonpartisan and each identifies universal values that should be adopted, though the number of values vary. Michael Josephson developed "Character Counts!," the most widely used character education program in the U.S. Josephson retired from careers in law, business, and education to run the Joseph and Edna Josephson Institute, named for his parents. He serves the organization without a salary and all proceeds from speaking engagements and written work are stated as going directly back into the nonprofit institute.[3] The Center for the 4th and 5th Rs is led by Thomas Lickona, a professor of educational psychology at the State University of New York-Cortland. The Center for the 4th and 5th Rs is a university bureau committed to "building a moral society and developing schools which are civil and caring communities."[4] Lickona is a widely published author who also serves on the board of the CEP. Josephson and Lickona, however, are not the only ones influencing character education programs. Truett Cathy also influences character education curriculum in the U.S.

Cathy is the founder and CEO of Chick-fil-A, the fast food restaurant headquartered in Georgia. Cathy is also an avowed Christian fundamentalist.[5] Accordingly, he donated an "age-appropriate" (protestant) Bible to every school library in the state of Georgia in 2003. He is also the financial resource behind the national "Core Essentials" character education initiative based in Georgia, and through his financing, Chick-fil-A sponsors the teacher's guides sent to each school.[6] In addition, Cathy teamed with William Bennett to offer wristbands and cassettes as part of "kid's meals" at various Chick-fil-A stores. The wristbands and cassettes tout such values as "respect," "courage," and "honesty." This essay explores three main lines of inquiry: (1) the specifics of

---

[2] See, for example, http://www.character.org, http://www.charactercounts.org, and http://www.cortland.edu/c4n5rs/.

[3] See http://www.charactercounts.org. See also Michael Josephson, "Character Education Is Back in Our Public Schools," *The State Education Standard* (Autumn 2002): 41-45.

[4] See also Thomas Lickona, *Character Matters: How to Help Our Children Develop Good Judgment, Integrity, and Other Essential Virtues* (New York: Simon and Schuster, 2004).

[5] See S. Truett Cathy, *Eat MOR Chikin: Inspire More People Doing Business the Chick-fil-A Way* (Nashville: Cumberland House Publishing, 2002); S. Truett Cathy, *It's Easier to Succeed Than Fail* (Nashville: Thomas Nelson Publishers, 1989); and Ken Blanchard and S. Truett Cathy, *The Generosity Factor* (Grand Rapids, MI: Zondervan, 2002). Both Thomas Nelson and Zondervan are Christian publishing houses.

[6] Core Essentials, *Core Essentials: A Strategy for Teaching Character* (Alpharetta, GA: Core Essentials, Inc., 2001).

"Core Essentials" as a strategy for teaching character; (2) the role (and ironies) of private businesses influencing public school curricula; and (3) the assumptions inherent in the kind of teaching of character outlined by Core Essentials. Girding this inquiry is a concern about the problematic enterprise of teaching character itself as if it is an unquestionable domain. Further, the larger contexts of childhood obesity findings and Christian influences on and in public spheres will be considered along with Theodore Brameld's *Ends and Means in Education*, John Dewey's *Moral Principles in Education*, and Pierre Bourdieu's *Acts of Resistance* and *Firing Back*.[7] Ultimately, this article offers a critique and raises questions that may be helpful when considering character education and school-business partnerships.

Since Truett Cathy is a fundamentalist Christian as well as a private businessman, this chapter questions the understanding demonstrated by the Georgia state superintendent of schools, Kathy Cox, in a July 1, 2003, letter to Georgia school principals. She wrote that Truett Cathy is "a pioneering businessman" whose "generosity" allowed for an "age-appropriate Bible" to be placed in every school library in the state. She also wrote that Truett Cathy's "initiative has been completely funded by Mr. Cathy. No state funds have been used to supply this book to your school. Mr. Cathy has a passion for helping children, [sic] and he sees this as another way to encourage the youth of our great state."[8] What does the distinction between state and private funds for Bible purchases and placement mean? Does the fact that a Christian fundamentalist funded a character education program represent any challenges or concerns for, say, students who are Jewish or agnostic or Muslim? Is there any connection between Kathy Cox's endorsement, nay, praise of Truett Cathy and Cox's claim that the term "evolution" is a "buzzword" that should be replaced in the state curriculum of Georgia?[9] If Truett Cathy were actually interested in the welfare of children, why would he promote unhealthy fast-food as part of a character education program that touts "honesty" as a virtue?

---

[7] Theodore Brameld, *Means and Ends in Education: A Midcentury Appraisal* (New York: Harper and Row Publishers, 1950); John Dewey, *Moral Principles in Education* (Carbondale, IL: Southern Illinois University Press, 1909); Pierre Bourdieu, *Acts of Resistance: Against the Tyranny of the Market* (New York: The New Press, 1998), trans. Richard Nice; and Pierre Bourdieu, *Firing Back: Against the Tyranny of the Market 2* (New York: The New Press, 2003), trans., Loïc Wacquant.

[8] Kathy Cox, letter to school principals, July 1, 2003.

[9] See Mary MacDonald, "Georgia May Shun 'Evolution' in Schools: Revised Curriculum Plan Outrages Science Teachers," *The Atlanta Journal-Constitution* (29 January 2004): A1.

Indeed, what assumptions are made by Truett Cathy, furthered by the state, and pushed into the hands of teachers by the private, nonprofit Core Essentials organization that Cathy's profits from Chick-fil-A support?

The Program Itself: An Overview of Various Aspects

A visit to the Chick-fil-A website reveals an interesting phenomenon. On the page displaying information regarding Chick-fil-A's support of "Core Essentials," the company also notes the following: "Amid our nation's growing concern for children's character development, Chick-fil-A has found a way to help. Since 2000 we've been a national sponsor of Core Essentials, an educational program that gives teachers and parents tools for imparting key values to elementary-age boys and girls. By teaching inner beliefs and attitudes such as honesty, patience, respect, orderliness and courage, Core Essentials helps children treat others right, make smart decisions, and maximize their potential. The entire program teaches 27 values over a three-year period. To learn more about Core Essentials, contact a Chick-fil-A franchisee in your area."[10]

When you go to the website page and begin reading the paragraph just cited, you are interrupted by the cartoon image of the back of a cow's head. The image then scrawls "eat mor chikin'" across the screen, the very screen that includes the words "character development." It seems inconsistent, at least, to (1) have "more" and "chicken" spelled incorrectly on the page devoted to children's schooling, and (2) for those who would support the general notion of character education and the ensuing lists that accompany the phrase, where do "graffiti" and "interruption" appear on those lists?

Once past the website interruption, however, one can find more information about the program, and it does not take long to understand the underlying point. The website indicates that there is a booklet for teachers to help in the teaching of character. In *Core Essentials: A Strategy for Teaching Character*, the first page of the booklet *qua* teachers' guide outlines three main elements of the program: Identifying Basic Components, Preparation, and Establishing a Routine. Each of the three main elements has subheadings identifying key features indicative of the main elements as well as the overall intent of the larger program. Under "Identify the Basic Components" exists "teacher's guide, bookmarks/tablecards, value-able card, and posters." The teacher's guide is the booklet and tells teachers what to do, when to do it, and how to do it. The subsection that explains elements in the teacher's guide notes that "each

---

[10] See http://www.chick-fil-a.com/CoreEssentials.asp. Accessed 21 January 2004.

month you have age-appropriate materials at two academic levels, K-2 and 3-5. Included in the guide are literature and video suggestions which may be displayed in the library by the media specialist."[11] For the bookmarks/tablecards, the booklet instructs that "the bookmark is perforated and should be separated from the tablecard, which is designed to be folded and placed in a convenient location at home (kitchen counter or table). The parents of each child may then use this tool to emphasize the value through family discussions and activities." For the value-able card, importantly, the booklet reveals that the ". . .card is a key component which leads to successful implementation of the program. It is designed as the incentive for children who are caught [sic] displaying the value. Each month you will see suggestions in the Teacher's Guide for 'Catching Kids.' Use these ideas to help you choose students who show they understand the value. The card rewards them with a FREE Chick-fil-A Kid's Meal. *Ideally, you should have enough cards to reward each student every month (if earned).*"[12]

Good, Old-Fashioned Character

With this overview, consider what happens to the students in classes that adopt the Core Essentials program. What I intend to do here is outline the specific instructions that are included in the teacher's guide and underscore the elements that make this character education plan a traditional, and thereby restrictive and troubling, approach to teaching children. One may argue that a traditional approach to character education is what is needed. Core Essentials relies heavily on the idea that values are to be "imparted," thus reinforcing a banking approach to teaching and learning whereby the teacher deposits data into the students' "empty vaults" (or minds).[13] This essay intends to problematize the banking approach and show that there are underlying ironies that make the program highly questionable. There are also elements of hypocrisy that make the entire enterprise suspect.

There is a different value for each month of the year represented by the guidelines in question. They include, beginning in September and ending in May: initiative, respect, uniqueness, peace, orderliness, kindness, courage, joy, and patience. For each month, the teacher's guide begins with the exact same formula: a definition of the term, a list of suggested books that represent the

---

[11] Core Essentials, p.1.

[12] Ibid., italics in the original.

[13] See Paulo Freire, *Pedagogy of the Oppressed* (New York: Continuum, 1970).

value, a list of quotes, a story about an animal that illustrates the value, and directions for teachers. Consider the directions for October. The value is "respect" and the teacher is given the definition: "responding with words and actions that show others they are important."[14] One of the "famous person" quotes given in the booklet is "Always respect your parents...Do whatever your parents say. They are your best friends in life." Aside from the obvious parallel to one of the Ten Commandments (Honor thy father and mother), there is also an irony in having the quote signify "respect." The quote is attributed to George Steinbrenner, the notorious baseball owner whose fights with managers and team members are legendary.

For December, the value is peace and is defined as "proving that you care more about each other than winning an argument." The booklet also indicates that "the first step toward living peaceably is one made quietly inside ourselves. We must decide that other people are worth more to us than our own selfish desires, and that the value of agreement is greater than the satisfaction of defeating an opponent."[15] While the moralistic sentiment may sound nice, I wonder about a possible hidden agenda. Much like the "always respect your parents...do whatever they say" quote from the October lesson, I wonder about the degree to which students are actually being subjugated under a logic of hegemony. As though a sexually abusive parent's directions are always to be followed, the underbelly of universalism may reveal itself given careful analysis. That a corporate fast-food chain arguably interested in increasing market share via competition supports a program that appears to want to produce docile, unquestioning students goes to the heart of the school-business intersection as well. To wit, are schools about producing unquestioning consumers via a character education program that appears to elevate passivity and dogma? This concern does not only apply to the students subjected to the program, however. Teachers, too, are under a hegemonic rationale that subjugates and marginalizes their expertise and professionalism under pre-ordained scripts.

Each week in December, for example, has a corresponding paragraph that begins "Our value this month is peace. The definition of peace is 'proving that you care more about each other than winning an argument.'"[16] Forget that the vast majority of schools are not in session for a full four weeks in December; the four-week script nevertheless reflects a kind of proletarianization or

---

[14] Core Essentials, 5.

[15] Ibid., 11.

[16] Ibid., 12.

de-skilling of teaching at the same time that it seems to mimic catechism-like recitations from Christian churches. For the "bulletin board" aspect of the teacher's guide for December, teachers are told to "design a bulletin board with a chimney made of craft paper. Give each child a stocking made out of construction paper. On the stocking, have the students write how they care for other people. The children may decorate their stockings afterwards. Hang their stockings on the chimney that you have made." The title given to the bulletin board assignment is "The Stockings Were Hung by the Chimney with Peace." Aside from the overly prescriptive directions that devalue teachers' autonomy and professionalism, stockings are typically hung by chimneys in Christian homes, not Jewish or Muslim homes. Furthermore, if stockings are hung in homes for the Christmas holidays, is the point of young children hanging the stockings to "care for other people" or to receive presents?

A Christian theme is able to be discerned in other parts of the Core Essentials handbook as well. For January, orderliness is the value, and while the paragraph begins with "a study of nature," the teacher is supposed to explain to the students that "the constellations are a beautiful example of the order which exists in the skies."[17] Given the recent controversy in Georgia concerning Kathy Cox and evolution, the "order in the skies" reference sounds eerily like creationist "grand design" assertions.[18] For February, the value is kindness, and the teacher is supposed to explain that a wise saying is "do to others as you would have them do to you."[19] Fine as far as it goes, the unhidden "Golden Rule" taken together with other religious themes raises concerns in my mind. Should elementary students hassle their parents into taking them to Chick-fil-A for their "free" meal during the month of X, they would receive a cassette and/or a bracelet/watch-type band that has a compartment to hold more information from the Core Essentials program. For "responsibility" the plastic holder on the wristband is a sheep dog and the insert of stickers includes statements like "guard sheep dogs are responsible for protecting sheep" and "shepherds trust their sheep dogs to do what is expected of them." While my intent is not to make too much of these points, it does seem to me to be another Christian theme. Sheep? Shepherds? Further, married with the religious and overwhelmingly Christian themes are themes about work and capitalism. For the month of April, for example, students read quotes from Dale

---

[17] Ibid., 14.

[18] See Mary MacDonald, "Evolution Furor Heats Up," *The Atlanta Journal-Constitution* (31 January 2004): A1.

[19] Core Essentials, 17.

Carnegie and Henry Ford Carnegie's quote is "when fate hands you a lemon, make lemonade" and Ford's is "there is joy in work."[20]

What these and other quotes within the curriculum arguably indicate is the nexus of Christianity and capitalism. By weaving a language of accommodation with a language of economics, contrived optimism becomes an unquestioned foundation for docile, naïve workers. The nexus results in a kind of confused nationalist mythology that takes Christian values for granted while accommodating the lauding of individualism and pretenses of participating in a democracy. The mythology of "anyone can be anything they want" given "free markets," "hard work," and entrepreneurialism masks the reality faced by increasing numbers of workers. As Bourdieu points out,

> there are more and more low-level service jobs that are underpaid and low-productivity, unskilled or underskilled (based on hasty on-the-job training), with no career prospects—in short, the *throwaway jobs* of what André Gorz calls a 'society of servants.' According to economist Jean Gadrey, quoting an American study, of the thirty jobs that will grow fastest in the next decade, seventeen require no skills and only eight require higher education and qualification. At the other end of social space, the *dominated dominant*, that is, the managers, are experiencing a new form of alienation. They occupy an ambiguous position, equivalent to that of the petty bourgeois at another historical stage in the structure, which leads to forms of organized self-exploitation.[21]

Part of the historical stage to which Bourdieu refers was outlined in 1926 by Richard Henry Tawney. In his classic text, *Religion and the Rise of Capitalism*, Tawney presaged that "rightly or wrongly, with wisdom or its opposite, not only in England but on the Continent and in America, not in one denomination but among Roman Catholics, Anglicans, and Nonconformists, an attempt is being made to restate the practical implications of the social ethics of the Christian faith, in a form sufficiently comprehensive to provide a standard by which to judge the collective actions and institutions of mankind [sic], in the sphere both of international politics and of social organizations."[22]

The scenario goes something like this: inculcate the youngest and most impressionable with externally contrived religious values and increasingly

---

[20] Ibid., 23.

[21] Bourdieu, *Firing Back*, 31. Italics in original.

[22] Richard Henry Tawney, *Religion and the Rise of Capitalism* (New York: Harcourt, Brace, and Company, 1926), 5.

mold the docile congregation of followers into workers who honor authority. In the process, remove opportunities for critique and questioning by championing *a priori* notions of consensus and the status quo. According to Lindblom, corporations are intimately tied to this very process and set up the nexus of and integration between capitalism and Christian moral codes at the expense of public debate and authentic democratic governance. He notes the key features in business terms and calls them "the grand issues of politico-economic organization: private enterprise, a high degree of corporate autonomy, protection of the status quo on distribution of income and wealth, close consultation between business and government, and restriction of union demands to those consistent with business profitability. . . .They try, through indoctrination, to keep all these issues from coming to the agenda of government."[23]   For the parallel to schools, I am reminded of Theodore Brameld's discussion of indoctrination when he was attempting to defend the notion of "partiality" in schools in his *Ends and Means in Education*.[24]

Brameld defined indoctrination as a "method of learning by communication which proceeds primarily in one direction. . .for the purpose of inculcating in the mind and behavior of the latter a firm acceptance of some one doctrine or systematic body of beliefs—a doctrine assumed in advance by its exponents to be so supremely true, so good, or so beautiful as to justify no need for critical, scrupulous, thoroughgoing comparison with alternative doctrines."[25]   Brameld's concern was that schools practiced indoctrination at the expense of the society. For the purpose of this essay, however, he went even further. He indicted "the Church" for establishing the very conditions that promoted learning of the kind he deplored (and this essay challenges). "For many centuries," Brameld wrote, "the Church has deliberately and frankly inculcated its own doctrine as alone true and good, its chief indoctrinators being priests vested with authority to communicate its tenets to receptive minds. . . .this kind of education flourishes oftener than not: inculcation of moral codes or social folklore, and especially of attitudes and programs identified with the traditional economic-political system, simply means that public schools, far more often than most of their personnel themselves realize, are under the heavy influence of the dominant ideology."[26]

---

[23] Charles E. Lindblom, *Politics and Markets: The World's Political-Economic Systems* (New York: Basic Books, 1977), 205.

[24] Brameld, *Means and Ends in Education*, 65ff.

[25] Ibid., 66.

[26] Ibid., 67.

When specifically looking carefully at the text of the Core Essentials teacher's guide, to link and illustrate Brameld's point, a series of questions comes to mind. When, in March, the theme is courage, teachers are told that "courage is the foundation of our democracy. Discover the courage of the young citizens in your class by using a few of these ideas: Watch for students who do the right thing even when it has consequences; Observe students who stand up for their beliefs; Notice those students who do not give in to peer pressure; and Let students write or discuss what courage means to them. Allow them to make a pledge about their courage and watch to see who lives up to that pledge."[27]   Given the preceding months that privileged meekness and obedience to authority, what should be "discovered" about the "young citizens" in the class? If citizenship has been crafted in a hierarchical and externally imposed fashion, with the teacher at the center—or more accurately, the Core Essentials program at the center—how serious are teachers supposed to take the task laid out for them? Further, in terms of power, if the teachers are the ones "allowing" students to make a pledge and "letting" students write and discuss what courage means to them, the idea of students as courageous citizens is further subjugated under the power and authority of the teacher via the Core Essentials curriculum.

Values and the Drive-Thru

Throughout the Core Essentials teacher's guide there are sections called "Catching Kids." These sections are ostensibly intended to "catch" children "doing good," so as to turn the idea of "catching" a student doing something into a positive rather than a negative action. Unique to the Core Essentials program, however, is that, because the program is underwritten by Truett Cathy and his Chick-fil-A fast-food chain, the "Catching Kids" sections have "value-able cards." These cards are considered "rewards" by the program and, when given out by the teacher to the student, enable the student to get a free "kid's meal" at Chick-fil-A. A couple of issues converge around this point. First, the students who "earn" the reward are specifically within grades K-2 and 3-5. What we have are the youngest and most impressionable students in schools being bribed to act in particular ways in order to get a meal that is unhealthy. As Carolyn Vander Schee has pointed out, childhood obesity is a concern that has direct links to schools and programs they sponsor (both via

---

[27] Core Essentials, 20.

in-school food services and out-of-school connections like Core Essentials).[28]
Other studies also conclude that fast-food intake among school children is
part of a growing obesity epidemic.[29]

By using an unhealthy meal as a reward for complying with a "character
education" program, one wonders about the hypocrisy. Where in the program,
for example, are students instructed to demonstrate courage by questioning
the corporate underwriting of the program itself? When are the students encouraged to consider the fact that, in order for them to redeem their "kid's
meal" voucher, they will have to be accompanied by an adult who most likely
will purchase food and provide profit for Chick-fil-A? Indeed, recall the direct
quote from the teacher's guide noted toward the beginning of this chapter.
The guide encourages teachers to "use these ideas to help...choose students
who show they understand the value... *Ideally, you should have enough cards to
reward each student every month (if earned)."* The point may not be to reward students for good character, even if we could agree on what good character
means. The point is to get as many children from grades K-5 into a fast-food
chain to eat greasy food with their parents. Can we imagine that the marketing
department at Chick-fil-A has not surmised the amount of business they
would generate over a three-year period of time? Differently, but related, when
are students asked about honesty in disclosing complete calorie and fat content in the food that is being used to lure them to behave in particular ways?
Chick-fil-A does have a section on its website where it lists the nutritional
value of *items* on their menu.[30] But even the way the documentation is presented is misleading. To consider the amount of fat and calories in a "kid's
meal," you have to know what actually comprises a "kid's meal." On the website, for example, both 4- and 6-ounce servings of chicken nuggets are provided

---

[28] See Carolyn Vander Schee, "Food Services and Schooling," in *Schools or Markets?: Commercialism, Privatization, and School-Business Partnerships*, ed. Deron Boyles (Mahwah, NJ: LEA, 2005),
1-30.

[29] Shanthy A. Bowman, Steven L. Gortmaker, Cara B. Ebbeling, Mark A. Pereira, and David S.
Ludwig, "Effects of Fast-Food Consumption on Energy Intake and Diet Quality Among
Children in a National Household Survey," *Pediatrics* 113, no. 1 (January, 2004): 112-118; Richard J. Deckelbaum and Christine A. Williams, "Childhood Obesity: The Health Issue,"
Obesity Research 9, suppl. 4 (November, 2001): 239S-243S; David S. Ludwig, Karen E. Peterson, and Steven Gortmaker, "Relation between Consumption of Sugar-Sweetened Drinks
and Childhood Obesity: A Prospective, Observational Analysis," *The Lancet* vol. 357 (17 February 2001): 505-508. See also Marion Nestle, *Food Politics: How the Food Industry Influences
Nutrition and Health* (Berkeley, CA: University of California Press, 2003).

[30] See http://www.chickfila.com/MenuTable.asp?Category=specialties. Accessed June 10, 2004.

on separate lines. A "kid's meal," however, includes more than just the chicken nuggets. The meal includes waffle fries and a drink. Why not be "honest" and include the combined caloric value of the entire meal (allowing for variants like whether the drink is a soda, lemonade, or water)? Is it easier to differentiate and parse the particulars so the whole is not easily discernible? Perhaps the most extreme evidence of Chick-fil-A's Janus-faced approach to the issue of caloric intake and nutrition is their stance that eating plenty of their fast food is not really the problem. The problem is lack of exercise. Indeed, and incredibly, Chick-fil-A offers a "Chick-fil-A 10-Second Tip" in the Children's Hospital's (Knoxville, TN) "Healthy Kids" newsletter. The tip is, "Rather than only focusing on decreasing a big eater's intake, try to increase activity and exercise."[31]

To illustrate the link between the previous claims concerning the problems with externally imposed ideology and health issues associated with fast-food intake, consider that students in the Core Essentials program are structurally inhibited from exploring the issue of healthy eating. The subject does not fall under any of the categories that are pre-ordained for and imposed on teachers. Furthermore, teachers are "sold" the idea that the program will "only take 15 minutes," so when would teachers find the time to go beyond the pre-packaged approach anyway? Missing is the kind of approach developed by Janet Cundiff. She suggests a general structure through which students can answer the question, "Can you 'eat healthy' by frequenting fast food restaurants?"[32] Her approach uses Web links and teams of students to investigate food pyramids and food facts. Teams are asked to learn more about various fast-food restaurants, including, among others, Taco Bell, Burger King, and Chick-fil-A. Teams search for healthy meals and individuals have roles regarding the various aspects of nutrition to be found on the various websites. Students then synthesize the information, present it to others, and reconsider, according the Cundiff, their own decisions, opinions, and arguments. Accordingly, the students are actively engaged in developing questions and critiques. The Core Essentials program does not foster these postures, as its primary concern is with external imposition of pre-ordained assumptions about charac-

---

[31] "Chick-fil-A 10-Second Tip," *Children's Hospital's Healthy Kids: A Quarterly Publication for Parents Preschoolers* [sic] (Knoxville, TN), volume IX (Winter, 2003): 3. That the hospital condones (and promotes) this kind of logic is fodder for further investigation.

[32] Janet Cundiff, "Living in the Fast (Food) Lane!" http://www.web-and-flow.com/members/jcundiff/fastfoods/webquest.htm. Accessed June 10, 2004. The movie *Supersize It!* also explores issues relating to and resulting from eating fast food.

ter.

I wonder what it would be like if, during the month of October (when "respect" is the value of the month), students would be encouraged to ask whether they, as a group, are actually being shown "respect" via the very program touting the value. Said differently, when is respect for the children shown by the teachers, Core Essentials executives, and Truett Cathy? What role did they have in determining whether they should be subjected to the overtly Christian themes embedded in the program? I also wonder whether the lessons being taught—regardless of whether they are ultimately valid—are also being demonstrated by the people who are promoting the program? How patient would Truett Cathy be of students demonstrating against his company? How respectful of students would Kathy Cox be if they refused to engage in surveillance of one another as the "catching kids" section of the program encourages?

Implications and Further Considerations

One point, then, is to discern the ironies and to tease out the inconsistencies related to the Core Essentials program. We have, in short, a program funded by a fundamentalist Christian whose company uses "kid's meals" as a bribe for behaving in docile, disempowered, uncritical ways. Might this actually be the motive for the program? That is, might it be the case that imposing hierarchy, developing non-questioning students, and privileging Christian-corporate values are intentional acts perpetrated by those wishing to maintain and increase their power, even at the expense of the very students to which they preach equality and kindness? To have Core Essentials and Chick-fil-A work in tandem with William Bennett's *Book of Virtues* raises an obvious question about hypocrisy. Bennett, of course, was revealed to have gambled away millions of dollars at the same time he was loudly proclaiming the vital importance of teaching "virtues" in schools. Is this a "do as I say, not as I do" quagmire? What does it mean that universalists like Bennett actually represent particularist and contextual realities that are not easy to generalize? What does it mean when the Georgia State Superintendent of Schools, Kathy Cox, wishes to delete "evolution" from the curriculum, but applauds Truett Cathy's donation of protestant versions of the Bible to all of the public schools in the state?

Beyond critique of those in power and control of the program, one has to consider the reality of classroom life. Teachers, in a perversely thankful way, simply do not have the time to spare to "add-on" the "curriculum" represented by Core Essentials. The state of Georgia already has a character education component. It also has a core curriculum that, given No Child Left Behind, is raising the degree to which teachers teach to end-of-year tests. Teachers simply do not have the time to alter their bulletin boards, monitor the Chick-fil-A vouchers, and "catch" students behaving in ways the authors of the program do not conduct themselves anyway. So, beyond exploiting the youngest students in schools, beyond the attempt to further proletarianize teaching, beyond attempting to mold obedient and subservient future workers, and beyond the irony and hypocrisy, is there anything valuable about the values valued by Core Essentials? Maybe.

If "Core Essentials" would be used as an object lesson itself, we might be able to reveal a kind of criticality that teaches about values while not externally imposing them without critique. Values exist in schools. Students bring values to the classroom just like their teachers. The question is whether those values are to be explored or whether they are to be assumed. Dewey makes it clear that "morals" are an important part of being a citizen (or any part of a group). He differs greatly from "Core Essentials," though, in that he is not interested in externally imposed, "specialist-"developed terms and themes spread out over three years as part of a preparation plan for future work or future citizenship. In *Moral Principles in Education*, Dewey puts it this way: "We need to see that moral principles are not arbitrary, that they are not 'transcendental'; that the term 'moral' does not designate a special region or portion of life. We need to translate the moral into the conditions and forces of our community life, and into the impulses and habits of the individual. All the rest is mint, anise, and cumin."[33] In another passage, Dewey writes that "the emphasis then falls upon construction...rather than upon absorption and mere learning."[34] As though he is aware of Core Essentials and other such programs, Dewey argues that children are rarely emergent and constructive creatures in classroom settings. Their intellectual life is stunted by the proceduralism of traditional expectations and methods. So, too, says Dewey, of morals in schools:

> The child knows perfectly well that the teacher and all his fellow pupils have exactly the same facts and ideas before them that he [sic] has; he is not *giving* them anything at all. And it may be questioned whether the moral lack is not as great as the intellectual. The child is born with a natural desire to give out, to do, to serve. When this tendency is not used, when conditions are such that other motives are substituted, the

[33] Dewey, *Moral Principles in Education*, 58.
[34] Ibid., 21.

accumulation of an influence working against the social spirit is much larger than we have any idea of—especially when the burden of work, week after week, and year after year, falls upon this side.[35]

Three years worth of value-able "kid's meal" cards externally dangled for Pavlovian results strikes me as the very thing Dewey would argue against. Importantly, Dewey is not arguing against morals. Instead, he is arguing against morals "in the air...something set off by themselves...[morals] that are so *very* 'moral' that they have no working contact with the average affairs of everyday life."[36] As a pragmatist and fallibilist, however, he argues that the utility that various values might have get their worth in their organic growth and development in context. Dewey again:

> Here, then, is the moral standard, by which to test the work of the school upon the side of what it does directly for individuals....Does the school as a system...attach sufficient importance to the spontaneous instincts and impulses? Does it afford sufficient opportunity for these to assert themselves and work out their own results? Can we even say that the school in principle attaches itself...to the active constructive powers rather than to processes of absorption and learning?[37]

I submit that the answers to Dewey's questions are "no," "no," and "no." Far too often in far too many schools, far too many teachers fall back on methods of teaching that are comfortable, traditional. Accordingly, students' natural tendencies to inquire become stifled in rooms that are organized (physically and in terms of curriculum) for convenience and platoon-style management.[38] While teachers are not primarily to blame for the external imposition of No Child Left Behind mandates and high-stakes testing that structure their lives, the very frustration they often feel with such external imposition is not recognized when they, in turn, impose upon their students. Core Essentials is simply another in a long line of impositions that teachers and students must navigate. The difference is the degree to which the program represents corporate infiltration under the guide of character education and the universalism it entails.

Extending Dewey, Bourdieu challenges the rhetoric of universalism that

---

[35] Ibid., 22.

[36] Ibid., 57.

[37] Ibid., 53.

[38] Herbert Kliebard, *The Struggle for the American Curriculum, 1893-1958* (New York: Routledge, 1995), 84, 162.

sets up the structures within which schools operate as stifling places for external imposition. For Bourdieu, "the effect of shared belief. . .removes from discussion ideas which are perfectly worth discussing."[39]

Indeed, Bourdieu envisions a kind of collective intellectualism that challenges deeply held beliefs. Long-standing assumptions become the focus of renewed critique and action. He is specifically interested in examining the major power brokers in modern society. As he puts it, "the power of the agents and mechanisms that dominate the economic and social world today rests on the extraordinary concentration of all the species of capital—economic, political, military, cultural, scientific, and technological—as the foundation of a symbolic domination without precedent. . . ."[40] This symbolic domination is difficult to critique, however, because of the power it has over members of society. For Bourdieu, students are also a direct target and engage in hegemonic practices that further subjugate them to the influence of the market. He claims, for example, "that the 'civilization' of jeans, Coca-Cola, and McDonald's [Chick-fil-A] has not only economic power on its side but also the symbolic power exerted through a seduction to which the victims themselves contribute. By taking as their chief targets children and adolescents, particularly those most shorn of specific immune defenses, with the support of advertising and the media which are both constrained and complicit, the big cultural production and distribution companies gain an extraordinary, unprecedented hold over all contemporary societies—societies that, as a result, find themselves virtually infantilized."[41]

Recall that Core Essentials is imposed on students in grades K-5. Bourdieu's suggestion that the larger society is infantilized by the hold corporate interests have over it is even more striking when we consider that the project of disempowerment literally begins with infants. Organic growth of student interests, for Dewey, paired with sociological critique of business influences, for Bourdieu, make for heady prospects when envisioning what schools—and their curricula—might look like during reformation. It would take, however, a sober reconsideration of the roles of students and teachers in schools to engage in substantive reconstruction of schools. It would require a collective "intellectualization" of various roles and, in order to do so, a sloughing off of the dead skin of corporate- and fundamentalist-sponsored, universalist edicts in

---

[39] Bourdieu, *Acts of Resistance*, 6.

[40] Bourdieu, *Firing Back*, 39.

[41] Ibid., 71.

the form of, among others, character education programs like Core Essentials.

What is not being advocated is a substitution of one kind of pre-ordained morality for another. There should not exist, in other words, a revised script that suggests "The value of the month is criticality. Criticality is defined as ..." This sort of "bait and switch" game has been played for too long in the history of curriculum. The function of indoctrination is the same, even though the forms may morph. Instead, students and teachers should develop their own versions of criticality as those versions emerge (and change) through the natural curiosity of students in K-5. In this way, a singular (Christian) view of character education is replaced with a pluralistic understanding of character and students, taking a cue from Dewey, would utilize their instincts and impulses to explore that variety with one another. No fries are necessary.

Bibliography

Blanchard, Ken and S. Truett Cathy. 2002. *The Generosity Factor*. Grand Rapids, MI: Zondervan.

Bourdieu, Pierre. 1998. *Acts of Resistance: Against the Tyranny of the Market*. New York: The New Press. Trans. Richard Nice.

Bourdieu, Pierre. 2003. *Firing Back: Against the Tyranny of the Market 2*. New York: The New Press. Trans. Loïc Wacquant.

Bowman, Shanthy A., Steven L. Gortmaker, Cara B. Ebbeling, Mark A. Pereira, and David S. Ludwig. 2004. "Effects of Fast-Food Consumption on Energy Intake and Diet Quality Among Children in a National Household Survey." *Pediatrics* 113, no. 1, January.

Brameld, Theodore. 1950. *Ends and Means in Education: A Midcentury Appraisal*. New York: Harper and Row Publishers.

Cathy, S. Truett. 2002. *Eat MOR Chikin: Inspire More People Doing Business the Chick-fil-A Way*. Nashville: Cumberland House Publishing.

Cathy, S. Truett. 1989. *It's Easier to Succeed Than Fail*. Nashville: Thomas Nelson Publishers.

Chick-fil-A. 2003. "Chick-fil-A 10-Second Tip." *Children's Hospital's Healthy Kids: A Quarterly Publication for Parents Preschoolers* [sic]. IX. Knoxville, TN: Children's Hospital. Winter.

Core Essentials. 2001. *Core Essentials: A Strategy for Teaching Character*. Alpharetta, GA: Core Essentials, Inc.

Cundiff, Janet. 2004. "Living in the Fast (Food) Lane!" www.web-and-flow.com/members/jcundiff/fastfoods/webquest.htm.

Deckelbaum, Richard J., and Christine A. Williams. 2001. "Childhood Obesity: The Health Issue." *Obesity Research* 9, suppl. 4. November.

Dewey, John. 1909. *Moral Principles in Education*. Carbondale, IL: Southern Illinois University Press.

Freire, Paulo. 1970. *Pedagogy of the Oppressed*. New York: Continuum.

Josephson, Michael. 2002. "Character Education Is Back in Our Public Schools," *The State Education Standard*. Autumn.

Kaestle, Carl F. 1983. *Pillars of the Republic: Common Schools and American Society, 1780-1860.* New York: Hill and Wang.

Kliebard, Herbert. 1995. *The Struggle for the American Curriculum, 1893-1958.* New York: Routledge.

Lickona, Thomas. 2004. *Character Matters: How to Help Our Children Develop Good Judgment, Integrity, and Other Essential Virtues.* New York: Simon and Schuster.

Linblom, Charles E. 1977. *Politics and Markets: The World's Political-Economic Systems.* New York: Basic Books.

Ludwig, David S., Karen E. Peterson, and Steven Gortmaker. 2001. "Relation between Consumption of Sugar-Sweetened Drinks and Childhood Obesity: A Prospective, Observational Analysis." *The Lancet* 357. February 17.

MacDonald, Mary. 2004. "Evolution Furor Heats Up." *The Atlanta Journal-Constitution.* January 31. A1.

MacDonald, Mary. 2004. "Georgia May Shun 'Evolution' in Schools: Revised Curriculum Plan Outrages Science Teachers." *The Atlanta Journal-Constitution.* January 29. A1.

Marty, Martin E. and R. Scott Appleby. 1997. *Fundamentalism and Society: Reclaiming the Science, the Family, and Education.* Chicago: The University of Chicago Press.

Mosier, Richard. 1965. *Making the American Mind: Social and Moral Ideas in the McGuffey Readers.* New York: Russell & Russell.

Nestle, Marion. 2003. *Food Politics: How the Food Industry Influences Nutrition and Health.* Berkeley, CA: University of California Press.

Spring, Joel. 2005. *The American School, 1642-2004.* Boston: McGraw-Hill.

Tawney, Richard Henry. 1926. *Religion and the Rise of Capitalism.* New York: Harcourt, Brace, and Company.

Vander Schee, Carolyn. 2005. "Food Services and Schooling." *Schools or Markets?: Commercialism, Privatization, and School-Business Partnerships.* Ed. Deron Boyles. Mahwah, NJ: Lawrence Erlbaum.

Williams, Mary M. 2000. "Models of Character Education: Perspectives and Developmental Issues," *Journal of Humanistic Counseling, Education, and Development* 39, no. 1, September.

www.character.org

www.charactercounts.org

www.chickfila.com/CoreEssentials.asp

www.chickfila.com/MenuTable.asp?Category=specialties

www.cortland.edu/c4n5rs/

Zarra, Ernest J. 2000. "Pinning Down Character Education," *Kappa Delta Pi Record* 36, no. 4, Summer.

CHAPTER SIX

Packaging Youth and Selling Tomorrow
Deconstructing the Myths of Marketalkracy

Carly Stasko and Trevor Norris,
Ontario Institute for Studies in Education

Consumption is now recognized as a defining characteristic of the lifestyle of the Western world.

–*Jane Kenway and Elizabeth Bullen*[1]

Playing off teen insecurities is a proven strategy. But even that won't get you very far if you're using a stale campaign and yesterday's slang.

–*Shelly Reese*[2]

In today's free market, children are increasingly less free to be kids as they are transformed through the gaze of marketers into profit-generating demographics. In the following chapter we explore the key characteristics and implications of the growing influence of marketing and the promotion of consumer values among America's youth. We define a "marketalkracy" as a political regime that is centered around the language of marketing and of the market itself. Its meaning is derived in part from the Greek *kratia*, meaning "power" or "to rule"[3]; thus, marketalkracy could mean the "rule by the language of marketing," or "rule by market discourse." As we will show, the language of the market is an increasingly central aspect of the daily lives of youth, as evidenced by the immense vocabularies of consumer products, logos, and the meanings

---

[1] Jane Kenway and Elizabeth Bullen, *Consuming Children: Education-Entertainment-Advertising* (Philadelphia: Open University Press, 2001), 94-95.

[2] Shelly Reese, "The Quality of Cool," *Marketing Tools* 3, no. 6 (1997), 27.

[3] http://www.etymonline.com/index.php?search=-cracy&searchmode=none [accessed June 28, 2007].

associated with them that youth have taken in and learned in order to participate in consumer society. An understanding of such a process is necessary if
we are to effectively address the challenges that consumer culture presents to
the lives of young people and to the larger society.

This chapter begins by considering the effect of marketalkcracy on youth
and society, then critiques several key presuppositions behind marketing, and
argues that these unquestioned presuppositions serve to help advance the
"rule" of the market and brands. We draw from recent literature in the field as
well as the transcription of a panel in which four marketers discussed the ethics of marketing to teens. As it will not be possible to present a comprehensive
account of all the key features,[4] implications, and presuppositions behind
marketalkcracy, we will select those which contribute to the formation and
perpetuation of a marketalkcracy as it relates to youth.

As it will become apparent, the undue influence of the market on society
renders us without political agency and construes the world as fixed and un-
changeable. Harvard theologian Harvey Cox aptly described how the market is
deified and elevated beyond reproach. American political theorist Benjamin
Barber describes how market totalism becomes dominant, and observes that
"When religion colonizes every sector of what should be our multidimensional
lives, we call the result theocracy; and when politics colonizes every sector of
what should be our multidimensional lives, we call the result tyranny. So why,
it might be asked, when the marketplace—with its insistent ideology of consumption and its dogged orthodoxy of spending—colonizes every sector of
what should be our multidimensional lives, do we call the result liberty?"[5] Perhaps this is because marketing is in the business of constructing reality, and as
linguist Susan Gal argues, "The strongest form of power may well be the ability to define social reality, to impose visions of the world."[6] And so it is with
this in mind that we attempt to adjust our gaze upon the gazers who hide behind the two-way mirrors of market research and the glossy images of advertising in our freest of free markets where nothing is free except for the cost of
our labor as consumers.

---

[4] Harvey Cox, "The Market as God," *Atlantic Monthly* (March, 1999): 18-23.

[5] Benjamin Barber, *Consumed: How Markets Corrupt Children, Infantilize Adults, and Swallow Citizens Whole* (New York: W. W. Norton and Company, 2007).

[6] Susan Gal, "Language, Gender, and Power: An Anthropological Review," *Gender Articulated:
Language and the Socially Constructed Self*, ed. Kira Hall and Mary Bucholtz (New York: Routledge, 1995), 178.

The Growth of Big Marketing

While corporations once focused on the production of concrete physical products, they are increasingly focused on the production of images and meanings in the form of brands and logos.[7] As a result, advertising and marketing have grown ever more prevalent, as more and more parts of our day involve exposure to these signs and images: while filling up our cars, riding elevators, or waiting for the subway. In schools, ads can increasingly be found in hallways, classrooms, and even on and in textbooks. What is the result? According to the Millward Brown Global Market Research Agency, "nowhere else in the world are 8- to 12-year-olds more materialistic or more likely to believe that their clothes and brands describe who they are and define their social status."[8] It is therefore essential for us to reflect on the influence of what has been called the "Captains of Consciousness"[9] or the "Hidden Persuaders"[10] in shaping our values and culture.

Marketers help deepen our attachment to commodities, reinforce the notion that happiness and a positive self-image come from acquisition, and help ensure that we associate products only with the symbolic meaning which marketers create and not with the conditions of their production or their effect on the environment after consumption. In so doing, they create a culture of consumers, a "consumer culture" that excludes alternatives from being presented. As marketing spreads, it is taking on new forms such as "buzz" marketing or "stealth marketing," which pays individuals for promoting products to friends and family or just to wear a new product in public. As if there were not already enough ads in the "real" world, advertising is now moving into the virtual world by putting ads and product placements in video games—what French philosopher Jean Baudrillard calls "hypersimulation."[11]

Soon it may be the case that more money is spent marketing to youth than educating them, as students become targeted more as present and future con-

---

[7] Naomi Klein, *No Logo: Taking Aim at the Brand Bullies* (Toronto: Vintage Canada, 2000).

[8] Juliet Schor, "Those Ads Are Enough to Make Your Kids Sick," *Washington Post* (11 September 2004): http://www.washingtonpost.com/wp-dyn/articles/A13374-2004Sep11.html. [accessed 12 September 2006].

[9] Stuart Ewen, *Captains of Consciousness: Advertising and the Social Roots of the Consumer Culture* (Toronto: McGraw Hill, 1976).

[10] Vance Packard, *The Hidden Persuaders* (New York: D. McKay Co., 1965).

[11] Jean Baudrillard, *The Consumer Society: Myths and Structures* (London: Sage, 1970/1998); Jean Baudrillard, *Simulacra and Simulation*, trans. Sheila Faria Glaser (Ann Arbor: University of Michigan Press, 1981/1994).

sumers than as future participants in the public world or agents of social change.[12] Statistics confirm this trend in which increases in advertising budgets far exceed increases in spending on education. In 2004, $266 billion was spent on advertising in the U.S.,[13] while it is estimated that "global advertising spending will increase at a robust 5.9% during the 2005-2009 period."[14] Not only is the total amount of spending on advertising increasing but also the total amount of exposure. Benjamin Barber notes that "teachers struggle for the attention of their students for at most twenty or thirty hours a week, perhaps thirty weeks a year, in settings they do not fully control and in institutions that are often ridiculed in the popular media, [while] the true tutors of late consumer capitalist society as measured by time are those who control the media monopolies...who capture sixty or seventy hours a week, fifty-two weeks a year, of children's time and attention."[15]

As a result, contemporary experiences of childhood and adolescence are increasingly the construct of consumer culture, and what has been referred to as Generation X or Y could in fact be called the "Branded Generation."[16] As marketer Anne Sutherland explains: "If the boomers were the 'me' generation, then Generation Y could be thought of as the 'more generation.' As one *New Yorker* cartoon glibly pointed out, these kids have only known a 'bull market.' The end result: More spending, more experiencing, more demands for more."[17] However, while such a long period of sustained economic growth itself promotes more consumerism and growth, it would also seem to imply that only a major economic depression or world war could do anything to alter consumerism. In the meantime, we are all encouraged to shop in the fight against terror. Consumerism has reshaped the world in its image—

---

[12] See, for example: Henry A. Giroux, *The Abandoned Generation* (New York: Palgrave, 2003); Jane Kenway and Elizabeth Bullen, *Consuming Children: Education-Entertainment-Advertising* (Philadelphia: Open University Press, 2001).

[13] Melanie Wells, "Kid Nabbing," *Forbes* (1 February 2004): http://www.commercialalert.org/issues/culture/buzz-marketing/kid-nabbing [Accessed May 5, 2007]

[14] M. Evans, "Canadian Advertisers Must 'Wake Up' to Internet," *National Post* (Toronto) (27 October 2005): B 7.

[15] Barber, *Consumed*, 231.

[16] Alissa Quart, *Branded: The Buying and Selling of Teenagers* (Cambridge: Perseus Publishers, 2003); Al Urbanski, "The Branded Generation," *Promo Magazine* (1 July 1998): http://promomagazine.com/mag/marketing_branded_generation/index.html. [accessed January 19, 2007].

[17] Ann Sutherland and Betty Thompson, *Kidfluence: Why Kids Today Mean Business* (Toronto: McGraw-Hill Ryerson, 2001), 77.

transforming childhood, parenting, education, and civic agency, just to name a few of the key elements in social life that have been rewritten in the marketalkracy.

Marketers know that teens are more influenced by their peers than by any other demographic, and to this end have attempted to recruit teens as marketers for each other. For example, Procter & Gamble recently established a subsidiary called "Tremor," which has "assembled a stealth sales force of teenagers—280,000 strong—to push products on friends and family."[18] Teenagers are invited to join a "network," described as a "way for kids to influence companies and find out about cool new products before their friends do."[19] While movies and television have long contained "product placement," more recently musicians have been approached to include references to McDonald's in their lyrics. "Eminem and 50 Cent could soon have a new lyrical weapon to add to their arsenal: the Big Mac."[20] With the growing popularity of video games luring youth away from the television screen, advertisers have begun placing products within the virtual world of games themselves.[21]

Children today are so thoroughly immersed in advertising's world of images and jingles that they have no trouble identifying dozens of consumer brands and corporate slogans; they have developed a new kind of literacy. Literacy discourse is characterized by tensions over what "literacy" means, who it serves, how it ought to be measured, and how it should be taught and learned. There is much written about emotional literacy, functional literacy, and so on. However, what is increasingly apparent in today's students is what could be called the literacy of marketalkcracy. Even at a very early age, many children can more readily identify countless logos and meanings associated with them than they can important historical figures. A provocative display of this dynamic occurs in the documentary, *Super Size Me*,[22] wherein several school children were shown dozens of corporate logos, and were more successful at identifying them than when shown pictures of Jesus, Martin Luther King Jr., and Mother Teresa. A 1986 study showed the popularity of Ronald McDon-

---

[18] Melanie Wells, "Kid Nabbing," *Forbes* (1 February 2004): www.commercialalert.org/buzzmarketing.pdf [Accessed March 10, 2007].

[19] Ibid.

[20] Keith McArthur, "Ronald McDonald Recruits New Posse," *The Globe and Mail* (29 March 2005): A 17.

[21] Tessa Wegert, "Advertisers Playing Video Game Card," *The Globe and Mail* (15 December 2004): B 8.

[22] www.supersizeme.com/

ald: "A poll of school-age children showed that 96% of them could identify Ronald McDonald, second only to Santa Claus in name recognition."[23]

Media theorist Carrie McLaren describes an exercise she undertook with high school students which demonstrates the extent to which students are increasingly "literate" in the language of marketing. "On the first day of class, I ask students to try and identify several plants and trees common in our Brooklyn neighborhood. They generally fail to name one. Then I show a slide of the alphabet comprised entirely from brand logos and they name almost all of them."[24] That students display such a remarkable literacy with respect to the language of marketing and comparably little knowledge of the natural world around them demonstrates the wide reach of marketing. This hegemonic literacy derived from such advertising is not traditional literacy but is an essential component of participation in marketalkcracy. However, while students may display this kind of "commercial literacy," they are limited in their ability to use this literacy to communicate beyond consumer activities.

Marketers can readily gain access to our minds, as the name of the marketing firm Mindshare indicates, whose website proudly proclaims that "we work collaboratively to enable our clients to gain a greater share of consumers' minds."[25] While Socrates called upon us to "know thyself," and Freud showed that we are largely "unknown to ourselves," marketers demonstrate that they often know more about us and our desires than we do. A new trend in marketing, perhaps its most extreme form, is called "neuromarketing," and uses magnetic resonance imaging (MRI) to map brain patterns and reveal how consumers respond to a particular advertisement or product. Researchers at the Brighthouse Institute for Thought Sciences[26] measure the discrepancy between a participant's stated preference and the pleasure centers of his or her brain which the product activated. The results confirm the greater impact of brands and images over physical sensations. Researchers can thereby determine the effectiveness of marketing campaigns and branding strategies, and plan new and more effective ones. A *Forbes* article states that the intention is to "find a

---

[23] Steven Greenhouse, "The Rise and Rise of McDonald's," *New York Times* (8 June 1986): section 3, 1.

[24] http://www.stayfreemagazine.org/ml/ [accessed June 2, 2007].

[25] Mindshare Web site: http://www.mindshareworld.com/output/Page2.asp [Accessed June 22, 2007].

[26] http://www.cognitiveliberty.org/neuro/Rushkoff_Neuromarketing.html [Accessed June 22, 2007].

buy button inside the skull."[27] Soon the search for this "buy button" will surpass the unreliability of surveys and focus groups as it turns from a "soft" social science to a "hard" neurological science wherein our preferences become understood at the molecular level. Mapping the shopper's mind in this way allows unlimited reach into the most private dimensions of human thought and desire. Researcher Adam Kovol contends that they're doing consumers a favor by helping determine what we like and want, and that their work is benign because "they only observe and learn."[28] However, it seems that if such work were truly benign, and no advantage could be gained from such observations, marketing companies would not fund it in the first place. It seems grossly inappropriate that while sick Americans wait months for cost-prohibitive medical MRI scans so that their doctors can observe and learn with the goal of healing them, private research facilities use the same tools to perform research that often has the end goal of selling unhealthy products such as cigarettes, alcohol, cars, and junk food to children.

All in the Family: Youth Marketing as Child Labor

MRI imaging of the consumer mind is only one of the ways that marketing is elbowing its way into the private lives of the public citizenry. Now more than ever, advertising is colonizing the private dreams, hopes, and self-concepts of children as well as the sanctity of the family. According to James U. McNeal, a professor of marketing at Texas A&M University, marketers currently target youth in three primary ways.[29] To begin, today's youth as a demographic has a sizable disposable income to be spent on technology, fashion, fast food, and media. Many teens in the West are taking on multiple part-time jobs just to support their consumer spending habits, in contrast to the majority of youth globally who are working as primary breadwinners for the family. Children have been described as marketers' "Trojan Horse"[30] in the

---

[27] Melanie Wells, "In Search of the Buy Button," *Forbes* (31 August 2003): http://search.forbes.com/search/find?MT=in+search+of+the+buy+button [Accessed June 22, 2007].

[28] Kelly, Margo, "The Science of Shopping," CBC *Marketplace* (2 December 2002). http://www.cbc.ca/consumers/market/files/money/science_shopping/ [accessed May 24, 2007].

[29] James McNeal, "Tapping the Three Kids' Markets," *American Demographics* (April 1998): 37-41.

[30] This is a term widely used by marketers. See the discussion by Erika Shaker of the Canadian Center for Policy Alternatives in her article "Individuality.com: Empowering Youth Through Consumption?" in *Our Schools/Ourselves* (July 2001): http://www.media-awareness.ca/

family, who influence their parents through what some call the "Nag Factor" or "Pester Power."[31] This is true not only of products that kids want for themselves but also for the products their parents buy. One need only stand at the checkout line of a grocery store where the candies and junk food are strategically positioned at children's eye level to hear the all too familiar begging, pleading, whining, and consumer-driven tantrums that further serve to separate parents from their money (and parental autonomy). Market researchers estimate that in 2003 "children age four to twelve influenced some $565 billion of their parents' purchasing each year."[32] One marketer observed that "The *influence market* is five to seven times the size of the primary market."[33] Thus, advertising may have influenced family dynamics in such a way that parents concede to their kids and their "expert" opinion. Marketers are not only interested in the ways that children can spend and influence spending today, they are also investing a great deal of resources into ensuring lifelong brand-loyal consumers for the future. At a time when children are developing their sense of identity and formulating their worldviews, they are targeted with multi-platform marketing campaigns that battle it out for the pinnacle of product placement—to be front and center in the foundational memories of childhood and adolescence.

Jonathan Rowe and Gary Ruskin argue that "corporations are literally alienating children from their parents, shifting children's loyalties more toward the corporations themselves."[34] In addition to creating animosity between children and their families, many marketing strategies seek to exploit the already tenuous emotional landscapes of today's dual income and/or divorced families. Parents who spend less time with their children because of work or divorce are compelled to show their love and ease their guilt through spending. Children in divorced families have extra sets of parents and grand-

---

english/resources/articles/advertising_marketing/empowering_youth.cfm

[31] See Joel Bakan, *The Corporation: The Pathological Pursuit of Power* (Toronto: Viking, 2004), 119-122; Ann Sutherland and Betty Thompson, *Kidfluence: Why Kids Today Mean Business*.

[32] Jonathan Rowe and Gary Ruskin, "The Parent's Bill of Rights: Helping Moms and Dads Fight Commercialism," *Mothering Magazine* Issue 116 (Jan/Feb 2003). http://www.mothering.com/articles/growing_child/consumerism/bill_of_rights.html See also Kim Campbell and Kent Davis-Packard, "How Ads Get Kids to Say I Want It!" *Christian Science Monitor* (18 September 2000). http://csmonitor.com/cgi-bin/durableRedirect.pl?/durable/2000/09/18/p1s1.htm [Accessed October 23, 2005].

[33] Sutherland and Thompson, *Kidfluence: Why Kids Today Mean Business*, 119.

[34] Rowe and Ruskin, "The Parent's Bill of Rights: Helping Moms and Dads Fight Commercialism."

parents to buy them stuff, and often children can play one parent against the other. In homes where parents cannot afford to satisfy the consumer tastes of their children, parents will often feel inadequate and kids can interpret the absence of consumer goods as an absence of affection. This equation is not simply an invention of the child but a media-constructed association. As Gary Ruskin, former director of Commercial Alert, has said of marketers, "These minds do not work to solve the nation's real problems; they work to create new problems for you."[35] It may seem overly suspicious to claim that marketers exploit these societal trends if it were not for the fact that "guilt money" and "pester power" were terms born from the marketing industry itself and entrenched in the discourse of marketalkracy. Sut Jhally, the founder and executive director of the Media Education Foundation, argues that youth marketing is a new form of child labor, as children become corporate spokespeople and unconsciously do the work of marketers within the family. Jhally goes so far as to suggest that, at the same time we make efforts to protect our children from bullying and physical molestation, "we have opened up our doors and allowed people to come into our homes to manipulate our children and draw value out of them."[36] Yet some marketers argue that they are performing a public service by educating children. For example, in *Kidfluence: Why Kids Today Mean Business*, Anne Sutherland and Betty Thompson argue that marketers are a part of a dramatic transformation of the traditional family: from an authoritarian, parent-centered structure to a "bi-directional relationship" more democratically centered around children's real needs and interests.[37] The authors suggest that baby boomers who grew up in authoritarian households are trying to raise their children differently by involving them in family discussions in a much more democratic manner. Parents will increasingly ask their children's opinion about consumer decisions because they are afraid of making a mistake. Thus, business responded by speaking to younger people, who are now the educated experts within the family and appreciated for their extensive product knowledge. Sutherland and Thompson explain:

---

[35] Gary Ruskin, "Why They Whine: How Corporations Prey on Our Children," *Mothering Magazine*. http://www.mothering.com/articles/growing_child/consumerism/whine.html [Accessed June 26, 2007].

[36] William O'Barr, "Advertising, Cultural Criticism & Pedagogy: An Interview with Sut Jhally," http://www.sutjhally.com/articles/advertisingcultura [accessed July 4, 2007].

[37] Sutherland and Thompson. *Kidfluence: Why Kids Today Mean Business*.

In the new family model, kids feel like a valuable part of the family unit and grow up believing they have the right to vote on all issues affecting their family, including purchasing decisions. Small questions like "What should we get Grandma for her birthday?" to weightier queries like "Where shall we spend our summer vacation?" are within the parameters of normal dialogue for most families. In fact, today's parents go as far as to say it is unfair not to include younger members of the family in buying decisions. Families who do not confer with their children about purchases, either of a daily nature or larger one-time acquisitions, deny their kids an opportunity to develop important life skills. Many families who have adopted these democratic practices like the dignity they give the family. They promote the concept that all family members are equally valued and given consideration regardless of age.[38]

According to these marketers, increased ability to make consumer choices is equated with increasing democratization of the family, and marketers are providing a service to society by spreading democracy. However, this may put the cart before the horse: While some parents may ask for their child's opinion, many others are simply overwhelmed by constant berating. Few parents will be grateful to marketers while walking through the candy section of a store or driving past a fast-food restaurant.

Marketization of Youth: Invention, Disappearance, and Extension

This trend towards the marketization of youth constitutes a form of objectification because it reduces children to a market. Gary Ruskin formerly of Commercial Alert argues that "There's been a shift in the predominant way our society thinks of children. Not long ago we considered children vulnerable beings to be nurtured. However, today we increasingly see kids through an economic lens. In our business culture, children are viewed as an economic resource to be exploited, just like bauxite or timber."[39] There is a constant pressure for this objectifying construction of youth as a market to happen at a younger and younger age. Kids-R-Us former president Mike Searles claims that "If you own this child at an early age, you can own this child for years to come...I want to own this kid younger and younger."[40]

Scholars who have researched employment trends argue that those children who worked outside of the home in earlier eras either did not go to school or turned their earnings over to the household. Melissa K. Lickteig as-

---

[38] Ibid., 18.

[39] Ruskin, "Why They Whine: How Corporations Prey on Our Children."

[40] Ibid.

serts that "historically, children who worked did so largely to help supplement their family's household income; their wages contributed to the collective needs of family maintenance."[41] She argues that, in contrast, teenagers today in many cases work to buy consumer products for themselves. Companies like Nike, Coke, MTV, and countless others would be much less successful were it not for the growth in discretionary spending money among this demographic cohort. Jane Kenway and Elizabeth Bullen argue that "This century has certainly seen sweeping changes in conceptions of childhood, and in child-rearing practices, family life and children's culture. The 'nature' of being young, the relationships of the young to adults, to the family and to other social institutions, such as the school, have changed considerably across time and place."[42] As a result, "we are entering another stage in the construction of the young as the demarcations between education, entertainment and advertising collapse and as the lines between the generations both blur and harden."[43]

Some scholars like Neil Postman argue that the invention of childhood is commonly attributed to the industrial revolution and the abolitionist movement against child labor,[44] while others attribute the creation of teenagers to demographic marketing, which first emerged during the 1950s as a "direct offspring of an incessantly increasing consumerism and a growing dependence upon the media for information and recreation."[45] Feminist author and baby boomer Susan Douglas describes how she was part of the "first generation of preteen and teenage girls to be relentlessly isolated as a distinct market segment....which cultivated in [them] a highly self-conscious sense of importance, difference, and even rebellion."[46] She explains that because "young women became critically important economically, as a market, the suspicion began to percolate among them, over time, that they might be important culturally, and then politically, as a generation."[47] If industrialization and marketing is in part responsible for the construction of the child and the teenager, it is with bitter

---

[41] M. K. Lickteig, "Brand Name Schools: The Deceptive Lure of Corporate-School Partnerships," *The Educational Forum* vol. 68 (Fall 2003): 46.

[42] Jane Kenway and Elizabeth Bullen, *Consuming Children: Education-Entertainment-Advertising* (Philadelphia: Open University Press, 2001), 2.

[43] Ibid., 3.

[44] Neil Postman, *The Disappearance of Childhood* (New York: Vintage, 1994).

[45] Marcel Danesi, *Cool: The Signs and Meanings of Adolescence* (Toronto: University of Toronto Press, 1994), 4.

[46] Susan Douglas, *Where the Girls Are: Growing Up Female with the Mass Media* (New York: Random House, 1994), 14.

[47] Ibid.

irony that its culminating task will be the disappearance of the child as it is construed as a "target market." In contrast, Benjamin Barber argues that even as childhood disappears it is extended into all age groups, creating "kidults" as adults are infantilized. Barber speaks of the "infantalist ethos" and "enduring childishness" promoted by marketers, and asserts that "a new cultural ethos is being forged that is intimately associated with global consumerism. Those responsible for manufacturing and merchandizing goods for the global marketplace, those who are actually researching, teaching, and practicing marketing and advertising today, are aiming both to sell to a younger demographic and to imbue older consumers with the tastes of the young."[48]

Youth ranging from preteens to emerging adults[49] are being taught to see themselves as "individual consumers" rather than as a "public citizenry," while the structures and supports once offered by governments and communities are increasingly replaced by privatized "services." For young people today, the precarious workforce devoid of security, health plans, and union protection has been repackaged as the "Me, Inc." economy where they are the creators of their own destiny—"free agents in an economy of free agents."[50] Today's youth are sold a narrative of individual power that is granted through choice, while at the same time their ability to challenge the true powers of this world have become increasingly limited. The branded images of products and politicians are ever present in the mediasphere as marketers seek to access public mindshare. Yet access to the CEOs and politicians behind these constructed and often contradictory images and messages has become dangerously difficult. Instead, the value of today's youth is to be found in their disposable income and "kidfluence." A disproportionate amount of resources is invested in developing and understanding today's youth as a market, while, in contrast, the limited and dwindling resources of governments and families interested in the "whole child" are under such threat that it is often believed that they can be

---

[48] Barber, *Consumed: How Markets Corrupt Children, Infantilize Adults, and Swallow Citizens Whole*, 7.

[49] "A generation ago, young people ...finished college, started careers, moved out of their parents' home and, in many cases, got married in their early 20s. These days, all of this is happening five to 10 years later as young people take longer to finish their schooling, are ambivalent about what they want to do with their lives and are not driven to start a career or a family. Many of them return to their parents' homes sometime during their 20s to regroup, save money and ponder their next steps." Quoted from "Emerging Adulthood," *Parenthood.com*, http://www.parenthood.com/ articles.html?article_id=9153 [accessed May 22, 2007].

[50] Tom Peters, "The Brand Called You," *Fast Company* 10 (August 1997): 83-92.

sustained only through commercial sponsorship. Thus, what choice is there for young people who wish to be valued, invested in, and perceived as more than just a market? To address this question we will now consider several key presuppositions among marketers, including the notions of choice, savvy, apathy, and impotence.

Choice Is Your Voice: Rights, Choice, and Freedom

It could be said that consumerism is our new ideology, the paradigm of postmodernity, in which the human being is dehumanized and depoliticized and "rights" are replaced with "tastes" as young consumers increasingly find their power in their pocket books. Because of the discrepancy in spending power between private marketing institutions and public democratic projects, our hopes, fears, and dreams are most commonly voiced before the two-way mirror of a market researcher, while we experience a false democracy through the limited scope of our consumer choices. Contemporary consumerism has become our primary language such that consumption has become our primary experience of participation in something beyond ourselves. Marketing is often defended as promoting choices and giving people what they need and want. "The market will provide a market solution," proclaims the marketalkracy.

However, consumerism is often portrayed by the marketing industry as a means of improving our collective "rights" and "choices" by arguing that we are increasingly free as we continue to be presented with more and more choices. However, the choices of others affect us each in very different ways, and the choices of a few people have wide-reaching effects on many others around the world. Furthermore, while we may have countless choices in our lives, from cars to candy, there are many choices which we simply do not have. For example, while it is true that we can choose to shop and consume less, we cannot choose to live in a society with less consumerism. And while consumers may have "rights," perhaps we also have a right to live in a *less* materialistic society. A large amount of financial resources are invested each year into market research so that business can better understand the desires, interests, concerns, and ideals of today's youth. While it is argued that this allows them to determine what choices young people will make, the true goal of market research is to determine which choices will bring financial reward. If a student chooses to have less bullying in her school, this is not a choice she will be offered by advertisers. If, however, the student wishes to purchase sneakers associated with a celebrity that she admires, that is the type of choice she can be sold.

Even more troubling are the ways in which a consumer-driven culture uses resources and creates waste in unsustainable ways and perpetuates unhealthy mental and physical lifestyles ranging from cynicism to obesity and diabetes. And yet the choice to choose less is simply not on the radar of marketers, for obvious reasons: Since there is little money to be made from such messages, it is not a choice that is promoted with equal vigor or persuasiveness. While it is the job of marketers to research and present choices that will be financially profitable, it tends to be in the interest of educators and parents to create choices for today's youth that exist beyond the limited paradigm of commodities. Notions of choice are influenced by the interests of those involved. There is a reason why many teachers refer to young people as students and the citizens of the future, while marketers (and, indeed, some teachers) tend to refer to youth as "shareholders," "stakeholders," and a "market" themselves—in other words, future loyal customers. Many important things simply cannot be understood in terms of choice or rights, as this market discourse speaks to us primarily as isolated individuals—as if we all consist primarily of needs and desires and are driven chiefly by the mentality of "looking out for number one" and concerned above all with "me and my stuff." What kind of a world is that? And what kind of people fill it?

Oh So Savvy: Flattery Will Get You Nowhere

In a panel discussion organized by the Association for Media Literacy (AML), which featured four experts from the youth marketing industry, there was clear agreement about how "savvy" today's youth are, suggesting that they are more media-literate than any generation before them. For example, marketer Debbie Gordon claims "children are doing a fabulous job now of understanding advertising, they have become so much more savvy."[51] Yet often what marketers call "savvy" among young consumers could in fact be referred to as simply cynical or media-saturated; savvy often means "hard to reach" rather than increasingly critical or resistant towards the reigning marketalkcracy. Being savvy in this sense means they can identify and differentiate between different products and brands. However, this does not necessarily indicate any

---

[51] Carly Stasko and Trevor Norris, "AML Panel on Youth Marketing: Transcript of Event." (November 2, 2005). http://www.aml.ca/articles/articles.php?articleID=349 [accessed July 12, 2007].

kind of critical understanding about how advertising works or the implications of consumer culture on health, politics, or the environment. Thus, when a panel of marketers addressed the critical eye of the "young consumer," it was in relation to tastes rather than opinions. Max Valiquette, the founder and president of Youthography, a leading Canadian youth marketing company, described to an audience of teachers and parents how difficult it was to sell to young people today because they have seen so much advertising: "If an ad isn't smart and funny, then they will reject it." His challenge as a marketer is to keep the ever-shortening attention span of today's youth focused on his commercial message long enough for the desirable associations to register. In contrast, a parent or teacher has a different challenge—to promote a kind of literacy that moves beyond "savvy" and into the realm of creative and critical thinking, beyond knowing what she likes or does not like yet understanding why she responds to commercial messages in certain ways, how that effect was achieved, and what implications this may have on her worldview or the world itself.

Debunking the Apathy Myth

Some marketers suggest that marketing might help increase political participation because it will mean that youth become more demanding and empowered and come to expect more of government. Present political apathy is said to result from "bad marketing" on the part of politicians because politics is not positioned as "cool." Marketing is thereby construed as the new standard by which politics is measured, voting is equated with buying, citizenship with consumption, and politicians are packaged and sold as a consumer good. As Max Valiquette explained at a panel on youth marketing, "Young people are being so engaged in every process right now *but* the political process. Your parents want to know what you think, your schools want to know what you think, marketers, for the love of god, always want to know what you think. Youth expect politics to be customized to them. This generation wants to be participatory because that's the way they've grown up; they expect it to be interactive."[52]

Yet ironically many people are disengaged because politics is already so over-marketed and image-oriented, and politicians and issues become slogans rather than providing genuine personal connections and identifications. Society becomes so thoroughly saturated with marketing that there is little room

---

[52] Ibid.

left over for politics; politics itself becomes subsumed under marketalkcracy. As McLuhan anticipated, "Politics will be replaced by imagery. The politician will be only too happy to abdicate in favor of his image because the image will be much more powerful than he ever could be."[53] Perhaps people might be more likely to gain interest in politics and be less cynical about their ability to influence the world around them in ways other than shopping if politicians and issues seemed to be more "real" and more human.

While consumerism is all about individual gratification and narcissistic self-preoccupation, politics is about collective social change based on the ability to think beyond one's own needs. Consumerism speaks to us only as isolated individuals but does not speak to us about larger social concerns, and problems are framed as purely individual issues that can be resolved only through individual acts of consumption. What is problematic is that marketing encourages us to think about the political world around us such that we engage in politics only so as to better protect "me and my stuff."

Will the answer to these concerns present itself as a consumer choice? Not likely. It is beyond the world of selling and choosing that such solutions will be created, beyond individual decisions and personal preferences. For example, the Canadian group Adbusters has been trying for years to have their "uncommercials" aired on TV and in newspapers—commercials that discourage shopping and overconsumption.[54] Networks declined airing these anti-ads because they conflicted with the interests of their other advertisers. From the perspective of the role of media in society, perhaps what is most unfortunate about this situation is that the dominant mode of communication communicates only one message. There is really only one kind of choice that is presented to us: the choice to consume.

Often, the media paints a picture of today's youth as self-centered-apathetic-consumption-obsessed-tycoon-wannabees. Considering all the money put into market research, cool hunting, and tailored marketing strategies, is anyone surprised that today's youth seem to care more about MTV than the possibilities of social change? Young people have quite an influence on MTV (just as it does upon them), and they know this. Cool Hunters follow them around the schoolyard desperately seeking the holy grail of youth "cool," and

---

[53] Quoted in: http://www.imediaconnection.com/content/3882.asp [Accessed June 21, 2007].

[54] See, for example, specific Adbusters clips, and their accompanying rejections: http://64.233.167.104/search?q=cache:TITFgTej7pgJ:www.adbusters.org/metas/psycho/mediacarta/rejected/+adbusters+uncommercial&hl=en&ct=clnk&cd=4&gl=ca

market researchers painstakingly devise questions to probe the teenage mind for ways of tapping into their disposable income.

Young people know that they have power as a market, that someone will listen whenever they are talking about their buying habits. On the other hand, in the political arena young people have considerably less power or influence. Many are too young or disillusioned to vote, and cannot afford to fund campaigns, hire lobbyists, or operate their own broadcast networks. If they have things to say or questions to ask about the state of the world, who besides marketers are listening? Their teachers, families, and friends may care, but they are overshadowed by the sheer size, funding, and slick packaging of commercial culture.

In spite of all this, today's young people still believe that change is possible, and are still demanding to take part in creating a more just and sustainable world. Ironically, it is some of North America's most well funded market researchers who are studying and exploiting this cultural trend towards civic agency among youth. The new marketer's bible is a 14-country survey of over 3,000 teens called "GenWorld: The New Generation of Global Youth."[55] This study calls today's teens "Interactivist Gen," and describes the growing desire among youth to contribute to society, to make a positive difference in the world, and to "do the right thing" both locally and globally. Yet, marketers are only interested in youth civic engagement insofar as it can be packaged into a profitable marketing campaign, rather than a genuine youth movement. In response to the complex desires of "Interactivist Gen," marketers struggle to forge links between their products and social and environmental causes—often spending more money to promote their ethics than on the issues they profess to care about. Young people feel empowered when they are told that their opinions matter, but what kind of power is it when only their consumer interests or their ability to influence their family and friends is valued? What happens to the notion of the citizen when only the consumer is of interest?

Feign the Victim/Blame the Victim

The divide between civic interests and financial interests regarding today's youth is most delineated when the issue of responsibility arises. This is perhaps one of the more contentious topics which most marketers prefer not to

---

[55] Gia Medeiros and Chip Walker, "GenWorld: The New Generation of Global Youth" *Energy BBDO Report* (2005): http://www.fresh-films.com/downloads/GenWorld_TeenStudy.pdf [accessed Sept 14, 2006].

discuss or debate. Among the tactics marketers use to address the ethical or political implications of marketing is evasion and deference to choice. For example, Anne Sutherland responded to ethical concerns by asking, "Is marketing deceitful? I'm not sure, I think we need to understand that it's one of the tools of the toolbox, and then we'll make our own choices."[56]   Perhaps with more honesty Valiquette claims that his job is to make sure his staff gets paid and his dog gets fed.[57] They readily reply with pat answers such as: "It's out of our hands" and "It's what people want." Responsibility is thereby passed on to governments, consumers, or their employers as they claim to be powerless before market forces. It is ironic that those who promote "empowerment" in fact claim that they themselves are powerless. On the one hand, the responsibility for any ethical or social problems associated with marketing is often passed on to the corporations that marketers work for, and marketing is construed as merely a part of a larger system over which it has little or no control. On the other hand it is youth as consumers who apparently have all the power. The relationship between marketing and society is portrayed as such a complicated game of chicken and egg that it is virtually incomprehensible, and those who create the advertising research or content are absolved of any responsibility for its effect on society. What is implied is that things should proceed as they have, that such a complicated system is best left untouched, and that it is better to simply benefit from the way things are than to try to imagine or initiate any alternative.

Marketers celebrate choice yet they often defer to their own limited choices; it is the consumers who are free, while the marketers are helpless. For example, marketer Anne Sutherland described a campaign in which Zellers, in the interest of mothers, attempted to offer fashions for young girls that were age-appropriate despite the influence of adult sexualized fashions on young girls fuelled by pop artists such as Christina Aguilera, Britney Spears, and the Pussycat Dolls. However, she explained that mothers instead took their daughters and dollars elsewhere, and hence Zellers had no choice but to offer similar styles if they were to remain competitive.[58] Sutherland also explained that their research showed that parents often ask their kids what specific brands of household products, such as cereal, they should buy. Sutherland argued that

---

[56] Carly Stasko and Trevor Norris, "AML Panel on Youth Marketing: Transcript of Event." (November 2, 2005).http://www.aml.ca/articles/articles.php?articleID=349 [accessed July 12, 2007].

[57] Ibid.

[58] Ibid.

since parents were asking their children such questions, the kids learned that it was important to pay attention to advertising, and hence advertisers had no "choice" but to target kids in their advertising campaigns.

Youth marketer Shelly Reese describes the teen audience as a "moving target" and explains that "as teens age, their preferences rapidly change. That means companies have to be ready to shift their focus at a moment's notice—over, and over, and over again."[59] Is this suggesting that it is the fault of children who are "moving targets" that marketing has become so pervasive? Are we really supposed to feel pity for the hard-working "hunters" in this metaphor? As Naomi Klein discusses in *No Logo*, with "so much competition, the agencies argue, clients must spend more than ever to make sure their pitch screeches so loud it can be heard over all the others."[60] She quotes David Lubars, a senior ad executive in the Omnicom Group, who explains candidly that consumers are "like roaches—you spray them and spray them and they get immune after a while."[61] Because of all the ad-spray and the increasing "immunity" of children to advertising, marketers profess to have no choice but to continue to colonize new virgin territories with commercial messages, ranging from product placement and "viral marketing" to school commercialism, where "the advertiser gets a group of kids who cannot go to the bathroom, who cannot change the station, who cannot listen to their mother yell in the background, who cannot be playing Nintendo, [and] who cannot have their headsets on."[62]

Advertising Consumerism and School Commercialism

Max Valiquette went on to say that "Advertising pays for most of the culture we consume."[63] This notion is very confusing to us: it seems to imply that advertising is a form of public service, without which we would not have culture. And yet culture has been around a lot longer than advertising. Perhaps what advertising brings is a particular kind of culture. Marketers help deepen our attachment to commodities, reinforce the notion that happiness and a

---

[59] Shelly Reese, "The Quality of Cool," *Marketing Tools* 3(6) (2005): 27.

[60] Klein, *No Logo*, 9.

[61] Ibid.

[62] Joel Babbit, "Channel One Vision," paper presented at the On the Youth Market Conference, Boston, Massachusetts, May 5-6, 1994. Quoted in *Children First*, 64.

[63] Carly Stasko and Trevor Norris, "AML Panel on Youth Marketing: Transcript of Event." (November 2, 2005) http://www.aml.ca/articles/articles.php?articleID=349 [accessed July 12, 2007].

positive self-image comes from acquisition, and help ensure that we associate products only with the symbolic meaning which marketers create and not the conditions of their production. In doing so they create a culture of consumers, a "consumer culture," at the same time that any alternatives are silenced by their invisibility. Rather than questioning what is represented in advertising, we must also consider what and whom is missing. Where have the non-commercial narratives gone? What about representations of women and men that do not fit into the beauty myth or gender and racial stereotypes? Perhaps it is advertising itself that consumes our culture. Marshall McLuhan once said that "all advertising advertises advertising."[64] But it may in fact be closer to the truth to say that what advertising advertises is not so much a specific product, but rather the values of a life centered around consumption. Advertising advertises consumer values.

Schools are increasingly used as sites for the advancement of marketalk-cracy. If there was any doubt about the extent to which marketers and advertisers had gained access to schools, this trend can be observed within the daily life of any and every student. Before they even set foot in a school building, students are exposed to advertising images as they begin their day, by boarding a school bus labeled with ads, inside and out, to get to a school that has been named after a corporation, as is their gymnasium, cafeteria, or other classrooms. In fact one Philadelphia school board president and self-proclaimed "director of corporate development" talks about "peddling the naming rights to the district's only school on eBay" and "instituting a school uniform policy and selling ads on the uniforms."[65] As these already inundated students enter the school building, posters in their bathrooms and hallways often replace their artwork and class projects with more advertising. Before their lessons begin, they are required to watch several minutes of Channel One, or in Canada the Youth News Network (YNN), an American broadcaster who "charges advertisers $200,000 per 30-second advertising spot."[66] Once the lesson begins some teachers may be "sponsored" by a candy company such as General Mills, who offered teachers $250 per month to act as "freelance brand managers" for

---

[64] http://www.marshallmcluhan.com/poster.html.

[65] Kristen A. Graham, "Is This Any Way to Pay for Public Education?" *The Philadelphia Inquirer* (22 February 2004): A01.

[66] E. Shaker, "Youth New Network and the Commercial Carpet-bombing of the Classroom," *Education, Ltd., No. 5* (Canadian Center for Policy Alternatives, 1999), 1; Sarah Elton, "Parental Discretion Advised," *This Magazine* (July/August 2001): 19-23. More about Channel One and YNN will be said below.

Reese's Puffs.[67] Textbook covers display advertisements provided by Cover Designs, and include math exercises which refer to consumer products, biology case studies which favorably profile a large pharmaceutical corporation, or nutrition lessons sponsored by Hershey's Chocolate. Their online research habits are monitored for market researchers. Classroom activities include brainstorming to develop new product ideas, or completing surveys and market research studies, as outlined by Melissa Lickteig: "Chips Ahoy gives schools a counting game where children count the number of chips in their cookies. Kellogg's sponsors an art project for children to make Rice Krispies sculptures. Campbell's Soups designed a science lesson comparing Prego sauce to Ragu to teach students about viscosity."[68] Some students receive one doughnut for every "A" on their report card,[69] or free pizza for improved reading skills.[70] Upon leaving their classroom they may find that their cafeteria serves unhealthy fast food and their sports teams wear uniforms dominated by corporate logos. While this would certainly be a dystopian day in the life, each of these activities has been well documented.[71]

Perhaps the fastest growing trend is the production of Sponsored Educational Materials (SEMs). This unsolicited advertising and promotional material

---

[67] http://www.commercialalert.org/index.php/category_id/2/subcategory_id/39/article_id/127 [accessed August 15, 2004].

[68] Melissa K. Lickteig, "Brand-Name Schools: The Deceptive Lure of Corporate-School Partnerships," *The Educational Forum* vol. 68 (Fall 2003): 46.

[69] Youthography, *If It's Big with You* (2004). www.youthography.com/aboutus/ press/news/25.html [accessed February 11, 2007].

[70] Alex Molnar, "The Commercial Transformation of American Public Education." *Philosophical Studies in Education* 31 (Phil Smith Lecture, Ohio Valley Philosophy of Education Society, 1991): 30-37. http://64.233.167.104/search?q=cache:En6Fi_9YMKoJ:www.asu.edu/educ/epsl/CERU/Documents/1999phil.html+Sut+Jhally+children+to+advertise+to+their+parents&hl=en&gl=ca&ct=clnk&cd=15 [accessed February 11, 2007].

[71] See, for example: Henry A. Giroux, *Stealing Innocence: Youth, Corporate Power, and the Politics of Culture* (New York: Palgrave, 2000); Henry Giroux, *The Mouse that Roared: Disney and the End of Innocence* (New York: Rowman & Littlefield Publishers, 1999); Joe Kincheloe and Shirley Steinberg, eds. *Kinder Culture: The Corporate Construction of Childhood* (Boulder, CO: Westview, 1997); Alex Molnar, *Giving Kids the Business* (Boulder, CO: Westview, 1996); Deron Boyles, *American Education and Corporations: The Free Market Goes to School* (New York: Falmer, 2000); Deron R. Boyles, ed., *Schools or Markets?: Commercialism, Privatization, and School-Business Partnerships* (Mahwah, NJ: Lawrence Erlbaum and Associates, Inc., 2005); Phyllis Sides, "Captive Kids: Teaching Students to Be Consumers," *Selling Out Our Schools: Vouchers, Markets, and the Future of Public Education* (Milwaukee: Rethinking Schools Publications, 1996); and Naomi Klein, *No Logo: Taking Aim at the Brand Bullies* (Toronto: Vintage Canada, 2000).

is sent directly to schools and targeted for particular grades and subject areas. Examples include "an environmental curriculum video produced by Shell Oil and concentrated heavily on the virtues of the internal-combustion engine while offering students pearls of wisdom like, 'you can't get to nature without gasoline or cars.'"[72] "Read-A-Logo" is a reading software program that uses corporate logos in place of some common words. Students are required to recognize corporate logos in magazines and newspapers and bring them into class. Their website proudly proclaims that their package "turns a logo-laden environment into an arena of print appreciation."[73]

Alex Molnar argues that the pedagogy of advertising reduces freedom to the "execution of impulses" rather than the "freedom of the intellect,"[74] and promotes "pseudo-communities based on consumerism or the uncritical acceptance of a particular policy or point of view."[75] Henry Giroux observes that

> ...schools are being transformed into commercial rather than public spheres as students become subject to the whims and practices of marketers whose agenda has nothing to do with critical learning and a great deal to do with restructuring civic life in the image of market culture. Civic courage—upholding the most basic non-commercial principles of democracy—as a defining principle of society is devalued as corporate power transforms school knowledge.[76]

The following is an examination of seven reasons marketers seek access to public schools:

(1) First, and most obviously, schools provide a direct opportunity for immediate profit, and corporations are in pursuit of the money spent every day by students. Market researchers approximate that "there are more than 60 million kids aged 5 to 19 with over $100 billion of their own money to spend."[77] It was estimated that 9- to 19-year-olds in Canada spent $13.5 billion in 1999.[78]

---

[72] Steve Manning, "The Corporate Curriculum," *The Nation* (1999).

[73] http://www.teachingk-8.com/archives/past_online_extras/logos_signs_of_the_times_help_beginning_readers_by_dr_shelley_b_wepner.html [Accessed March 10, 2007].

[74] Alex Molnar, *School Commercialism: From Democratic Ideal to Market Commodity* (New York: Routledge, 2005), 82.

[75] Ibid., 83.

[76] Giroux, *Stealing Innocence*, 173.

[77] The 8th Annual Kid Power Food and Beverage Conference, 2006. http://www.iqpc.com/cgi-bin/templates/singlecell.html?topic=334&event=11140 [accessed March 10, 2007].

[78] "How Teens Got the Power: Gen Y Has the Cash, the Cool—and a Burgeoning Consumer Culture," *Macleans* (22 March 1999).

(2) Schools are vast sorting sites, where students are not only held captive but also organized by age and grades, which facilitates "very refined and specific targeting and message segmentation."[79] Marketing firm Youthography happily notes on their website that schools provide a much more targeted market than that available to TV broadcasters as schools contain specific age groups and are also organized by income, race, and language, reflecting the local ethnicity and economic status of the surrounding population.[80] Kenway and Bullen ask, "What better place than an all-girls school, for instance, for gender-targeted marketing such as Johnson & Johnson's 'Follow Your Dream' Promotion?"[81] Thus, schools help assemble a target audience, which is in turn sold to corporations.

(3) Marketers seek access to schools because schools are sites where cultural values are taught and ideological messages internalized. Youth have been called "consumers in training"; they are developing "brand loyalties" which may last for their entire lifetime, and may include lifelong addiction to tobacco, cola, and other physical substances. As one marketing journal asserts, "Millions of people, especially young people, identify with certain brands the way they once did only with film stars and sports heroes."[82] Considering how young they are, and that they have years of consuming to look forward to, they are a much more sought after demographic than older consumers. Because "they have a lifetime of spending ahead of them,"[83] which marketers measure in terms of "CLV," or "customer lifetime value," they are able to calculate the total amount of money they expect to make from a customer through their lifetime.

(4) Marketers capitalize on the social legitimacy accorded to schools. Corporate involvement in schools can often be construed as benevolent, and thereby improve their image. A 2006 *New York Times* article quoted Molnar as noting that "One standard goal corporations have in their marketing programs is making the corporation itself seem more desirable and good, and it's hard

---

[79] Calvin Curran, "Misplaced Marketing," *Journal of Consumer Marketing* 16, no. 6 (1999): 534-535, 534.

[80] Youthography, *If It's Big with You* (2004). www.youthography.com/aboutus/press/news/25.html [accessed March 10, 2007].

[81] Kenway and Bullen, *Consuming Children*, 94-95.

[82] "The Branded Generation," *Promo Magazine* (1 July 1998). http://promomagazine.com/mag/marketing_branded_generation/index.html [accessed March 10, 2007].

[83] Michele Jacobsen and Louise Mazur, *Marketing Madness: A Survival Guide for a Consumer Society* (Boulder: Westview Press, 1995), 21.

to find something more desirable and good than public schools."[84] Erica Shaker of the Canadian Center of Policy Alternatives argues that "merely by being associated with the school, the product and the sponsoring corporation appear to have additional legitimacy and the implicit endorsement of the educational system."[85] Such partnerships are a "cheap and effective way for corporations to gain goodwill in the community, and in return...the schools can give them an enormous amount of exposure."[86] Often not only is their image improved, but at the same time corporations are often eligible for a tax deduction. This revenue could have gone to the schools in the first place, which would have made school-business partnerships less necessary. The Canadian Center for Policy Alternatives explains how this constitutes a loss to taxpayers in several ways: "Partnerships usually represent a financial loss to taxpayers. The donation is always tax-deductible, which means less tax revenue for education...Taxpayers pay for educational time being diverted to activities to promote the corporation...as we accept these donations, we can expect an exponential loss through a reduction in the funds we receive from the Ministry of Education."[87] However, rather than permitting schooling to succumb to this trend, Ruth Jonathan argues that "in any open society the social practice we call education must represent the limiting case of the free market."[88]

Resistance, Creativity, and Being Beyond Buying: Alternatives to the Shopping Solution

While it is the goal of society to ensure the well-rounded development of our youth and the future they will inherit, the goal of advertising is unapologetically and narrowly focused on encouraging consumption and brand loyalty. Choice is encouraged insofar as choice is a product. "Media literacy" is encouraged insofar as children are able to use the technologies that expose them to the messages of advertisers and are able to differentiate between the different brands of choice for sale. As media literacy educators we are equally, if not more, interested in the ability of students to create new choices for

---

[84] Tamar Lewin, "In Public Schools, the Name Game as a Donor Lure," *New York Times* (26 January 2006): A1.

[85] Erica Shaker, "Corporate Content: Inside and Outside the Classroom," *Education, Limited: CCPA Education Project* 1, no. 2 (1998): 4.

[86] Tamar, "In Public Schools, the Name Game as a Donor Lure."

[87] Dianne Dunsmore, "Losses Often Outweigh Gains: 12 Reasons to Say 'No' to Corporate Partnerships," *Canadian Center for Policy Alternatives Education Monitor* (2000), 2.

[88] Ruth Jonathan, "Illusory Freedoms: Liberalism, Education and the Market" (1997), 6.

themselves in addition to making wise choices from the options made available to them. Like the classic "choose your own adventure" book, consumer culture offers a variety of choices that can present the illusion of adventure and freedom. However, authentic freedom comes when the reader does not just "choose," but rather imagines, designs, and creates her own story.

How are young people able to get their voices heard beyond voting with their dollars? Increasingly, they are discovering their own powers as producers, turning their media-saturated childhoods into media-literate action.[89] Growing up immersed in consumer culture, many young people have shifted their relationship with commercial culture and have learned to deconstruct the commercial messages that dominate their environment as they explore new ways to co-opt and subvert such messages to express new alternatives. The spirit of DiY (do-it-yourself) media has inspired many young activists whose tactics range from culture jamming (creatively subverting the messages of advertising),[90] to indymedia production, global street-parties, and protest. In the book *We Don't Need Another Wave: Dispatches from the Next Generation of Feminists*, Jennifer Pozner calls her young peers to action when she says, "Don't like the media? Be the media. Do your own reporting on Indymedia.org web sites, make your own films with www.PaperTiger.org or DykeTV.org, and host your own college, community or cable access TV or radio show."[91] DiY culture nurtures communities where people share skills, ideas, and creative expression, thereby fueling connectivity. It has been described by zine publisher Liz Worth as "an ever-expanding movement rooted in anti-consumerist ideals" that "gives people possibilities" because it is "a way for them to take a political stance, start up a scene, or accomplish something on their own terms."[92] *Hey Kidz! Buy This Book*, a self-described "radical primer on corporate and governmental propaganda and artistic activism for short people,"[93] is just one example of the kinds of resources that are made by youth for youth to challenge the marketalkracy.

---

[89] Carly Stasko, "Action Grrrls in the Dream Machine," in *Turbo Chicks: Talking Young Feminisms*, Lara Karaian, Allyson Mitchelle and Lisa Rundle, eds. (Toronto: Sumach Press, 2001), 273-284.

[90] Trevor Norris, "Cultivating Sweet Things: An Interview with Culture Jammer Carly Stasko," *Orbit: OISE/UT's Magazine for Schools* 35, no. 2 (2005): 22-24.

[91] Jennifer Pozner, "Reclaiming the Media for a Progressive Feminist Future," in *We Don't Need Another Wave: Dispatches from the Next Generation of Feminists*, Melody Berger, ed. (Emeryville, CA: Seal Press, 2006), 287-302.

[92] Liz Worth, "Just Do It –Yourself," *The Toronto Star* (15 August 2006): C1.

[93] Anne Elizabeth Moore, *Hey Kidz! Buy This Book: A Radical Primer on Corporate and Governmental Propaganda and Artistic Activism for Short People* (Chicago: Soft Skull Press, 2004).

This chapter exemplifies a clear bias towards emphasizing the civic responsibility of empowering today's youth with media literacy skills, and the opportunities to express their perspectives that reside beyond their consumer preferences held so dominant in marketalkcracy. While the power and numbers of marketing messages can seem overwhelming, it is clearly a challenge to successfully market to today's youth. It is also clear that while great amounts of money are spent to understand and influence them, much of that research provides data that is ineffective for explaining unpredictable and changing young people. Perhaps it is because the true desires of young people—or all people for that matter—cannot be simply rewarded with commodities.

Advertisers are having an increasingly difficult time standing out and being heard within the cacophony of consumer messages. For a brand to acquire "mindshare" has become a notable challenge now that the mind itself is becoming more and more occupied by market messages. Some marketers suggest that this barrage of commercial messages makes it even more paramount that they devise increasingly effective ways to market, so that their products are "attracting their relevant audiences like a beacon in a fog,"[94] as if we are otherwise lost at sea. While the end result of this plan is to promote a culture of general consumerism, regardless of particular brand loyalties, it equally results in more and more criticism of consumerism as it becomes clear that products do not reward shoppers with the happiness they desire, and that such happiness is fleeting as the symbols of success become obsolete with increasing speed, pushing us to buy more—or perhaps to give up instead.

Many marketers claim that it is their task simply to meet our "identity needs" in the context of identity fragmentation, destabilization, and disorientation, professing to serve society as they help us to find meaning. "Value-based corporate branding provides strong support to consumers' identity projects, serving 'to structure our experiences' at a time of societal transformation. It successfully addresses the growing desire for orientation. [As] a generator of values and meaning, a sophisticated brand narrative helps to reconstruct identities damaged by social change."[95] However, this overlooks the extent to which this very identity crisis is in part caused by the very features of marketalkcracy itself. Furthermore, it implies that marketing is the solution to this very crisis. The "we meet all your identity needs" approach to assisting "iden-

---

[94] Guido Palazzo and Kunal Basu, "The Ethical Backlash of Corporate Branding," *Journal of Business Ethics* 73, no. 4 (July 2007), 337.

[95] Ibid.

tity projects" reveals that marketers market marketing as the solution to life in a marketalkcracy.

Young people who are critical of the excessive commercialization of their lives may present new challenges to marketers, but are always seen as a new demographic—*as a market rather than a movement*. Marketers imply that activism as a strategy of resistance is an "identity project" equivalent to consumerism, and assert that their task is to devise strategies to draw all identity projects into the realm of consumption. "Individuals associated with such forms of civic engagement are seen as deriving value and recognition from their actions, thereby reconstructing and reinforcing aspects of their identity."[96] Resistance through the lens of marketalkracy is not about political engagement or social transformation, but merely self-expression—which often could in fact be better met by consumerism. "Individuals participating in acts of instant solidarity, linking their life stories to the narratives written by activist groups, often discover that consumption decisions are an efficient means to communicate moral and political statements. They shop for a better world."[97] Yet an alternative to marketalkcracy cannot be bought. Cultural theorist Joshua Gamson argues that what "is truly disturbing is that it's hard for people to imagine alternative ways to make themselves known to each other [because] the symbolic tools in our society are largely about consuming."[98] We can ask: what kind of identities does the market offer? Perhaps our notion of media literacy needs to be expanded to include the ability to create meaning, identity, culture, and community rather than simply buying products that communicate as well as shape our worldviews and sense of self. As Gamson puts it, "The point is to create alternatives rather than just expose manipulation."[99] In addition to encouraging critical literacy we must also support creative literacy so that young people are empowered with the skills, opportunities, and mentors they need to engage in the project of being beyond buying.

Conclusion

In conclusion, this chapter has sought to demonstrate some of the key features, presuppositions, and implications of marketing to youth as a contributing factor in the formation and perpetuation of what we are calling a

---

[96] Ibid.

[97] Ibid.

[98] Carrie McLaren, "Celebs, Freaks, Media Lit: Interview with Joshua Gamson," *Stay Free!* 15 (1998). http:..www.stayfreemagazine.org/archives/15/josh.html [Accessed June 22, 2007].

[99] Ibid.

marketalkcracy. The reason advertisers are interested in youth is the same reason educators, activists, and optimists are so determined to work with young people: they are energetic, open-minded, and are still forming their worldviews. Will today's youth accept unsustainable consumerism as a cooked frog accepts the increasing temperature of the water in its cooking pot, or will they discover new ways of creating a balance between consumption and preservation, choice and creation, markets and movements? Perhaps we are too adaptive for our own good. Often whatever is most prevalent and dominant within a society becomes normalized and unquestioned: children growing up with their own cell phone at age five do not think it is strange that they are the target of marketers, just as many of us do not question why we now buy our water in bottles. While the increasing influence of youth marketing is dramatic, it is also easy for kids and teens to accept if they have never known it any other way. Children and their overwhelmed parents and teachers need the opportunity to know a commercial-free refuge in order to develop the critical and creative thinking skills required to participate fully within a democratic society. It may be tempting to think nostalgically about "the good old days" before BIG MARKETING, or likewise to surrender to the belief that the rule of marketalkracy is inevitable. If we are truly to adapt rather than pine for the past or simply accept things as they are, we must create new ways of understanding and addressing youth commercialism within the broader context of consumer culture. We are inundated by choices and yet if we truly intend to empower youth—and not just profit from them—new choices will need to be created, not consumed. However, there is hope: the very marketers who may be responsible for promoting cynicism and insecurity among today's youth have found out through their own costly research that today's young people, more than ever, want to help to create a better world.[100] They are hopeful, idealistic, multitalented, and globally connected. They are all these things while at the same time they struggle with their own apathy and superficiality. Today's youth believe that they can be, do, and have anything they want. What will happen when they realize that what they want most is not for sale? Let us not underestimate the power that we have as parents, teachers, and concerned citizens. Hopefully, with the help of our collective action, compassion, creativity, and com-

---

[100] Gia Medeiros and Chip Walker, "GenWorld: The New Generation of Global Youth" *Energy BBDO Report.* http://www.freshfilms.com/downloads/GenWorld_TeenStudy.pdf [Accessed September 14, 2006].

mitment to education, our next generation will have the support and skills they need to forge a brighter future for the generations that follow.

Bibliography

Babbit, Joel. 1994. "Channel One Vision," paper presented at the "On the Youth Market Conference," Boston, Mass., May 5-6.

Bakan, Joel. 2004. *The Corporation: The Pathological Pursuit of Power.* Toronto: Viking.

Barber, Benjamin. 2007. *Consumed: How Markets Corrupt Children, Infantalize Adults, and Swallow Citizens Whole.* New York: W.W. Norton and Company.

Baudrillard, Jean. 1970/1998. *The Consumer Society: Myths and Structures.* London: Sage.

Baudrillard, Jean. 1981/1994. *Simulacra and Simulation.* Sheila Faria Glaser, trans. Ann Arbor: University of Michigan Press.

Boyles, Deron. 2000. *American Education and Corporations: The Free Market Goes to School.* New York: Falmer.

Boyles, Deron R., ed. 2005. *Schools or Markets?: Commercialism, Privatization, and School-Business Partnerships.* Mahwah, NJ: Lawrence Erlbaum and Associates.

Campbell, Kim and Kent Davis-Packard. 2000. "How Ads Get Kids to Say I Want It!" *Christian Science Monitor.* 18 September. http://www.csmonitor.com/2000/0918/p1s1.html. Accessed 22 June 2007.

Cox, Harvey. 1999. "The Market as God." *The Atlantic Monthly.* March. vol. 283, no. 3: 18-23.

Curran, Catherine. 1999. "Misplaced Marketing." *Journal of Consumer Marketing.* vol. 16, no. 6: 534-536.

Danesi, Marcel. 1994. *Cool: The Signs and Meanings of Adolescence.* Toronto: University of Toronto Press.

Douglas, Susan. 1994. *Where the Girls Are: Growing Up Female with the Mass Media.* New York: Random House.

Dunsmore, Dianne. 2000. "Losses Often Outweigh Gains: 12 Reasons to Say 'No' to Corporate Partnerships." *Canadian Center for Policy Alternatives Education Monitor.*

Elton, Sarah. 2001. "Parental Discretion Advised." *This Magazine.* July/August.

Evans, M. 2005. "Canadian Advertisers Must 'Wake up' to Internet." *National Post* [Canada]. 27 October: B7.

Ewen, Stuart. 1976. *Captains of Consiousness: Advertising and the Social Roots of Consumer Culture.* Toronto: McGraw Hill.

Gal, Susan. 1995. "Language, Gender, and Power: An Anthropological Review." *Gender Articulated: Language and the Socially Constructed Self.* Kira Hall and Mary Bucholtz, eds. New York: Routledge.

Giroux, Henry A. 1999. *The Mouse that Roared: Disney and the End of Innocence.* New York: Rowman and Littlefield.

Giroux, Henry A. 2000. *Stealing Innocence: Youth, Corporate Power, and the Politics of Culture.* New York: Palgrave.

Giroux, Henry A. 2003. *The Abandoned Generation.* New York: Palgrave.

Graham, Kristen A. 2004. "Is This Any Way to Pay for Public Education?" *The Philadelphia Inquirer.* 22 February.

Greenhouse, Steven. 1986. "The Rise and Rise of McDonald's." *New York Times.* 8 June. Section 3, 1.

"How Teens Got the Power: Gen Y Has the Cash, the Cool, and a Burgeoning Consumer Culture." 1999. *Macleans.* 22 March.

Jacobsen, Michele and Louise Mazur. 1995. *Marketing Madness: A Survival Guide for a Consumer Society.* Boulder: Westview Press.

Jonathan, Ruth. 1997. *Illusory Freedoms: Liberalism, Education and the Market.* London: Blackwell.

Kenway, Jane and Elizabeth Bullen. 2001. *Consuming Children: Education-Entertainment-Advertising.* Philadelphia: Open University Press.

Kincheloe, Joe and Shirley Steinberg, eds. 1997. *KinderCulture: The Corporate Construction of Childhood.* Boulder: Westview.

Klein, Naomi. 2000. *No Logo: Taking Aim at the Brand Bullies.* Toronto: Vintage Canada.

Lewin, Tamar. 2006. "In Public Schools, the Name Game as a Donor Lure." *New York Times.* 26 January: A1.

Lickteig, M.K. 2003. "Brand Name Schools: The Deceptive Lure of Corporate-School Partnerships." *The Educational Forum.* Fall, vol. 68. http://findarticles.com/p/articles/mi_qa4013/is_200310/ai_n9341370/pg_1. Accessed 22 June 2007.

Madeiros, Gia and Chip Walker. 2005. "GenWorld: The New Generation of Global Youth." *Energy BBDO Report.* www.freshfilms.com/downloads/GenWorld_TeenStudy.pdf. Accessed 14 September 2006.

Manning, Steve. 1999. "The Corporate Curriculum." *The Nation.* 27 September.

McArthur, Keith. 2005. "Ronald McDonald Recruits New Posse." *The Globe and Mail.* 29 March: A17.

McLaren, Carrie. 1998. "Celebs, Freaks, Media Lit: Interview with Joshua Gamson." *Stay Free!* vol. 15. www.stayfreemagazine.org/archives/15/josh.html. Accessed 22 June 2007.

McNeal, James. 1998. "Tapping the Three Kids' Markets," *American Demographics.* April: 37-41.

Molnar, Alex. 1996. *Giving Kids the Business.* Boulder: Westview Press.

Molnar, Alex. 1999. "The Commercial Transformation of American Public Education." *Philosophical Studies in Education.* vol. 31: 30-39.

Molnar, Alex. 2005. *School Commercialism: From Democratic Ideal to Market Commodity.* New York: Routledge.

Moore, Anne Elizabeth. 2004. *Hey Kidz! Buy This Book: A Radical Primer on Corporate and Governmental Propaganda and Artistic Activism for Short People.* Chicago: Soft Skull Press.

Norris, Trevor. 2005. "Cultivating Sweet Things: An Interview with Culture Jammer Carly Stasko." *Orbit: OISE/UT's Magazine for Schools.* vol. 35, no. 2: 22-24.

O'Barr, William. 2005. "Advertising, Cultural Criticism & Pedagogy: An Interview with Sut Jhally." http://muse.jhu.edu/journals/asr/v003/3.2jhally.html

Packard, Vance. 1965. *The Hidden Persuaders.* New York: D. McKay Co.

Palazzo, Guido and Kunal Basu. 2007. "The Ethical Backlash of Corporate Branding." *Journal of Business Ethics.* vol. 73: 337.

Peters, Tom. 1997. "The Brand Called You." *Company.* vol. 10, August: 83-92.

Postman, Neil. 1994. *The Disappearance of Childhood.* New York: Vintage.

Pozner, Jennifer. 2006. "Reclaiming the Media for a Progressive Feminist Future." *We Don't Need Another Wave: Dispatches from the Next Generation of Feminists.* Melody Berger, ed. Emeryville, CA: Seal Press: 287-302.

Quart, Alissa. 2003. *Branded: The Buying and Selling of Teenagers.* Cambridge: Perseus.

Reese, Shelly. 1997. "The Quality of Cool." *Marketing Tools.* vol. 3, no. 6.

Rowe, Jonathan and Gary Ruskin. 2003. "The Parent's Bill of Rights: Helping Moms and Dads Fight Commercialism." *Mothering Magazine.* Jan/Feb. Issue 116. http://www.mothering.com/articles/growing_child/consumerism/bill_of_rights.html. Accessed 27 June 2007.

Rushkin, Gary. 1999. "Why They Whine: How Corporations Prey on Our Children." *Mothering Magazine* 97. November/December.

Schor, Juliet. 2004. "Those Ads Are Enough to Make Your Kids Sick." *Washington Post.* 11 September.

"The Science of Shopping." 2002. *CBC Marketplace.* 2 December.

Shaker, Erika. 1998. "Corporate Content: Inside and Outside the Classroom." *Education Limited: CCPA Education Project.* vol. 1, no. 2. Canadian Center for Policy Alternatives.

Shaker, Erika. 1999. "Youth New Network and the Commercial Carpet-Bombing of the Classroom." *Education, Ltd., No. 5.* Canadian Center for Policy Alternatives.

Shaker, Erika. 2001. "Individuality.com: Empowering Youth Through Consumption." *Our Schools/Ourselves.* July.

Sides, Phyllis. 1996. "Captive Kids: Teaching Students to Be Consumers." *Selling Out Our Schools: Vouchers, Markets, and the Future of Public Education.* Robert Lowe and Barbara Miner, eds. Milwaukee: Rethinking Schools Publications.

Stasko, Carly. 2001. "Action Grrrls in the Dream Machine." *Turbo Chicks: Talking Young Feminisms.* Lara Karaian, Allyson Mitchelle, and Lisa Rundle, eds. Toronto: Sumach Press: 273-284.

Sutherland, Anne and Betty Thompson. *Kidfluence: Why Kids Today Mean Business.* Toronto: McGraw-Hill Ryerson.

Urbanski, Al. 1998. "The Branded Generation." *Promo Magazine.* 1 July.

Wegert, T. 2004. "Advertisers Playing Video Game Card." *The Globe and Mail.* B8.

Wells, Melanie. 2003. "In Search of the Buy Button." *Forbes.* 31 August.

Wells, Melanie. 2004. "Kid Nabbing." *Forbes.* 1 February.

Worth, Liz. 2006. "Just Do It—Yourself." *The Toronto Star.* 15 August: C1.

www.adbusters.org/metas/psycho/mediacarta/rejected/+adbusters+uncommercial&hl=en&ct=clnk&cd=4&gl=ca. Accessed 22 July 2007.

www.cognitiveliberty.org/neuro/Rushkoff_Neuromarketing.html. Accessed 22 June 2007.

www.commercialalert.org/index.php/category_id/2/subcategory_id/39/article_id/127. Accessed 15 August 2004.

www.commercialalert.org/issues/culture/buzz-marketing/kid-nabbing. Accessed 5 May 2007.

www.csmonitor.com/cgi-bin/durableRedirect.pl?/durable/2000/09/18/pls1.htm. Accessed 23 October 2005.

www.etymonline.com/index.php?search=-cracy&searchmode=none. Accessed 28 June 2007.

www.fresh-films.com/downloads/GenWorld_TeenStudy.pdf. Accessed 14 September 2006.

www.imediaconnection.com/content/3882.asp. Accessed 21 June 2007.

www.iqpc.com/cgi-bin/templates/singlecell.html?topic=334&event=11140. Accessed 27 June 2007.

www.marshallmcluhan.com/poster.html. Accessed 27 June 2007.

www.mediaawareness.ca/english/resources/articles/advertising_marketing/empowering_youth. cfm. Accessed 2 June 2007.

www.mindshareworld.com/output/Page2.asp. Accessed 22 June 2007.

www.mothering.com/articles/growing_child/consumerism/bill_of_rights.html. Accessed 27 June 2007.

www.mothering.com/articles/growing_child/consumerism/whine.html. Accessed 26 June 2007.

www.muse.jhu.edu/journals/asr/v003/3.2jhally.html. Accessed 4 July 2007.

www.parenthood.com/articles.html?article_id=9153. Accessed 22 May 2007.

www.stayfreemagazine.org/ml. Accessed 2 June 2007.

www.supersizeme.com. Accessed 2 June 2007.

www.youthography.com/aboutus/press/news/25.html. Accessed 22 May 2007.

CHAPTER SEVEN

BusRadio
Music to a Captive Audience?

Dennis Attick, Georgia State University

Marketing to youth has become a lucrative business that is an increasingly conspicuous aspect of modern life. Corporations understand the value of capturing the youth market such that annual conferences are dedicated to helping companies develop and hone their youth marketing activities. The "Kid & Tweens Power 2007" conference held at the Disney Yacht Club in May 2007 is one such conference.[1] This conference, conducted by the Kid Power Xchange, a division of the International Quality and Productivity Center (IQCP), featured companies such as Disney, Frito-Lay, Pepsico, and PBS sharing their youth marketing strategies. The conference provided opportunities for the companies to assist each other, as well as other emerging companies, in developing "new strategies and tools to help them achieve their youth marketing goals."[2] It appears that the participating companies and attendees are aware of the profits that can be made from marketing their products to children. Why else would multinational companies expend the resources needed to participate in a three-day conference on the topic?

While advertisers and marketers are increasingly targeting youth, it is most troubling to consider the role that public schools play in allowing corporations to advertise to children and adolescents. In the past 25 years, there has been a

---

[1] The Kid and Tweens Power 2007 conference information can be found at http://www.iqpc.com/cgi-bin/templates/genevent.html?topic=445&event=12748&. Last accessed June 18, 2007. According to the conference brochures, this conference will "Offer participants the new Kid Power Experience that is focused on brands and the people behind their success: Brand Managers, Marketers, Creative Directors, Agencies and more." It should be noted that BusRadio was one of the companies to have a demonstration booth at this conference.

[2] Ibid.

marked increase in partnerships between public schools and private businesses and multinational corporations.[3] The Center for the Analysis of Commercialism in Education reports that during the last decade of the twentieth century, instances of school-business partnerships increased by over 300 percent as school systems searched for new ways to raise money.[4] Equitable funding for public schools is a highly contested issue, and one that is beyond the scope of my current argument. However, in this chapter I will examine one currently developing school-business partnership to shed light on the fact that there are companies that continue to see public schools, and in this case school buses, as marketing arenas. This chapter will also discuss the overarching problems associated with using public schools as markets in which to advertise to youth.

I extend the ongoing critique of school-business partnerships by examining a current initiative by BusRadio, a Boston-based startup company that plans to install radios in public school buses across the United States. According to their business model, BusRadio installs the radio systems for free in exchange for providing the content that will be played on these radio systems. BusRadio plans to generate profits by selling advertising time to corporations whose ads will run throughout the programming. I argue that BusRadio's plan is a conspicuous example of the problematic nature of school-business partnerships as they plan to use public school students in their quest to generate profits for themselves and the companies that advertise on BusRadio. Further, I argue that BusRadio's attempt to access the student market is grounded in a consumerist ideology that holds the ongoing possession and consumption of material items as an essential human activity.

Schools as Markets

Joel Spring argues that throughout the twentieth century, public schools in the United States have played an increasingly important role in promoting consumerism in children.[5] In fact, as early as the 1920s, the National Educa-

---

[3] See, for example, Alex Molnar, *School Commercialism: From Democratic Ideal to Market Commodity* (New York: Routledge, 2005); and Deron Boyles, *American Education and Corporations: The Free Market Goes to School* (New York: Falmer, 2000).

[4] Alex Molnar, "Cashing in on Kids: The Second Annual Report on Trends in Schoolhouse Commercialism," *Center for the Analysis of Commercialism in Education.* Document 99-21, (September, 1999): 3. The report can be found at http://www.asu.edu/educ/epsl/CERU/Annual%20reports/cace-99-21.htm. Accessed June 27, 2006.

[5] Joel Spring, *Educating the Consumer-Citizen* (Mahwah, NJ: Lawrence Erlbaum Associates, Publishers, 2003). Spring contends that public schools have throughout the 20th century become

tion Association was concerned enough about commercialism in schools to develop a committee that investigated corporate propaganda in schools.[6] In the 1930s, Harold Rugg's textbooks were the first texts to be critical of advertising directed at children and the corporate encroachment on public schools.[7] More recently, Juliet Schor argues that corporate influence in schools is not a new phenomenon, as agricultural and food companies have sponsored health and nutrition classes in public schools for decades.[8] While the commercialization of public schools has been evident since the early twentieth century, partnerships between schools and private businesses have escalated exponentially in the past 25 years. Further, and perhaps most problematic, is the fact that school-business partnerships are often understood by the general public as beneficial and indicative of the private sector's support for the community.

Deron Boyles argues that school-business partnerships have become a widely accepted practice in education, as cash-strapped schools continue to welcome financial support regardless of the consequences.[9] While there is a larger issue at play regarding a community's responsibility for the funding of public schools, as noted earlier, that issue is beyond the scope of this chapter. However, the concern over school-business partnerships is worthy of ongoing investigation, as these partnerships continue to occur. Alex Molnar argues that schools are considered fertile territory for marketers and advertisers because students represent a captive audience that is already segregated by age and geographic location, which increases the advertisers' ability to market to distinct subgroups of students.[10] In this sense, schools that maintain partnerships with private business actually perform an important market function categorizing and subdividing students according to age, grade level, and often, socioeconomic status.

It is troubling to consider that children are increasingly understood as a subgroup to be marketed to when childhood is a time that should be free of

---

an integral component of the training of children to be consumers. Spring sees public schools as working in conjunction with businesses and the media to reinforce consumerist attitudes in students instead of teaching students to be critical of the consumer culture.

[6] Alex Molnar, *School Commercialism: From Democratic Ideal to Market Commodity*, 7.

[7] Joel Spring, *Educating the Consumer-Citizen*, 132-133. It should be noted that Rugg's textbooks were branded as un-American, un-Christian, and unpatriotic for promoting criticality regarding advertisers, corporations, and American capitalism.

[8] Juliet B. Schor, *Born to Buy: The Commercialized Child and the New Consumer Culture* (NewYork: Scribner, 2004), 85-86.

[9] Boyles, *American Education and Corporations*, 4-5.

[10] Molnar, *School Commercialism*, 7.

market notions of consumerist behavior. Molnar argues, "Since children are generally understood to be a protected class, it is hard to justify marketing to them under any circumstance."[11] Extending from Molnar, I would argue that it is impossible to justify allowing corporations to advertise to students in a school setting, or in an activity related to schooling such as riding the school bus. However, as Joel Spring argues, schools are now part of our advertising-driven economy that sees schools as spaces where young people are trained to be consumers from a very young age.[12]

The BusRadio Concept

BusRadio is the latest brainchild of two businessmen who already have a history of profiteering off of public school students. Steve Schulman and Michael Yanoff, the creators of BusRadio, are also responsible for the creation of Cover Concepts, a company that distributes free textbook covers embossed with advertisements from multinational corporations to schools.[13] The "free" textbook covers distributed to students by Cover Concepts feature paid advertisements for products such as Coca-Cola, Champs Sports, and Frito-Lay.[14] Cover Concepts now provides textbook covers to over 30 million school-aged children in public schools in the United States.[15] Boyles argues that Cover Concepts is another example of businesses using schools as "captive markets where they can test new merchandise, advance their public relations, and appear philanthropic by 'donating' materials to schools."[16] As Boyles points out, this corporate philanthropy is, in fact, contrived philanthropy, as the corporations and private businesses reap large profits from the support they offer schools.

---

[11] Ibid.

[12] Joel Spring, *Educating the Consumer-Citizen*, 207-208.

[13] Deron Boyles, "Uncovering the Coverings: The Use of Corporate-Sponsored Textbook Covers in Furthering Uncritical Consumerism," *Educational Studies* 37, 3 (2005): 255-266. In his examination of textbook covers Boyles argues that corporations often "sell" established (often sexist) norms back to young girls through various social institutions. Where schools provide textbook covers to students for "free," the cost of the covers is actually "paid" for by the students whose consumerist tendencies are reinforced by the covers.

[14] Alexander Soule, "BusRadio Targets a Captive—and Raucous—Audience," *Boston Business Journal*, March 31-April 6, 2006, 8.

[15] Boyles, "Uncovering the Coverings: The Use of Corporate-Sponsored Textbook Covers in Furthering Uncritical Consumerism."

[16] Ibid.

It appears that BusRadio is another opportunity for Schulman and Yanoff to use public schools and public school students in their quest to make money. While Yanoff and Schulman have been successful in previous efforts to market and advertise to children, they claim that BusRadio will "take targeted student marketing to the next level."[17] While BusRadio first established contracts with schools in Massachusetts, by June of 2007, schools in 11 states had signed contracts with BusRadio.[18] BusRadio plans to establish contracts with schools throughout the U.S., with a goal of having 100,000 students exposed to BusRadio programming during the 2007-2008 school year.

According to BusRadio's business plan, school systems get free radio equipment for their fleet of buses, but those buses must broadcast BusRadio programming whenever the school bus is in operation. BusRadio's format includes forty-four minutes of music per hour, along with eight minutes of commercials, six minutes of public service announcements, and two minutes of contests.[19] However, within much of BusRadio's programming are market-driven notions of consumption intertwined within the product demonstrations and music presented on the radio programs. Further, a close examination reveals that the public service announcements and contests on BusRadio are embedded with advertisements and consumerist language. In the next sections of this chapter I will examine BusRadio's programming content and advertising, as well as BusRadio's claim that it promotes safety for children and schools.

BusRadio's Content

According to BusRadio, the majority of its programming will be music that is "age-appropriate, unoffensive, and relevant" to a school-aged population:

> Buses currently equipped with AM/FM radios have a poor selection of formats to choose from. It is virtually impossible to listen to commercial radio for thirty minutes without being offended by a song's lyrics or DJ's talk. Commercial radio was not designed to address a school system's transportation needs and as a result may not always be appropriate for school aged children.[20]

---

[17] Caroline E. Mayer, "The Next Niche: School Bus Ads," *Washington Post* (6/4/2006), B1.

[18] Ibid.

[19] Information on BusRadio's format and business plan can be found at www.busradio.org. Last accessed June 1, 2007.

[20] Ibid.

BusRadio offers that the music presented in its programming will provide an alternative to the offensive nature of regular AM/FM radio. As BusRadio CEO Michael Yanoff states, "We want a safer ride. We don't approve in what's being played now."[21] Yanoff's comment seems to indicate that, while in his opinion regular radio programming is unsuitable for children, the programming and advertising BusRadio will direct at children is more appropriate. However, an examination of the music artists featured on BusRadio reveals that the claims made by Yanoff regarding appropriate music for children and teens are specious. Contrary to Yanoff's comments regarding appropriate music for children and teens, several of the music artists promoted by BusRadio have long histories of producing music that is designed for a mature audience and may not be "suitable" for the audience BusRadio targets.

In 2007, Obligation, Inc., an organization that monitors corporate encroachment in the lives of children, released a public statement regarding concern for several of the music artists advertised on and supported by BusRadio.[22] Again, contrary to BusRadio's claims regarding their concern for children listening to appropriate music, the artists advertised on BusRadio include Wu-Tang Clan, and 'Lil John. Both artists are well known for songs that are replete with expletive-ridden lyrics often featuring sexist and racist language.[23] Not only are these artists featured on BusRadio, the artists' CD releases are promoted with contests and advertisements on the BusRadio website. I argue that this indicates that BusRadio does not actually care about the welfare of children and simply advertises that which is popular and will generate revenue. Further, BusRadio maintains strict control over the music played on its system, therefore allowing BusRadio to further advertise by playing only those artists who are part of the extended BusRadio advertising empire.

Along with the music programming, BusRadio claims it will also provide six minutes of public service announcements (also referred to as safety messages) each hour. The public service safety messages cover such topics as traffic safety, the importance of getting to the school bus on time, and participating in after-school programs. However, a review of the sample safety messages available for demonstration on the BusRadio website reveals advertisements for BusRadio embedded in each of the public service announcements. One of

---

[21] Wendy Koch, "School Buses in 11 States Tune In to Radio Programming," *USA Today* (9/17/06). N34.

[22] Information regarding Obligation, Inc.'s efforts to resist BusRadio can be found at http://www.obligation.org/busradiohome.php. Accessed June 1, 2007.

[23] Ibid.

the sample public service announcements for junior and senior high school students asks students not to be late to the bus stop. Not being late to the bus stop is indeed a good idea. However, the reason BusRadio does not want students to be late is so they can consume more BusRadio. The demonstration public service announcements on the website ask students to

> Try and get to the school bus stop five minutes before your scheduled pick-up time. That way, everybody gets to school on time, and you won't miss any of our BusRadio show.[24]

Here, the concept of punctuality is conjoined and conflated with consuming more BusRadio programming. While promoting punctuality in school children could be considered a public service, consuming more BusRadio programming is hardly a reason for a student to be punctual.

Another BusRadio public service demo available on the website, this one directed at elementary school students, tells students they shouldn't "run after the bus if you miss it," and "not to worry because BusRadio will be here the next day."[25] In this example, the safety of children is conflated with an advertising message that promotes further consumption of BusRadio programming. In fact, examining all of the safety messages available for demonstration on BusRadio's website reveals that, although BusRadio claims only eight minutes of advertisements per hour, the six minutes of public service announcements could be considered advertising, as the announcements feature clear advertising messages. In this sense, the actual amount of advertising is nearly doubled given that the safety messages are also advertisements for BusRadio.

BusRadio is advertised to schools and parents as beneficial under the premise that it increases bus safety by providing music for students to listen to while on the bus. According to Steven Schulman, BusRadio is designed to "soothe the beast on the bus, and at the same time, offer safety features that are so important."[26] Schulman's referring to students as "beasts" is troubling in its own right, but his equating the playing of music to safety is equally problematic. Edison Research was hired by BusRadio to study safety on buses that were equipped with BusRadio. Edison surveyed bus drivers who reported that

---

[24] Information on BusRadio can be found at www.busradio.org. Accessed September 20, 2006.

[25] Ibid.

[26] Leslie A. Maxwell, "School BusRadio Venture Raises Safety, Commercialism Concern," *Education Week* (9/20/06). Article can be found at www.edweek.org/ew/articles/2006/09/20/05bus _ wed.h26.html? Accessed 10/6/06.

students stayed in their seats and noise levels were reduced when BusRadio was used. Several bus drivers welcomed BusRadio as a replacement for regular AM/FM radio, and numerous bus drivers reported using BusRadio as a behavior management technique.

While BusRadio cites research showing their programming makes buses safer, the company makes no mention of the fact that radios on school buses have been tied to fatal accidents involving school buses in recent years. Fatal school bus accidents in Illinois in 1995, and Tennessee in 2000, were found by the federal safety board to have most likely been caused by bus drivers being distracted by radios on the bus.[27] Both accidents caused the deaths of several elementary school children. Further, in the wake of the accidents, the National Transit Safety Board (NTSB) recommended that states create strict guidelines limiting radios on school buses. However, BusRadio does not cite these incidents in its claims that it increases safety on school buses.

In regard to advertising, BusRadio refuses to offer specific information about which corporations will advertise on their programming; however, they do state that products advertised will focus on items that are popular with students such as TV shows, sneakers, cell phones, and bottled water.[28] Several of the early ad campaigns did feature advertisements for popular teen movies and television shows. In fact, during an early trial run of BusRadio, the WB network reported a significant increase in viewership of one of its popular teen shows after ads for the show ran on BusRadio the day the show was broadcast.[29]

One of the recurring advertisements on BusRadio directs students to visit the BusRadio website to participate in contests, and be exposed to more advertising. The BusRadio teen website (teen.busradio.com) features advertisements for current TV shows and movies, Sony products, and Amazon.com. There are also profiles of athletes such as Super Bowl quarterback Peyton Manning, and music artists such as Jessica Simpson, Wu-Tang Clan, and Pink. Again, throughout the BusRadio programming are ads that direct students to log on and continue the fun once they get home from school. However, the website contains more advertising, more product demos, and further promotion of the musicians and celebrities BusRadio endorses. BusRadio has forged a website

---

[27] Ibid.

[28] "Take the Bus, And Leave the Radio to Us," *Taunton Gazette* (10/1/06), Editorial. A10.

[29] Ibid.

wholly designed to offer students further opportunity to consume the BusRadio brand, as well as the products of BusRadio's corporate sponsors.

The Captive Audience

Using public schools as an arena in which to advertise to students who have little choice as to whether or not they attend school is a conspicuous example of captive audience marketing. As Juliet Schor argues, students are as close as advertisers can get to a truly captive audience, as schools are mostly secure facilities that offer students few opportunities to control what goes on within a school's walls.[30] BusRadio, by their own admission, embraces the idea of captive audience marketing in their plans to take captive audience marketing to its most extreme. While using public schools and school buses as arenas for marketing to a captive audience is a growing trend, the idea of captive audience marketing has a rich history in the United States.

In 1953, Charles L. Black, a Professor of Law at Columbia University, wrote an article that reviewed the "captive audience" case that was brought before the District of Columbia Court of Appeals.[31] The case involved the violation of public bus riders' rights by forcing them to listen to radio programming and advertisements while using public transportation.[32] The court held that the programming was not in violation of the riders' rights, but the case sparked controversy regarding forced listening and the ethics involved in such activities. Charles Black was one of the first scholars to write about captive audience advertising and marketing in the modern era. As Black argues, advertisers were quick to embrace the idea of captive audience marketing, which birthed the new advertising mantra "if people can hear, they can hear your commercial."[33] In this sense, any captive audience member who is not deaf has no choice but to hear advertisements once they choose to be in the captive environment.

Black argues that captive audience marketing not only privileges private corporations over public interest, but it also contradicts notions of liberty and erodes critical thinking. Black argues:

---

[30] Juliet B. Schor, *Born to Buy: The Commercialized Child and the New Consumer Culture*, 85.

[31] Public Utilities Commission v. Pollak, 343 U.S. 451 (1952).

[32] Charles L. Black, "He Cannot Choose But Hear: The Plight of the Captive Auditor," *Columbia Law Review*, 166 (1953).

[33] Charles L. Black, "He Cannot Choose But Hear: The Plight of the Captive Auditor," p. 961

Subjecting a man, willy-nilly and day after day, to intellectual forced-feeding on trivial fare, is not itself a trivial matter; to insist, by the effective gesture of coercion, that a man's right to dispose of his own faculties stops short of the interest of another in forcing him to endure paid-up banality, is not itself banal, but rather a sinister symbol of relative weighting of the independence of the mind of man and the lust to make a buck.[34]

Black equates forced listening of advertisements to an erosion of personal liberty and the privileging of material profit over humanity. Forced listening subverts the public good for the interest of the private owners, who can use public spaces as new arenas in which to generate profit.

Black's argument against forced listening here is applicable to an argument against BusRadio today. Consider Black's comments in regard to public transportation companies forcing riders to listen to radio programming:

The bus company is paid by entrepreneurs (a group whom operates on a national scale) for allowing them to install FM receivers in (and loudspeakers inescapably throughout) its vehicles. The entrepreneurs line up an FM station, which broadcasts special programs to which the bus radios are fixed-tuned. The passengers listen to what the people at the station want them to hear, whether they like it or not.[35]

The scenario critiqued here by Black speaks to BusRadio's business plan that offers school systems free radio equipment in exchange for control over what is broadcast over those radios. Like the riders in Black's scenario, students who are subject to BusRadio's programming have no control over the content provided. Further, the act of forced listening takes advertising beyond message placement. The listener has few options but to listen. As Black argues,

Forced listening rigs the market in ideas, for it heavily and arbitrarily favors those communications agreeable to its managers. Since its managers are advertisers or those who act in the interest of advertisers, the tendency of the market-rigging cannot be guessed at without some reference to advertising itself.[36]

Forced listening subverts an individual's ability to be free from outside distraction as well as one's ability to control what auditory messages are thrust into one's consciousness.

---

[34] Ibid., 961.

[35] Ibid., 968.

[36] Ibid., 968

The Youth Market

Children and adolescents are increasingly being targeted by advertisers and corporations as they represent a lucrative market. BusRadio is another recent example of a corporate entity attempting to gain access to the youth market. As Juliet Schor argues, "Kids and teens are the epicenter of American consumer culture. They command the attention, creativity, and dollars of advertisers. Their tastes drive market trends."[37] The youth market Schor describes is so valuable to corporations that advertising increasingly targets younger children in sundry new ways. Schor argues that the average first-grader can identify 200 brands and accumulates 70 new toys per year.[38] In 2006, the Walt Disney Company advertised its Little Einstein DVD's for preschoolers on the paper liners of examination tables in 2,000 doctors' offices.[39] It should be noted that, in this case, the doctors received free medical supplies for allowing their examination tables to be branded. Cultivating young customers is essential for advertisers and corporations, as selling to children and youth not only creates current profit, it develops brand loyalty that will also pay future dividends for the corporations.

While one could argue that adults possess the knowledge and awareness needed to discriminate about advertising messages, the same argument does not hold true in regard to children and adolescents. Maxine Greene has offered that children are unable to interpret their own reality in relation to media messages and cannot separate themselves from media-created notions of reality.[40] Further, Rick Fox and Victor Strasburger have argued that children demonstrate an inability to interpret and comprehend the complex messages embedded in television and radio advertising.[41] Fox's research reveals that even adolescents cannot understand the motives behind advertising and many adolescents are prone to buy that which is advertised to them. Because children and adolescents often do not fully comprehend advertising messages, they rep-

---

[37] Schor, *Born to Buy: The Commercialized Child and the New Consumer Culture*, 9.

[38] Ibid., 19.

[39] Louise Story, "Anywhere the Eye Can See, It's Likely to See an Ad," *New York Times* (1/15/07), B1.

[40] Maxine Greene, *The Dialectic of Freedom* (New York: Teachers College Press, 1988).

[41] See Victor C. Strasburger, "Children and TV Advertising: Nowhere to Run, Nowhere to Hide," *Journal of Developmental & Behavioral Pediatrics*, 22, 185-187 and Rick Fox, *Harvesting Minds: How TV Commercials Control Kids* (Westport, CT: Praeger, 2000). Fox's book examines adolescents' ability to decipher advertisements on Channel One, another example of a problematic school-business partnership.

resent a subgroup of the population that holds great value for advertisers and corporations. I argue that this is one of the main reasons why corporations, and companies like BusRadio, expend the resources needed to advertise to children and adolescents.

Resisting BusRadio

Throughout 2006 and 2007, numerous advocacy organizations, including the National Parent Teacher Association (NPTA), the Campaign for a Commercial Free Childhood (CCFC), and Commercial Alert, have voiced public opposition to BusRadio. In early 2007, Commercial Alert, an organization of concerned parents and scholars that resists corporate intrusion in public life, submitted a letter to over 100 advertisers asking them to refuse to advertise on BusRadio.[42] The Commercial Alert newsletter states that the organization opposes BusRadio's "exploitation of students through commercial operations," which is clearly what BusRadio promotes.[43] Further, Commercial Alert wrote letters to then governor of Massachusetts, Mitt Romney, asking him to consider prohibiting BusRadio on Massachusetts school buses, where BusRadio signed its first contracts. Commercial Alert has also organized picketing campaigns opposing BusRadio near the company's headquarters in Massachusetts.[44] While these actions have increased public awareness of BusRadio, the demonstrations have done little to alter the contracts of the Massachusetts schools that have contracts with BusRadio.

While resistance has mounted against BusRadio, school systems in 11 states are still choosing to move ahead with their BusRadio contracts.[45] BusRadio proposes to reach 100,000 bus riders in the 2006-2007 school year, with plans to grow that number to one million students in the next three years.[46]

---

[42] "Children's Advocate Asks Companies Not to Advertise on BusRadio or Channel One," *National PTA Newsletter* (9/19/06). Newsletter is available at www.pta.org/ia_newsletters_issue_1158681127343.html. Accessed 10/5/06.

[43] Ibid.

[44] "Commercial Alert Urges Gov. Romney to Expel Radio Ads from Mass. School Buses." Article can be found at http://www.commercialalert.org/issues/education/busradio/ commercial-alert-urges-gov-romney-to-expel-radio-ads-from-mass-school-buses. Last accessed June 1, 2007.

[45] Wendy Koch, "School Buses in 11 States Tune In to Radio Programming."As of June 2007, the eleven states maintaining contracts with BusRadio are California, Georgia, Indiana, Massachusetts, Michigan, New Jersey, Ohio, Oklahoma, Pennsylvania, Tennessee, and Washington.

[46] Ibid.

By choosing to expose their students to BusRadio and its advertisers, these school systems are privileging the raising of money above protecting a segment of the population that needs the most protection from advertisers and marketers. These school systems are allowing BusRadio to use public schools, our society's most important public service, as a partner in their quest to profit off of children and adolescents.

While numerous school systems are standing by their contracts with BusRadio, some, such as Jefferson County Public Schools in Kentucky, have rejected relationships with BusRadio. In May of 2007, the Jefferson County School Board refused a contract with BusRadio despite the fact that the school system would have earned up to $150,000 per year in shared advertising revenue.[47] The school system's NPTA president argued that the "NPTA opposed the exploitation of students through commercial operations that require students to view advertising...as a condition of the school's receiving a donation of money or loan of equipment."[48] I'm left to wonder why the criticality of Jefferson County's NPTA president is lacking in so many other educators and parents across the country who quickly accept the latest soft drink contract, computer contract, or BusRadio contract at the expense of their students, who become exploited subjects in the process.

The fact that arguments against BusRadio come mostly from outside of public schools should not be overlooked here. As I write this chapter in the spring of 2007, I can find no public comments or written arguments against BusRadio from principals, superintendents, or teachers. As I have cited here, the majority of the resistance to BusRadio has come from parents and public interest groups. A possible reason for this lack of internal response is that the professional educators who serve within our public schools have become acculturated to school-business partnerships to the degree that these educators readily accept contrived philanthropy as a given in modern education.

Closing

In this chapter I have argued against BusRadio and their attempt to direct advertise to a captive audience of public school children. Further, what I have also attempted to illustrate is the problematic relationship that exists between public schools, corporations, parents, teachers, and students. We are living in an age that is increasingly saturated by media and media-driven notions of re-

---

[47] "School Board Drops Proposal for BusRadios," *Louisville Courier-Journal* (5/18/07), A4.
[48] Ibid.

ality and existence. Where public schools could be arenas where students exist as active subjects investigating the roles that media play in their lives, public schools are increasingly partnering with corporations in the commodification and objectification of students. As Henry Giroux argues:

> The commercial logic that fuels this market-based reform movement is also evident in the way in which corporate culture targets schools not simply as investments for substantial profits but also as training grounds for educating students to define themselves as consumers rather than as social actors.[49]

Following this consumerist logic, school-aged children are no longer understood as students; they are, instead, seen as consuming objects that can be continually bombarded with advertising messages regarding the latest fads, trends, and styles. BusRadio is another recent example of corporations finding ways to use public schools as accomplices in their effort to develop young people into materialist consumers.

In closing, I consider again the writing of Charles Black, who warned of the encroachment of advertising and marketing on human beings in the mid-twentieth century. Black wrote of the dangers of advertising and marketing over 50 years ago, but his comments hold today. Black writes:

> ...that a human being, if he happens to be in a crowd, is properly to be treated as a means rather than as an end, as a commodity rather than as a person, not as a unique subject but as a fungible object, promised for daily delivery guaranteed...the aim and effect of which is to make of our people a herd handily corralled for whatever purpose certain resourceful gentlemen may think proper and of profit...[50]

Black's comments here speak to the heart of our consumption-driven society. We increasingly live in a world that is replete with advertising messages urging people of all ages to consume the latest "thing." While advertising is not a new idea, the growth in the amount of advertising directed at children continues to be of great concern. BusRadio represents a glaring example of a private business finding a new means by which to reach the growing youth market. What is especially disconcerting is the fact that BusRadio endeavors to use public schools as an accomplice in its effort to reap profits from youth.

---

[49] Henry Giroux, *Stealing Innocence: Corporate Culture's War on Children* (New York: Palgrave, 2000), 95.

[50] Charles L. Black, "He Cannot Choose But Hear: The Plight of the Captive Auditor," 966.

As BusRadio continues to extend its reach to an increasing number of public school students, concerned teachers, students, school administrators, and parents need to become leaders in the fight against BusRadio. If BusRadio's desire to offer up youth as a captive market to advertisers is to be countered, then those most directly impacted by BusRadio must find ways to speak out against it. As noted earlier, there is currently little public outcry regarding BusRadio aside from the actions of several activist organizations and a few school systems. Perhaps the lack of resistance is due to school-business partnerships being so conspicuous today that these partnerships are being accepted as an inherent aspect of modern public schooling. However, what is now needed is ongoing debate and inquiry into the role that corporations and businesses such as BusRadio play in U.S. public schools by anyone concerned with the welfare of schools and students.

Bibliography

Black, Charles L. 1953. "He Cannot Choose But Hear: The Plight of the Captive Auditor," *Columbia Law Review*, 166.

Boyles, Deron. 2005. "Uncovering the Coverings: The Use of Corporate-Sponsored Textbook Covers in Furthering Uncritical Consumerism," *Educational Studies*, Fall, pp. 255-266.

Boyles, Deron. 2000. *American Education and Corporations: The Free Market Goes to School.* New York: Falmer.

BusRadio. Information on BusRadio's format and business plan can be found at www.busradio.org. Last accessed June 1, 2007.

Commercial Alert. 2006. "Commercial Alert Urges Gov. Romney to Expel Radio Ads from Mass. School Buses," June 5. Article can be found at http://www.commercialalert.org/ issues/education/busradio/commercial-alert-urges-gov-romney-to-expel-radio-ads-from-mass-school-buses.

Fox, Rick. 2000. *Harvesting Minds: How TV Commercials Control Kids.* Westport, CT: Praeger.

Giroux, Henry. 2000. *Stealing Innocence: Corporate Culture's War on Children.* New York: Palgrave.

Greene, Maxine. 1998. *The Dialectic of Freedom.* New York: Teachers College Press.

Kid Power Xchange. "Kid and Tweens Power 2007." conference information can be found at http://www.iqpc.com/cgi-bin/templates/genevent.html?topic=445&event=12748&.

Koch, Wendy. 2006. "School Buses in 11 States Tune In to Radio Programming," *USA Today*, September 17, N34.

Louisville Courier-Journal. 2007. "School Board Drops Proposal for Bus Radios," May 18, A4.

Maxwell, Leslie A. 2006. "School Bus Radio Venture Raises Safety, Commercialism Concern," *Education Week*, September 20, 8-9. Article can be accessed at www.edweek.org/ew/ articles/2006/09/20/05bus_wed.h26.html?

Mayer, Caroline E. 2006. "The Next Niche: School Bus Ads," *Washington Post*, June 4, B1.

Molnar, Alex. 2005. *School Commercialism: From Democratic Ideal to Market Commodity* New York: Routledge.

Molnar, Alex. 1999. "Cashing in on Kids: The Second Annual Report on Trends in School-house Commercialism," *Center for the Analysis of Commercialism in Education.* Document 99-21, September. The report can be accessed at http://www.asu.edu/educ/epsl/CERU/Annual%20reports/cace-99-21.htm. Accessed June 27, 2006.

Schor, Juliet B. 2004. *Born to Buy: The Commercialized Child and the New Consumer Culture.* New York: Scribner.

Soule, Alexander. 2006. "Bus Radio Targets a Captive—And Raucous—Audience," *Boston Business Journal,* March 31-April 6, 8.

Spring, Joel. 2003. *Educating the Consumer-Citizen.* Mahwah, NJ: Lawrence Erlbaum Associates, Publishers.

Story, Louise. 2007. "Anywhere the Eye Can See, It's Likely to See an Ad," *New York Times,* January 15, B1.

Strasburger, Victor C. "Children and TV Advertising: Nowhere to Run, Nowhere to Hide," *Journal of Developmental & Behavioral Pediatrics, 22,* pp. 185-187.

CHAPTER EIGHT

Uncovering the Coverings
The Use of Corporate Supplied Textbook Covers to Further Uncritical Consumerism

Deron Boyles, Georgia State University

The Center for Science in the Public Interest (CSPI) released a report in 2003 charging that corporations in the food industry are increasing their efforts to market unhealthy foods to children.[1] Part of the concern the report raises involves the techniques used to market certain foods to students in schools. From Krispy Kreme promotions that offer students a donut for every A to "the Oreo Adventure game [called an 'advergame'] on Kraft Foods' Nabisco-world.com web site. . .[that has children's] 'health' ratings reset to '100 percent' when kids acquire golden cookie jars on a journey to a Temple of the Golden Oreo," marketing is big business and health seems to be marginalized or overlooked.[2]

"No amount of eye-rolling can capture how hypocritical it is for food company flacks to talk about 'moderation, balance, and exercise," said CSPI executive director Michael F. Jacobson. "Anyone who looks at these marketing techniques can see that they encourage excess, not moderation. Almost exclusively, they encourage consumption of an unbalanced diet of high-cal and low-nutrient foods. And to link junk foods like Oreos or Pepsi to physical fitness or athletic prowess has to be one of the most cynical and unfair marketing strategies I've ever seen."[3]

This essay extends the critique of business influences in schools by examining one specific medium for corporate marketing—textbook covers. It is not

---

[1] See <http://www.Cspinet.org> Accessed 18 November 2003.
[2] Ibid.
[3] Ibid.

unusual for businesses to supply schools with "free" textbook covers, to be sure. The covers are typically handed out by schools via teachers and are ostensibly offered at no cost. Yet the covers often feature cartoon characters, snack foods, sport drinks, athletes, celebrities, and television shows. These elements of the marketing campaign are precisely the kind of features CSPI criticized businesses for using. But is the criticism justified?

In this chapter, I wish to explore the various kinds of book covers that exist to see if a meta-narrative can be discerned. I also wish to question the degree to which the various covers indicate, inscribe, or otherwise represent cultural values that might be—consistent with the CSPI report—problematic. In a basic and general sense, my intent is to investigate what symbols are actually represented on the dust jackets. What meanings do they foreclose or "cover" over? What messages might they send? This chapter, therefore, highlights and describes a series of textbook covers, from over 100, that have been provided to me by various students, colleagues, and friends. Accordingly, this is not an exhaustive review of book covers. I am analyzing what I have been given with the intention of analyzing the symbols, meanings, and the pros and cons of using book covers in schools. Ultimately this chapter questions the role teachers play in promoting, wittingly or not, commercialism in schools.

Food and Nutrition: Toucan Sam and Friends

Picture "Toucan Sam," the cartoon mascot for Froot Loops cereal whose "nose" helps him "find fruity flavors."[4] The book cover on which Toucan Sam appears has the mock title "Birds Weekly." As with some magazines, titles of articles appear on the cover. In this case, the dust jacket philosophically asks, as one of the "subheadings," "Chicken or Egg: Which Came First?" Other "stories" purporting to appear inside "Birds Weekly" include "Building Your Nest Egg" and the added bonus of "Beak of the Month." Above the title appears the question "What's the Best Birdseed?" and in larger letters, next to the cartoon figure himself, is the promise that the "magazine" has the "Inside Story of *Toucan Sam*."[5] The back cover of the dust jacket provides background on toucan birds, via the cartoon character. Five pictures appear, along with a graphic in the background. The caption next to the first picture proclaims: "Toucan birds love fruit. And Toucan Sam is no exception—his big nose helps

---

[4] Kellogg Company, "Birds Weekly" book cover (New York: Cover Concepts, 2000), cover #99483.

[5] Ibid., italics in original.

him find it anywhere." The caption beside the next two pictures reads: "He goes to great lengths tracking down the most delicious fruit flavor." The final caption notes: "And that fruity flavor usually ends up being Kellogg's Froot Loops cereal. This is one taste this bird can't resist." The graphic behind all of the pictures and captions appears to be a large, twisted tree. It has a line drawn to it with the claim that the "Background photo—[is the] home of Toucan Sam."

A cursory glance at the dust jacket might give the impression that it represents a magazine, one that has stories inside. Because it is only a book cover, however, there are no actual stories. In fact, the only "information" vaguely related to the "articles" listed on the front cover is the singular claim on the back of the dust jacket that toucan birds love fruit. What is pictured, however, is a cartoon character and mascot for a sugary cereal. Supplied to students for "free," this book cover is obviously a not-too-covert advertising campaign. Images of the cereal appear on the front cover, the registered name and iconography appear on what would be the spine of the book (next to a student's name), and the product is featured again on the back cover, equating fruit to the cereal.

What makes it somewhat unique among book covers is that it uses a magazine format (rather than the more common "games" or illustrations of sports). It even purports to provide "factual" information. That toucan birds love fruit may be true, but the narrative Kellogg's provides is one that subsumes the tidbit of factual information within the story of the cartoon character's search for food. Forget that "fruit" is spelled "f-r-o-o-t." Forget that the fruit pictured actually has a collection of nonproportional illustrations of fruit.[6] Forget even that the bird is claimed to have a nose rather than a beak. The book cover represents what is so problematic about market logic masquerading as philanthropy in schools—misinformation, image as reality, and commercialism. I return to these issues and explore them in more detail at the end of this article, but other "food" examples of book covers further the point.

In addition to Kellogg's, Wyler's and Mondo have a book cover touting their soft drink mix and squeeze bottle products. The feature of the cover is the product, with two figures of young people skateboarding and rollerblading. Like other book covers, this cover promotes consumerism and specifically encourages students to take coupons home to their parents. In fact, the cover

---

[6] Of the lime, orange, and cherry pictured, the cherry is more than half the size of the lime.

states, "Hey Kids, Bring Savings Home!"[7] This concept of "savings," however, belies the fact that the only kind of savings you get is when you actually spend money. "Savings" via spending is one view of "savings," but a consumerist one void of alternatives such as not buying the product in the first place and *really* saving on the cost of the product not purchased. "Saving" one's teeth by not consuming that much sugar is also not relayed in the concept proffered here.

The Quaker Oats Company has a chewy granola-bar-strewn cover with bits of trivia: "It would take 4,042,105 Quaker Chewy Granola Bars to fill up a soccer field!"; "Over 3 billion pounds of chocolate are eaten every year in the U.S.!"; "The fastest speed ever achieved on a bicycle is 152.284 miles per hour!"; "The world record for bouncing a soccer ball on one's head is 7 hours and 16 minutes!"; "A worker bee makes only 1/12 of a teaspoon of honey in its entire lifetime!"[8] Aside from the incessant exclamation points after each point of trivia, one wonders about the choice of the trivia. Why is chocolate featured? Why are bouncing soccer balls and bicycle speeds included? When the company claims that it takes 4,042,105 of their bars to fill up a soccer field, what do they mean? Are the bars covering the field at a depth of only one bar or does "fill" mean bars stacked on top of one another until they reach the upper bar of the goal net structure? The tidbit about honey appears next to a picture of a pot of yellow-gold liquid that is part of the purported production line of the Quaker Oats Company, but is the honey trivia supposed to spark students' interests in entomology or something else?

No subtlety exists when the snack company Frito-Lay encourages students to "blast off for lunch" by eating any variety of chips. They use a labyrinthine puzzle that requires students to "decode" messages (e.g., "you rule," "no limits," "planet lunch," etc.). They note, "Also scattered throughout the maze are bags of Doritos. . .Ruffles. . . Lay's. . .potato chips, Chee-Tos, and Fritos. . . Grab 'em up for a quick snack and for their coded clues."[9] As Carolyn Vander Schee points out, the existence of marketing of snack foods is not solely re-

---

[7] Jel Sert Company, "Taste the Difference" and "It's Your World!" book cover (West Chicago, IL: The Jel Sert Company, 1997). In what may be an odd theme among fruit represented on book covers, the Wyler's portion of the book cover has four pieces of fruit pictured (kiwi, cherry, pineapple, and strawberry), with the cherry equal in size to the slice of kiwi.

[8] Quaker Oats Company, Chewy Granola Bars book cover (Braintree, MA: Cover Concepts, 1997).

[9] Frito-Lay, Inc., "Blast Off for Planet Lunch" book cover (Braintree, MA: Cover Concepts, 1997), cover #99739.

sponsible for the marked increase in childhood obesity.[10] Still, she points out, efforts such as marketing via book covers exacerbate the problem. Consider now some examples that might be connected with food and nutrition, but seem to me to have different messages in addition to nutritional issues.

Sports: Well, Basketball Anyway

The Powerade drink company and Gatorade drink company are extensions of the food topic, but the marketing of Powerade and Gatorade are universally sports oriented. Gatorade provides a cover that, at a distance, appears much like a traditional cover for a notebook (one with a black and white pattern all over it). They note on their cover, however, that the dust jacket contains sports figures—symbolic characters engaged in various sport activities. Two assignments are given: "Assignment #1—There are 126 athletes playing sports on this cover (Betcha can't find 'em all). Fill in the athlete's shapes with different colored pens. No two book covers look alike! Assignment #2—Play sports. Drink Gatorade. Cool down. Keep playing sports. Repeat 6,395,917 times."[11]

Another Gatorade book cover features the professional basketball player Michael Jordon. The cover features Jordon's head and what appears to be an x-ray of the basketball star's body. His "drive gear" is a hamster, his heart is a basketball, and his fuel is, of course, Gatorade. The book cover also features ranked characteristics such as "confidence," "focus," "motivation," and the like. The number one characteristic is "energy." Gatorade's website is listed, too, along with graphics that appear to reflect an interest in human anatomy and physiology—save the basketball heart and hamster stomach. Clearly an advertisement, this book cover reflects the message that sports are important and that drinking Gatorade is what a successful athlete drinks.

Perhaps one of the most interesting book covers advertising sport drinks is the Gatorade cover featuring a battle between basketball star Vince Carter and a dinosaur. Illustrated to mimic a movie titled "Raptor vs. Raptor" (i.e., a dinosaur versus a basketball player on the team called the Raptors), the book cover has an image of a ferocious-looking, blood-spattered animal on one side and a cartoon version of an overly muscled, sweat-spattered basketball player

---

[10] Vander Schee, Carolyn. 2005. "The Privatization of Food Services in Schools: Undermining Children's Health, Social Equity, and Democratic Education." in *Schools or Markets?: Commercialism, Privatization, and School-Business* Partnerships. ed. Deron Boyles. Mahwah, NJ: Lawrence Erlbaum Publishers. pp.1-30.

[11] Gatorade book cover (Braintree, MA: Cover Concepts, 1998).

on the other side. For each "star" or "character" there are specifics listed such as date of birth (January 26, 1977, for Carter; around 6 million years ago for "Ike" the dinosaur), interests (playing the saxophone for Carter; playing basketball for the dinosaur), and drinks (new Gatorade fierce grape for Carter; new Gatorade fierce berry for the dinosaur).[12] According to the cover, Carter's choice of drink is "the perfect way to replenish lost fluids while kicking velociraptor butt."[13] Clearly, the company is advertising its product. Equally clearly, however, is the competitive theme conveyed in the book cover. "Fierce," "kicking butt," "vs." are key terms used alongside a clearly confrontational image of a bloody dinosaur attacking a sweaty basketball player. What messages, besides drinking Gatorade, are being sent? To what degree are competition, ferocity, and winning constitutive features of market logics and capitalist expectations? Are "battles" represented as "normal" or "expected" elements of reality?

Powerade's book cover features the message that its "Powerflo" drink is fast and that, by extension, if you drink it, you too will be fast. In all, speed and going faster than others is a valuable goal. Hockey, track, soccer, basketball, and baseball are among the primary images featured on the cover. Words in large print reinforce the message. "The new Powerflo is fast. It's faster than your mother, your father, your dog, your cat, you car, boat, bike, or best friend . . ."[14] Of the fifteen images of people featured in the ad, six have their backs to the camera or are in silhouette (a little league baseball player, two firefighters, a race car driver, and two hockey players). Everyone else is unmistakably male and the imagery suggests that the other figures are also male. Might this book cover indicate that competition is central? Might the cover also suggest that males are the ones to compete, since females are, with near certainty, not even represented on the cover at all?

The gender issue raised in the Powerade cover pales in comparison to a book cover from Champs Sports.[15] On this book cover, more basketball players are featured—on one side as bobble-head-like figurines and on the other as actual images of people engaged in some aspect of playing basketball. Professional basketball jerseys are pictured on the edges of the cover and the "Champion" label is identified as "the only *guys* who make NBA replica jer-

---

[12] Gatorade book cover (New York: Cover Concepts, 1999-2000), Spring 2000 cover # 99491.

[13] Ibid.

[14] Coca-Cola Company, Powerade book cover (Braintree, MA: Cover Concepts, 1997).

[15] Champs Sports book cover (Braintree, MA: Cover Concepts, 1997), cover # 99779.

seys."[16] Most interesting and arguably most troubling, however, are the four groupings of people featured on the cover itself. In each of the four groups, there are four people photographed separately and then added together to show what appears to be a younger child, an older child, a teenager or young adult, and then a professional basketball player. Each of the positions or movements featured (i.e., two groups about to shoot the ball, the other two groups dribbling) start at what appears to be the beginning or basic step (featuring the images of the youngest players) and then gradually advances through the motion of shooting the ball or dribbling (featuring the images of professional basketball players).

Forget for moment that of the sixteen people pictured, two appear to be Euro-American or Anglo males, five appear to be African American or Mixed Race females, and nine appear to be African American or Mixed Race males.[17] The numbers of representation become less important when one looks closely at the two groups featuring women. Of the two, both begin with two young women. In one of the groups, however, the third woman featured actually has one female arm and one male arm—each of a different color but the male arm featured on the female matches the color and shape of the male pictured at the end of the process. Quite simply, the women pictured in the two groupings morph into men. Given the stage-like or developmental nature of the illustration, it appears that the women represent only the beginning stage while the men illustrate the pinnacle or fully developed form. What message does the Champion brand of clothing wish to send? What do students take away from seeing such imagery? What values, if any, are being suggested by having women transform into men? Why, for example, are professional basketball players who happen to be women *not* featured as the pinnacle? It is difficult to know what messages are actually received or understood (if any). Yet, why are the sports and sports drink book covers primarily in deep hues of blues and greens—with plenty of black as a primary color—while the book covers obviously marketed to girls are primarily pink, purple, and pastel blue?

"Secret Paths," Not so Secret Gender Identity Construction

Of the book covers I received, three clearly seem directed at girls. The first of these covers advertises "Purple Moon," a girls-only website that apparently

---

[16] Ibid., italics added.

[17] Clearly, there are also racial messages within the representation that reinforce assumptions about African Americans, basketball, and sports.

provides a place for girls to "collect treasures. . .play cool activities and meet other girls!"[18] The cover features butterflies, angels, hummingbirds, flowers, and "secret stone" jewels. The cover also includes an advertisement from a clothing store ("Fun Times and Fun Clothes...Wear the Coolest from Jonathan Martin Girls. . .at a mall near you"), and a lip gloss company ("Win fruitlicious lip gloss from LipSmacker. . . .The original fun flavored lip gloss that's good for your lips"). Unfamiliar with Purple Moon, I heeded their advice to visit their website (purple-moon.com). When I did, however, I found a page noting that the site was under construction. "In the meantime," the message on the website read, "visit one of our sister sites: Barbie.com, DivaStarz, and GenerationGirl.com."[19]

The other two covers directed at girls are Mary-Kate and Ashley covers, advertising their videos and fan-club website. Puzzles appear on the covers, including the maze "Can you find your way through the mall?" and the letter scramble "Search for 7 costume party words hidden in the square below." Each of the puzzles corresponds to videos by the actresses ("Mall Party" and "Costume Party," for example), but the messages seem to be that if you are a girl, you should shop, dress up, and "party." Whether there is a cause-effect relationship between young women viewing a book cover and shopping at the mall is not the point. My claim is not that viewing *x* means *y* will happen. My point is that the construction of identities is already so pervasive in general society that for corporations to use book covers as sales tools in schools seems to me to be overkill and a particularly specious form of exploitation. Corporations also manipulate societal norms and sell them back to girls; in essence the girls get the norms "for free" when they participate in societal institutions, but the norms make it incumbent upon girls to consume (and such consumption is not "free"). Indeed, the larger claim here is that sexism is a commodity and an ideology deeply rooted in and deeply valued by corporate interests.

Beyond the Mary-Kate and Ashley videos, other book covers tout the lineup for morning cartoons on the Cartoon Channel. Pokemon book covers advertise various movies. The Fox Family Channel plugs four shows in their morning lineup and four in their afternoon lineup. One group starts at 7 am and the other at 3 pm, which happens to coincide with the times just before and just after many elementary schools start and finish the day. PlayStation

---

[18] Purple Moon Media, Purple Moon book cover (Braintree, MA: Cover Concepts, 1997), cover #99789.

[19] See <http://www.purple-moon.com> Accessed 20 September 2002.

has a book cover, as well. It urges the viewer to "Give History a Wedgie" by playing their various action-adventure games.

To be as judicious as I can, there *are* book covers that might be perceived by some to be more valid or defensible than what has been described above. In the pile of book covers I received, three urged students not to smoke and one featured endangered species and geography games for identifying where endangered animals reside. The problem, of course, is that the no-smoking campaign is underwritten by the Phillip Morris company due to a court order and the endangered species book cover carries with it advertisements for Johnson & Johnson soap products (albeit with dispensers of the soap carrying pictures of animals).

Misinformation, Image as Reality, and Commercialism in Schools

The book cover has become the mini-billboard students carry around with them. Of course not all students use the book covers and not all students pay attention to the graphics, symbolism, and meanings behind the messages they see. But when schools hand out book covers, one wonders whether students receive the message that the covers are sanctioned by the school and hence have some form of validity or acceptance. When teachers pass book covers out to students, do the teachers' actions imply that they sanction the messages, symbols, and meanings embedded (or embossed) in the book covers? What responsibility, if any, do teachers have in such a process? What opportunity do the book covers represent to develop or further develop critical thinking and critical consumerism on the part of students?

Some may protest that the analysis of book covers provided here is overblown. On this view, too much attention is being paid to a form of hyper-analysis and we should simply relax. Students are already bombarded with commercial images and messages in their lives, so book covers are only an extension of the world in which they live. I believe many parents and many teachers would articulate such a view, either out of a defensive sense that they are being blamed for everything as it is (and this issue is another straw on the camel's back) or out of a general malaise which uncritical consumerism yields.

After pointing out such a possible objection to this overall inquiry, I want to pre-empt the point by maintaining that teachers and schools have different obligations to their students than to advance a private, corporate, commercial series of interests. I am not arguing that schools do not already advance such interests, but that they should not. Said more directly, I am asserting that schools should not be places where teachers allow the uncritical acceptance of any narrative, much less the clearly lopsided narrative put forward by corporate advertising campaigns *qua* book covers. By not investigating with students (and others?) the possible symbols and cultural messages that are featured in book covers like the ones detailed in this chapter, two points seem clear: (1) teachers may be committing a form of educational malpractice or intellectual negligence; and (2) teachers may be hegemonically reinforcing the very stereotypes and power structures that cause them to struggle in their daily lives as teachers. Ironically, what may at first appear to be a set of teacher-bashing claims is actually intended to advance a form of teacher power that comes from raising questions.[20]

At what point should individuals consider it appropriate to question the corporate influence over public schooling? When should teachers ask questions of principals, school boards, and politicians about corporate influence? The idea of using critical analyses of book covers as one aspect of an ongoing and never-ending process aimed toward developing critical transitivity and democratic responsibility does not seem to me to permeate current U.S. society nor the sub-society of teachers in U.S. schools. Instead, schools are seen by businesses, business advocates, and consumer materialists as the place for children to "get" an education in order to "get" a job. Further, businesses use schools as captive markets where they can test new merchandise, advance their public relations, and appear philanthropic by "donating" materials to schools. This is part of the problem with the book covers. They are "free," so they are either eagerly sought after or merely accepted since the hegemonic message so deeply reinforced in the U.S. is that schools are now and forever underfunded, so anything free must be accepted (and because it is accepted is good?). Teachers are often grateful, even for book covers.

I cannot help but wonder about the perversity of championing book covers as helping, in an economic sense, extend the life of textbooks that, on their own, are arguably corporate vehicles for reinforcing particular values, histories, and ideologies over others—but in covert ways. On this view, we have corporate covers covering corporate curriculum. Aside from this point, however, we

---

[20] I also wish to point out that while I am focusing on teachers, students are also a prime concern. Indeed, students are at times the barrier to corporate messages. Those messages and their entailing meanings, after all, require interpretation on the part of the receiver. Students may parody the symbols, reject the book covers out of hand, or give so little attention to their meaning that no effect takes hold.

are faced with students accepting donated goods (tax deductible for businesses) and for what educational value? I am not denying the possibility that students may question the covers on their own, reject them out of hand, or use them in subversive ways. I am claiming, however, that they are put in positions where reality is presented to them and, if unchallenged, sets in motion (or a form of non-motion) a pattern of non- or even anti-criticality.

It is as though teachers are acting as surrogate telemarketers. Imposing the corporate covers on students without reflection or critique of their roles, it is taken as a given part of many (though not all) teachers' jobs. Unlike telemarketing, however, students have no mechanism to opt out of being "called" in the first place. There is no "no call list" for them to save themselves from teachers passing out covers—even if they do not wish to accept one. They are still at the place where they have to answer the "call," even if they reject the "call" to take and use the cover and even if they reject the "calls" the covers represent. In terms of book covers, I believe teachers too often ask students to raise their hands if they *want* one, not engage students in *analyzing and critiquing* them.

Let me try to make clear that a call for analysis and critique in schooling, multiple ways of knowing, and critical transitivity should not be associated, to any degree of seriousness, with superfluous references to student choice in current classrooms. In current classrooms, students many times "choose" between booklets from Time, Inc., or the advertisement-riddled Channel One programming station. They also get to choose whether they want the Gatorade book cover featuring Michael Jordon or the Secret Path book cover featuring Barbi, lipstick, and clothing. But is this choice? If so, what kind of choice is it? To paraphrase Kozol, current schooling may answer the charge of promoting anti-intellectual and anti-democratic values by pointing to the aforementioned "choices," as well as to their learning centers, baby rabbits, and $3,000 vouchers. This is offered as evidence of freedom. But is it, really? Kozol writes:

> They have the right to choose without constraint among a thousand paths of impotence, but none of power, the right to demonstrate their sense of ethical surrender in ten different innovative "resource areas" and at twelve separate levels of proficiency. Like first class passengers on board a jet flight to a distant city, they have their choice of any drink or food or magazine or padded seat they prefer; but they are all going to the same place, they are all going there at the same rate of speed, and the place that they are going is a place neither they, nor you, nor I, but someone else they do not know has chosen for them. They have no choice about the final destination. They have no choice about the flight, the price, the pilot or the plane; but they can stretch

their legs, and walk along the aisle, and select their magazine, and they can call this freedom.[21]

My desire is to fashion a view of teaching and learning that legitimates schools as contested, public spheres and teachers as critically transitive agents who work toward forms of social justice, multiple forms of knowing, and critical considerations of the merits and demerits of capitalism and the corporate state. The need is to broaden the definition of teachers, authority, and ethics to include and legitimate educational practices linking democracy, intellectualism, teaching, and practical learning. It means, in part, that book covers should be used as object-lessons—a "free" and available tool to engage students in revealing, reworking, questioning, and possibly even re-appropriating the symbols and cultural values they are confronted with daily. Giroux contends the substantive nature of this task takes as its starting point the ethical intent of initiating students into a discourse and pedagogical process that advances the role of contestation within the school while addressing market logic masquerading as philanthropy in schools, misinformation, image as reality, and the commercialism that structures the daily lives of people in the United States and the world.[22]

Extending Giroux, Pierre Bourdieu calls for bringing together "specific individuals" (a la Foucault) in a collective form ("collective intellectual" for Bourdieu) to confront the production of pro-market, pro-careerist, pro-globalization narratives. "This collective intellectual," he writes, "can and must, in the first place, *fulfill negative functions*: it must work to produce and disseminate instruments of defense against symbolic domination that relies increasingly on the authority of science (real or faked)."[23] If the intellectual is "buttressed by the specific competency and authority of the collective thus formed, it can submit dominant discourse to a merciless logical critique aimed not only at its lexicon ("globalization," "flexibility," "employability," etc.) but also at its mode of reasoning in particular at the use of metaphors (e.g., the anthropomorphization of the market)."[24] Teachers and students as collective

---

[21] Kozol, Jonathan. 1975/1986. *The Night is Dark and I Am Far From Home: A Political Indictment of the U.S. Public Schools*. New York. The Continuum Publishing Corporation.

[22] See Henry Giroux, *Schooling and the Struggle for American Life* (Minneapolis: University of Minnesota Press, 1988).

[23] Bourdieu, Pierre. 2003. *Firing Back: Against the Tyranny of the Market 2*. Loïc Wacquant trans. New York: The New Press. p. 20.

[24] Ibid.

intellectuals, accordingly, should be able to take the discourse represented in items such as book covers and "subject this discourse to a sociological critique aimed at *uncovering* the social determinants that bear on the producers of dominant discourse. . .and on their products."[25] We would do well, then, to focus teacher and student energy on deconstructing and reconstructing the economic, corporate, and capitalist assumptions surrounding and infiltrating schools. The values that are transmitted, or at least symbolically represented, are too pervasive to let that very pervasiveness be an excuse not to grapple with and engage things such as newspaper advertisements, magazines, websites, television news programs—and, yes, textbook covers.

Bibliography

Bourdieu, Pierre. 2003. *Firing Back: Against the Tyranny of the Market 2*. Loïc Wacquant, trans. New York: The New Press.

Champs Sports book cover (Braintree, MA: Cover Concepts, 1997), cover #99779.

Coca-Cola Company, Powerade book cover (Braintree, MA: Cover Concepts, 1997).

Frito-Lay, Inc., "Blast Off for Planet Lunch" book cover (Braintree, MA: Cover Concepts, 1997), cover # 99739.

Gatorade book cover (Braintree, MA: Cover Concepts, 1998).

Gatorade book cover (no attribution, in author's possession).

Gatorade book cover (New York: Cover Concepts, 1999-2000), Spring 2000 cover #99491.

Giroux, Henry A. 1988. *Schooling and the Struggle for American Life*. Minneapolis: University of Minnesota Press.

Jel Sert Company, "Taste the Difference" and "It's Your World!" book cover (West Chicago, IL: The Jel Sert Company, 1997).

Kellogg Company, "Birds Weekly" book cover (New York: Cover Concepts, 2000), cover #99483.

Kozol, Jonathan. 1975/1986. *The Night Is Dark and I Am Far from Home: A Political Indictment of the U.S. Public Schools*. New York. The Continuum Publishing Corporation.

Purple Moon Media, Purple Moon book cover (Braintree, MA: Cover Concepts, 1997), cover #99789.

Quaker Oats Company, Chewy Granola Bars book cover (Braintree, MA: Cover Concepts, 1997).

Vander Schee, Carolyn. 2005. "The Privatization of Food Services in Schools: Undermining Children's Health, Social Equity, and Democratic Education." In *Schools or Markets?: Commercialism, Privatization, and School-Business* Partnerships. ed. Deron Boyles. Mahwah, NJ: Lawrence Erlbaum Publishers. pp.1-30.

---

[25] Ibid.

CHAPTER NINE

Schooling in Disaster Capitalism
How the Political Right Is Using Disaster to Privatize Public Schooling

Kenneth J. Saltman, DePaul University

Introduction

Around the world, disaster is providing the means for business to accumulate profit. From the Asian tsunami of 2005 that allowed corporations to seize coveted shoreline properties for resort development to the multi-billion dollar no-bid reconstruction contracts in Iraq and Afghanistan, from the privatization of public schooling following Hurricane Katrina in the Gulf Coast to the ways that No Child Left Behind sets public schools up to be dismantled and made into investment opportunities—a grotesque pattern is emerging in which business is capitalizing on disaster. Naomi Klein has written of

> ... the rise of a predatory form of disaster capitalism that uses the desperation and fear created by catastrophe to engage in radical social and economic engineering. And on this front, the reconstruction industry works so quickly and efficiently that the privatizations and land grabs are usually locked in before the local population knows what hit them.[1]

Despite the fact that attempts to privatize and commercialize public schools proceed at a startling pace,[2] privatization increasingly appears in a new form that Klein calls "disaster capitalism" and that David Harvey terms "accumulation by dispossession." This article details how in education the politi-

---

[1] Naomi Klein, "The Rise of Disaster Capitalism," *The Nation* (May 2005).

[2] For the most recent update on the state of educational privatization see the research provided by the Educational Policy Studies Laboratory at Arizona State University available at www.schoolcommercialism.org.

cal Right is capitalizing on disaster from Chicago's Renaissance 2010 to the federal No Child Left Behind Act, from educational rebuilding in the Gulf Coast of the U.S. to education profiteering in Iraq. The new predatory form of educational privatization aims to dismantle and then commodify particular public schools. This conservative movement threatens the development of public schools as necessary places that foster engaged critical citizenship. At the same time, it undermines the public and democratic purposes of public education; it amasses vast profits for few, and even furthers U.S. foreign policy agendas.

Educators committed to defending and strengthening public education as a crucial public sphere in a democratic society may be relieved by several recent failures of the educational privatization movement. By 2000 business publications were eyeing public education as the next big score, ripe for privatization and commodification, likening it to the medical and military industries and suggesting that it might yield $600 billion a year in possible takings.[3] However, it has become apparent that only a few years later, Educational Management Organizations (EMO) that seek to manage public schools for profit have not overtaken public education (though EMOs are growing at an alarming rate of a five-fold increase in schools managed in six years). The biggest experiment in for-profit management of public schooling, The Edison Schools, continues as a symbol, according to the right-wing business press, of why running schools for profit on a vast scale is not profitable.[4] The massive EMO Knowledge Universe, created by junk bond felon Michael Milken upon his release from prison from nearly a hundred counts of fraud and insider

---

[3] "Reading, Writing, and Enrichment: Private Money Is Pouring into American Education—And Transforming It," *The Economist* (January 16, 1999): 55. I detail a number of business publications that were salivating over privatizing public schooling in "Junk King Education," chapter one of Robin Truth Goodman and Kenneth J. Saltman, *Strange Love, Or How We Learn to Stop Worrying and Love the Market* (Lanham: Rowman and Littlefield, 2002). In academic circles Paul Hill was striving to make education an investment opportunity. Paul Thomas Hill, Lawrence C. Pierce, James W. Guthrie. *Reinventing Public Education: How Contracting Can Transform America's Schools* (Chicago: University of Chicago Press, 1997). Hill appears at the forefront of calls for Katrina profiteering in 2005.

[4] See, for example, William C. Symonds, "Edison: An 'F' in Finance," *Business Week*, 3806 (November 4, 2002): 2, and Julia Boorstin, "Why Edison Doesn't Work," *Fortune*, 146 (December 9, 2002): 12. For a detailed discussion of Edison's financial problems and the media coverage of them, see Kenneth J. Saltman, *The Edison Schools: Corporate Schooling and the Assault on Public Education* (New York: Routledge, 2005).

trading, is in the midst of going out of business.[5] By the autumn of 2005, the school voucher movement, which the Right has been fighting to implement for decades, had only succeeded in capturing the Washington, D.C. public schools (through the assistance of Congress), and that experiment is by all accounts looking bad. The charter school movement, which is fostering privatization by allowing for publicly funded schools managed by for-profit companies, and is being pushed by massive federal funding under No Child Left Behind, has also taken a hit from NAEP scores that, in traditional terms of achievement, suggest charters do not score as high as the much-maligned public schools. Even school commercialism has faced a sizable backlash from a public fed up and sickened by the shameless attempts of marketers to sell sugar-laden soft drinks and candy bars to U.S. schoolchildren who are suffering epidemic levels of type II diabetes and obesity. Although commercialism continues putting ads in textbooks and playing fields, on buildings and buses, a growing number of cities, states, and provinces have put in place anti-commercialism laws. Such laws limit the transformation of public space into yet more commercial space for corporations, which have succeeded in infiltrating nearly every bit of daily life with advertisements and narratives that proselytize the elements of corporate culture: celebrating consumerism, possessive individualism, social Darwinism, authoritarianism, and a corporate vision for the future of work, leisure, politics, and the environment.

It would be difficult to assert that most public schools currently foster the best alternative to corporate culture, that is, democratic culture, what Dewey called "creative democracy." Nurturing a democratic culture and a democratic ethos demands of educators continual work, practice, and attention.[6] The present historical moment is seeing the radical erosion of democratic culture by not only the aforementioned onslaught of commercial culture but also the state-led dismantling of civil liberties under the new dictates of the security state, the resurgence of jingoistic patriotism under the so-called "war on terror," and demands for adhesion to a militarized corporate globalization.[7] If many public schools do not presently foster a democratic ethos necessary for developing in citizens habits of engaged public criticism and participation, the

---

[5] See "Junk King Education" in Robin Truth Goodman and Kenneth J. Saltman, *Strange Love, Or How We Learn to Stop Worrying and Love the Market* (Lanham: Rowman and Littlefield, 2002).

[6] See Richard J. Bernstein's important discussion of the need for a democratic ethos based on Dewey's notion of Creative Democracy in *The Abuse of Evil* (New York: Verso, 2005).

[7] See William I. Robinson, *Critical Globalization Studies* (New York: Routledge, 2003).

public nature of public schools makes them a crucial "site and stake" of struggle for the expansion of democratic social relations. Privatizing public schools does not simply threaten to skim public tax money to provide rich investors with profit. Public schools differ from privately controlled schools in that they harbor a distinct potential for public deliberation and oversight that privately owned and controlled educational institutions limit. Privately controlled institutions are captured by private interests. For example, freedom of speech is protected on the public space of a town common but is privately regulated in a shopping mall. In a public school, learning and knowledge can be engaged in relation to pressing public problems in ways that can be limited within privatized schools. Consider, for example, the following threats to the public: the threats posed by the expanded corporate control over a biotechnology giant such as Monsanto that can patent life, own and control the genetic makeup of all crops, and infect biodiverse crops with potentially devastating genetically modified Franken-food; the threats posed to the global environment by a multinational corporation such as McDonald's that participates in destroying the rainforests for cattle grazing land; the threats to public life as a national security state expands to enable the U.S. government to continue to surround strategically the world's oil supplies with permanent military bases to benefit oil corporations, military corporations, and to continue to project a capitalist model of development that is most often, despite the rhetoric, thoroughly at odds with democracy, particularly in the states alleged to be U.S. allies: Egypt, Pakistan, Jordan, Uzbekistan, etc. When a for-profit corporation runs schools, it will share ideological commitments to corporate globalization that frame public problems in ways compatible with ever-expanding corporate profit despite the risks to people. Public problems such as the weakening of the public sphere resulting from the corporate takeover of knowledge and schooling is not likely to be taught by corporations such as The Edison Schools. At stake in the struggle for public education is the value of critical and public education as a foundation for an engaged citizenry and a substantive democracy.

Capitalizing on Disaster in Education

Despite the range of obvious failures of multiple public school privatization initiatives, the privatization advocates have hardly given up. In fact, the privatizers have become far more strategic. The new educational privatization might be termed "back door privatization"[8] or maybe "smash and grab" privatization. A number of privatization schemes are being initiated through a process involving the dismantling of public schools followed by the opening of for-profit, charter, and deregulated public schools. These enterprises typically despise teachers' unions, are hostile to local democratic governance and oversight, and have an unquenchable thirst for "experiments," especially with the private sector.[9] These initiatives are informed by right-wing think tanks and business organizations. Four examples that typify back-door privatization are (1) No Child Left Behind, (2) Chicago's Renaissance 2010 project, (3) educational rebuilding in Iraq, and (4) educational rebuilding in New Orleans.

No Child Left Behind

No Child Left Behind sets schools up for failure by making impossible demands for continual improvement. When schools have not met Adequate Yearly Progress (AYP), they are subject to punitive action by the federal government, including the potential loss of formerly guaranteed federal funding and requirements for tutoring from a vast array of for-profit Special Educational Service providers. A number of authors have described how NCLB is a boon for the testing and tutoring companies, while it does not provide financial resources for the test score increases it demands.[10] (This is aside from the cultural politics of whose knowledge these tests affirm and discredit.[11]) Send-

---

[8] The editors of *Rethinking Schools* describe the federal voucher scheme after Hurricane Katrina as "back door privatization." "Katrina's Lesson's," *Rethinking Schools* (Fall 2005): 4-5.

[9] David Hursh offers an important discussion of how neoliberal educational policies destroy democratic public educational ideals in "Undermining Democratic Education in the USA: The Consequences of Global Capitalism and Neo-liberal Policies for Education Policies at the Local, State, and Federal Levels." *Policy Futures in Education* 2, nos. 3 and 4 (2004): 607-620.

[10] For an excellent collection of criticisms of No Child Left Behind see Deborah Meier and George Wood (eds.), *Many Children Left Behind* (Boston: Beacon, 2004). In relation to what Henry Giroux has called the "war on youth" being waged in the U.S., see his important chapter on NCLB in Henry A. Giroux, *Abandoned Generation* (New York: Palgrave, 2003). See also the collection of writings on NCLB on the rethinkingschools.org website.

[11] School rewards professional and ruling class knowledge and dispositions and disaffirms and punishes the knowledge and dispositions of working class, poor, and culturally non-dominant groups. See, for example, the work of Antonio Gramsci, Pierre Bourdieu and Jean Passeron, Louis Althusser, Raymond Williams, Michael Apple, Henry Giroux, Peter McLaren, Stephen Ball, Sonia Nieto, Jean Anyon, Gloria Ladson-Billings, Michelle Fine, Lois Weis, to name just a few.

ing billions of dollars of support toward the charter school movement, NCLB pushes schools that do not meet AYP to restructure in ways that encourage privatization, discourage unions, and avoid local regulations on crucial matters. One study has found that by 2013 nearly all of the public schools in the Great Lakes region of the U.S. will be declared failed public schools and subject to such reforms.[12] Clearly, NCLB is designed to accomplish the implementation of privatization and deregulation in ways that open action could not.

A study of the Great Lakes region of the U.S. by educational policy researchers found that 85 to 95 percent of schools in that region would be declared "failed" by NCLB AYP measures by 2014.[13] These implications are national. Under NCLB, "The entire country faces tremendous failure rates, even under a conservative estimate with several forgiving assumptions."[14] Under NCLB, in order for Illinois, for example, to get much needed federal Title I funds, the school must demonstrate adequate yearly progress. Each year Illinois has to get higher and higher standardized test scores in reading and math to make AYP. Illinois schools, and specifically Illinois schools already receiving the least funding and already serving the poorest students, are being threatened with: (1) losing federal funds; (2) having to use scarce resources for under-regulated and often unproven supplemental educational services(SESs) (private tutoring) such as Newton, a spin-off company of the much criticized for-profit Edison Schools; or (3) being punished, reorganized, or closed and reopened as a "choice" school (these include for-profit or nonprofit charter schools that do not have the same level of public oversight and accountability, that often do not have teachers' unions, and that often have to struggle for philanthropic grants to operate). Many defenders of public education view remediation options 2 and 3 under NCLB as having been designed to undermine those public schools that have been underserved in the first place in order to justify privatization schemes.[15] Public schools need help, investment,

---

[12] See Edward W. Wiley, William J. Mathis, David R. Garcia, "The Impact of Adequate Yearly Progress Requirement of the Federal 'No Child Left Behind' Act on Schools in the Great Lakes Region," *Education Policy Studies Laboratory*, September 2005, available at <edpolicylab.org>.

[13] Ibid., "Executive Summary," 3.

[14] Ibid.

[15] See, for example, the contributors in Meier and Wood, *Many Children Left Behind*. Also see, for example, the writing of Stan Karp and Gerald Bracey on NCLB. A number of excellent

and public commitment.

NCLB is setting up for failure not just Illinois public schools but public schools nationally by raising test-oriented thresholds without raising investment and commitment. NCLB itself appears to be a system designed to result in the declaration of wide-scale failure of public schooling to justify privatization.[16] Dedicated administrators, teachers, students, and schools are not receiving much needed resources along with public investment in public services and employment in the communities where those schools are situated. What they are getting instead are threats.

The theoretically and empirically dubious underlying assumption of NCLB is that threats and pressure force teachers to teach what they ought to teach, force students to learn what they ought to learn. In terms of conventional measures of student achievement, Sharon Nichols, Gene Glass, and David Berliner found in their empirical study, *High-Stakes Testing and Student Achievement: Problems for the No Child Left Behind Act*, that "there is no convincing evidence that the pressure associated with high-stakes testing leads to any important benefits for students' achievement... [The authors] call for a moratorium on policies that force the public education system to rely on high-stakes testing."[17] These authors find that high-stakes testing regimes do not achieve what they are designed to achieve. However, to think beyond efficacy to the underlying assumptions about "achievement," it is necessary to raise theoretical concerns. Theoretically, at the very least, the enforcement-oriented assumptions of NCLB fail to consider the limitations of defining "achievement" through high-stakes tests, fail to question what knowledge and whose knowledge constitute legitimate or official curricula that students are expected to master, fail to interrogate the problematic assumptions of learning modeled on digestion or commodity acquisition (as opposed to dialogic, constructivist or other approaches to learning), and such compartmentalized versions of knowledge and learning fail to comprehend how they relate to the broader social and political realities informing knowledge-making both in schools and in society generally.

---

resources on privatization and commercialism implications of NCLB can be found at the site of the Educational Policy Studies Laboratory at www.schoolcommercialism.org.

[16] Alfie Kohn, "NCLB and the Effort to Privatize Public Education" in *Many Children Left Behind*, Deborah Meier and George Wood (eds.), (Boston: Beacon, 2004), 79-100.

[17] Sharon L. Nichols, Gene V. Glass, David C. Berliner, "High-Stakes Testing and Student Achievement: Problems for the No Child Left Behind Act," Educational Policy Studies Laboratory available at http://edpolicylab.org, "Executive Summary," 3.

Renaissance 2010

In Chicago, Renaissance 2010, essentially written by the Commercial Club of Chicago, is being implemented by Chicago Public Schools, a district with more than 85 percent of students who are poor and non-white. It will close 100 public schools and then reopen them as for-profit and nonprofit charter schools, contract schools, and magnet schools, and will bypass important district regulations. The right-wing Heartland Institution hailed the plan "Competition and (public private) Partnerships Are Key to Chicago Renaissance Plan," while the president of the Chicago Teacher's Union described it as a plan to dismantle public education.[18] These closings are targeting neighborhoods that are being gentrified and taken over by richer and whiter people who are buying up newly developed condominiums and townhomes. Critics of the plan view it as "urban cleansing" that principally kicks out local residents.[19]

Like NCLB, Renaissance 2010 targets schools that have "failed" to meet Chicago accountability standards defined through high-stakes tests. By closing and reopening schools, Renaissance 2010 allows the newly privatized schools to circumvent NCLB AYP progress requirements, making the list of Chicago's "need improvement" schools shorter. This allows the city to claim improvement by simply redefining terms.

NCLB and Renaissance 2010 share a number of features including not only a high-pressure model, but also reliance on standardized testing as the ultimate measure of learning, threats to teacher job security and teachers' unions, and a push for experimentation with unproven models, including privatization and charter schools, as well as a series of business assumptions and guiding language. For example, speaking of Renaissance 2010, Mayor Daley stated, "This model will generate competition and allow for innovation. It will bring in outside partners who want to get into the business of education."[20]

Beyond its similarities to NCLB, Renaissance 2010 is being hailed as a national model in its own right across the political spectrum. The Bill and Melinda Gates Foundation is the most heavily endowed philanthropy in history, worth about $80 billion, with projects in health and education. Its focus on

---

[18] For an important scholarly analysis, see Pauline Lipman, *High Stakes Education* (New York: Routledge, 2004).

[19] Activist groups include: Parents United for Responsible Education, Teachers for Social Justice, and Chicago Coalition for the Homeless, among others.

[20] Deb Moore, "A New Approach in Chicago," *School Planning and Management* (July 2004): 8.

school reform is guided by the neoliberal Democratic Leadership Council's Progressive Policy Institute. Though it offers no substance, argument, or evidence for why Renaissance 2010 should be replicated, the economically unmatched Gates Foundation praises Renaissance 2010 as a "roadmap" for other cities to follow.[21] As Pauline Lipman, a progressive urban education scholar at the University of Illinois at Chicago, writes:

> If Chicago's accountability has laid the groundwork for privatization, Renaissance 2010 may signal what we can expect nationally as school districts fail to meet NCLB benchmarks. In fact, failure to make "adequate yearly progress" on these benchmarks, and the threat of a state takeover, is a major theme running through the Commercial Club's argument for school choice and charter schools. Business and political leaders seem to believe turning schools over to the market is a common sense solution to the problems in the schools.[22]

Both NCLB and Renaissance 2010 involve two stages of capitalizing on disaster. The first stage involves the historical underfunding and disinvestment in public schooling that has resulted in disastrous public school conditions. For those communities where these schools are located, it is the public and private sectors that have failed them. However, the corporate sector is usually represented not only in mass media but also much conservative and liberal educational policy literature as coming to rescue the incompetent public sector from itself. As Dorothy Shipps points out in her book *School Reform, Corporate Style: Chicago 1880-2000*, the corporate sector in Chicago and around the nation has long been deeply involved in school reform, agenda setting, and planning in conjunction with other civic planning. As she asks, "If corporate power was instrumental in creating the urban public schools and has had a strong hand in their reform for more than a century, then why have those schools failed urban children so badly?"[23]

---

[21] "Snapshot: Chicago Renaissance 2010," *Possibilities: An Education Update*, page 2, The Bill and Melinda Gates Foundation, available at http://www.gatesfoundation.org/Education/RelatedInfo/Possibilities/Possibilities2004.

[22] Pauline Lipman, "'We're Not Blind. Just Follow the Dollar Sign,'" *Rethinking Schools Online* 19, no. 4 (Summer 2005). available at www.rethinkingschools.org.

[23] Dorothy Shipps, *School Reform, Corporate Style: Chicago 1880-2000* (Lawrence: The University of Kansas Press), x.

Creative Associates International, Incorporated

In Iraq, Creative Associates International, Incorporated (CAII), a for-profit corporation, has made over a hundred million dollars from no-bid contracts with the U.S. Agency for International Development (USAID) to rebuild schools, develop curriculum, develop teacher training, and procure educational supplies. The company has avoided using local contractors and has spent the majority of funds on security while the majority of schools continue to languish in squalor. Educational privatization typifies the way the U.S. invasion has been used to sell off Iraq. Privatization and the development of U.S.-style charter schools are central to the plan (conservative consultants from the right-wing Heritage Foundation have been employed), despite the fact that these are foreign to Iraq's public education system; and members of right-wing think tanks have been engaged to enact what invasion and military destruction has made a lucrative opportunity financially and ideologically. Privatization of the Iraqi schools is part of a broader attempt to privatize and sell off the Iraqi nation while for-profit educational contractor CAII appears as the spearhead of U.S. foreign policy to "promote democracy."[24] As I discuss at length elsewhere[25] the claims for "democracy promotion" in Iraq appear to have more to do with using this human-made disaster for promoting the interests of corporations and transnational capital and nothing to do with expanding meaningful and participatory democracy.

Hurricane Katrina

Likewise, following the natural disaster of Hurricane Katrina in the U.S. Gulf Coast, a for-profit educational contractor from Alaska, named Akima, won a no-bid contract to build temporary portable classrooms in the Gulf Coast. But for-profit education's big haul in the Big Easy was the U.S. Department of Education imposing the largest ever school voucher experiment for the region and nation. Right-wing think tanks had prepared papers advocating such an approach, describing public school privatization as a "silver lining" and a "golden opportunity."[26]

---

[24] Pratap Chaterjee, *Iraq, Inc.: A Profitable Occupation* (New York: Seven Stories Press 2004).

[25] Kenneth J. Saltman, "Creative Associates International, Inc.: Corporate Education and Democracy Promotion in Iraq," *Review of Education Pedagogy Cultural Studies* 28 (2006): 25-65.

[26] For example, Clint Bolick of the Alliance for School Choice described privatization as the "silver lining" of the cloud that was Hurricane Katrina. His op-ed or quote was then carried by countless publications, including the neoconservative *The National Review* and The Heart-

Six months after Hurricane Katrina, the destroyed New Orleans public schools sat slime-coated in mold, debris, and human feces, partially flooded and littered with such detritus as a two-ton air conditioner that had been on the roof and the carcasses of dead dogs.

> All 124 New Orleans Public Schools were damaged in some way and only 20 have re-opened with more than 10,000 students registered. There were 62,227 students enrolled in NOPS before the storm.[27]

The devastation nearly defies description.

> ... Katrina roared in, severely damaging about a quarter of the schools: Roofs caved in. Fierce winds blew out walls and hurled desks through windows. Floodwaters drowned about 300 buses. Computers, furniture and books were buried in mud. Dead dogs and rotting food littered hallways.[28]

Yet days after the disaster *The Washington Times* quoted long-standing advocate of school vouchers Clint Bolick of the Alliance for School Choice. Bolick used the tragedy to propose wide-scale privatization of the New Orleans public schools in the form of a massive voucher scheme. He said, "If there could be a silver lining to this tragedy, it would be that children who previously had few prospects for a high-quality education, now would have expanded options. Even with the children scattered to the winds, that prospect can now be a reality—if the parents are given power over their children's education funds."[29] Calling for the privatization of public schools, Bolick's metaphor of the "silver lining" would be repeated over and over in the popular press immediately after the storm. Karla Dial in the *Heartland News* wrote, "emergency vouchers could be the silver lining in the storm clouds that brought Hurricane Katrina to the Gulf Coast on August 29."[30]   Reuters quoted Louisiana State Superintendent of Education Cecil Picard as saying, "We think this is a once-in-a-lifetime opportunity. I call it the silver lining in

---

land Institute and *The Washington Times, USA Today,* etc. The quote was picked up and re-peated by others advocating the same.

[27] April Capchino, "More than 100 N.O. Schools Still Closed," *New Orleans City Business* (February 27, 2006).

[28] Sharon Cohen, "New Orleans' Troubled Schools Get Overhaul," Associated Press, March 4, 2006. YahooNews, news.yahoo.com.

[29] Clint Bolick, "Katrina's Displaced Students," *The Washington Times,* September 15, 2005.

[30] Karla Dial, "Emergency School Vouchers Likely for Katrina Victims," *Heartland Institute School Reform News* (November 2005). available at www.heartland.org.

the storm cloud."[31]   Jack Kemp, who served in the Reagan administration, a
longtime proponent of business approaches to urban poverty, took poetic license but stayed with the theme of precious metal, "...with the effort to rebuild after Katrina just getting underway, the Right sees, in the words of Jack
Kemp, a 'golden opportunity' to use a portion of the billions of federal reconstruction funds to implement a voucher experiment that, until now, it has
been unable to get through Congress."[32]   The governor of Louisiana saw gold
too. Although, before the storm, the state legislature had rejected the governor's attempt to seize control of the public schools from the city, "legislation
proposed by Governor Blanco in November allows the state to take over any
New Orleans school that falls below the statewide average on test scores and
place it into the state's Recovery School District. Under this low standard,
management of 102 of the 115 Orleans Parish schools operating before Katrina would be transferred to the state. The governor sees it as an effort to grasp
what she called a "golden opportunity for rebirth."[33]

Brian Riedlinger, the director of the Algiers Charter Schools Association
that would control all but one of the reopened New Orleans schools six
months after the tragedy, employed a creative variation on the theme, invok-
ing the poetry of Coleridge and the discourse of hygiene, "I think the schools
have been a real albatross. And so I think what we're giving parents is the possibility of hope, a possibility of wiping the slate clean and starting over."[34]
Long-standing advocates of public school privatization Paul T. Hill and Jane
Hannaway carried the hygienic metaphor a step further, writing in their Urban Institute report, "The Future of Public Education in New Orleans," that
"[e]ducation could be one of the bright spots in New Orleans' recovery effort,
which may even establish a new model for school districts nationally."[35]   This
"bright spot," according to Hill and Hannaway, which should be a national
model, calls for refusing to rebuild the New Orleans public schools, firing the

[31] Sharon Cohen, "New Orleans' Troubled Schools Get Overhaul" Associated Press, March 4,
2006. YahooNews, news.yahoo.com.

[32] People for the American Way, "Hurricane Katrina: A 'Golden Opportunity' for the Right-
Wing to Undermine Public Education" 11/14/05, available at www.pfaw.org.

[33] Paul Hill and Jane Hannaway, "The Future of Public Education in New Orleans," *After Katrina: Rebuilding Opportunity and Equity into the New New Orleans* (The Urban Institute, January
2006).

[34] Online NewsHour, "Rebuilding New Orleans Schools" December 19, 2005, available at
www.pbs.org/newshour/bb/education.

[35] Hill and Hannaway, "The Future of Public Education in New Orleans."

teachers and by extension dissolving the teachers' union, eradicating the central administration, and inviting for-profit corporations with sordid histories such as The Edison Schools[36] and other organizations to take over the running of schools.[37] Sajan George is a director of Alvarez & Marsal, a Bush administration-connected business-consulting firm that is making millions in its role subcontracting the rebuilding of schools. George, a "turnaround expert" contracted by the state, brought these metaphors together, stating, "This is the silver lining in the dark cloud of Katrina. We would not have been able to start with an almost clean slate if Katrina had not happened. So it really does represent an incredible opportunity."[38]

An incredible opportunity indeed.

Hurricane Katrina in New Orleans typifies the new form of educational privatization. The disaster has been used to enrich a predominantly white, tiny business and political elite while achieving educational privatization goals that the Right has been unable to achieve before: (1) implement the largest ever experiment in school vouchers; (2) allow for enormous profits in education rebuilding by contracting firms with political connections; (3) allow the replacement of a system of universal public education with a charter school network designed to participate in the dispossession of poor and African American residents from their communities. Such documents as those by the Urban Institute and the Heritage Foundation discuss strategies to make the temporary voucher scheme permanent and even how to take advantage of future disasters.

Vouchers use public money to pay for private schools and thus stand as a potentially lucrative business opportunity. Right-wing think tanks and advocates of educational privatization have been calling for wide-scale voucher schemes for decades, alleging that the competition for consumers' money will drive up quality and drive down costs. For example, the Heritage Foundation has been lobbying for vouchers for decades and published a report immediately after the hurricane calling for vouchers, as did the Urban Institute.[39] Support for vouchers comes largely from the neoliberal ideological belief that applying business ideals to the necessary bureaucratic public sector guarantees

---

[36] See Kenneth J. Saltman, *The Edison Schools: Corporate Schooling and the Assault on Public Education* (New York: Routledge, 2005).

[37] Hill and Hannaway, "The Future of Public Education in New Orleans."

[38] Cohen, "New Orleans' Troubled Schools Get Overhaul."

[39] People for the American Way, "Hurricane Katrina: A 'Golden Opportunity' for the Right-Wing to Undermine Public Education," November 14, 2005. available at www.pfaw.org.

efficiencies. Critics of vouchers have contended that (1) encouraging parents to "shop" for schools will take scarce federal resources away from those public schools most in need of them—schools that have historically been underfunded by having resource allocations pegged to local property taxes[40]; (2) vouchers have traditionally been used to maintain or worsen racial segregation in the face of desegregation policies[41]— particularly relevant legacy to the racial dispossession going on in New Orleans; (3) vouchers undermine universal public schooling by redefining a public good as a private commodity and stand to exacerbate already existing inequalities in funding; (4) vouchers undermine the public democratic purposes of public schooling by treating citizens as consumers; and (5) vouchers undermine the constitutional separation of church and state.

Not only was the voucher agenda being pushed unsuccessfully for years before the storm, but also until Katrina the only federally funded voucher scheme was implemented by the U.S. Congress in the District of Columbia.

> One that has been "marked by a failure to achieve legislatively determined priorities, an inability to evaluate the program in the manner required by Congress, and efforts by administrators to obscure information that might reflect poorly on the program."[42]

This voucher scheme was surreptitiously inserted into federal legislation by being rolled into a budget bill, and it was aggressively supported by one of the richest people on the planet, Wal-Mart inheritor John Walton of the Walton Family Foundation, one of the largest spenders pushing privatization of public education.[43]

---

[40] Linda Baker makes this important point about the embedded funding implications of "choice" in the context of how No Child Left Behind allows students to choose any school, "All for One, None for All," *In These Times*, October 24, 2005.

[41] For an excellent discussion of the history of voucher debates see Jeffrey Henig, *Rethinking School Choice* (Princeton: Princeton University Press, 1994).

[42] People for the American Way, "Hurricane Katrina: A 'Golden Opportunity' for the Right-Wing to Undermine Public Education" 11/14/05, available at www.pfaw.org.

[43] See the eulogy for Walton, who died in a private airplane crash, in the right-wing Hoover Institution in the Fall 2005 issue of *Education Next* magazine, p. 5. It is important to mention that Walton's multi-billion dollar inheritance was the result of Wal-Mart's spectacular growth that came not only from the entrepreneurial savvy of Sam Walton but also his commitment to union-busting, displacing the cost of health care onto public coffers by refusing to offer adequate health insurance to employees, the destruction of small businesses throughout the U.S. through monopolistic practices, and of course being a significant contributor to the vast

Not only did New Orleans not have a voucher scheme prior to Katrina, but a K-12 voucher bill had just been defeated in the Louisiana state legislature just before the hurricane.[44] The bill would have allowed for public tax money to fund private or religious schooling.

Despite public democratic deliberation on the issue concluding against vouchers, conservative privatization advocates moved quickly to take advantage of the disaster. Within two weeks after the hurricane struck, the Heritage Foundation released a "special report" refashioning their long-standing agenda as "principled solutions" for rebuilding. "Heritage has been pushing school vouchers since 1975 and so it is no surprise that the organization now strongly believes that a voucher proposal that would fund private schools constitutes a successful response to the crisis."[45]

The Bush administration, so slow to provide federal emergency aid to residents, was nonetheless quick to respond to extensive media criticism by following the privatization proposals of such right-wing think tanks. The administration proposed $1.9 billion in aid to K-12 students with $488 million designated for school vouchers. The editors of *Rethinking Schools* accurately wrote, "This smells like a back-door approach to get public funding for private schools and would essentially create the first national school voucher plan."[46]

Privatization advocates were quite explicit in their desire to undermine local control over educational decision-making and to create a situation in which it would be very difficult to reverse the implementation of vouchers. For example, Karla Dial reporting in the right-wing Heartland Institute *School Reform News*, quotes Chris Kinnan of Freedom Works, a D.C. organization fighting for "smaller government" and more "personal freedom."

> 'Having those vouchers for a couple of years would change the way parents and students and even educators think about them,' Kinnan said. 'The impact would be so powerful that if you did it right, [school] systems would be competing to attract these

---

loss of manufacturing sector work to China. See the excellent documentary film *Wal-mart: The High Cost of Low Prices*.

[44] Bolick, "Katrina's Displaced Students."

[45] People for the American Way, "Hurricane Katrina: A 'Golden Opportunity' for the Right-Wing to Undermine Public Education," 11/14/05. available at www.pfaw.org.

[46] The Editors, "Katrina's Lessons," *Rethinking Schools*, Fall 2005, p. 5.

[kids with vouchers]. It's all about changing the incentive. Once you have that freedom it would be very difficult to go back to the community control system.[47]

For Kinnan and his ilk, "freedom" means privatizing public control over
public resources so that fewer people with more wealth and power have more
political control over said resources. The genius of framing the amassing of
political and economic control over public resources as individual consumer
choice is that it takes on the deceptive appearance of increasing individual
control while it actually removes individuals from collective control. Privatizers
aim to treat the use of public resources as "shopping" by "consumers," thereby
naturalizing the public sector as a market—as a natural, politically neutral entity ruled by the laws of supply and demand rather than as a matter of public
priority, political deliberation, and competing values and visions. Such metaphors of consumer culture not only conceal the ways that public goods and
services are different from markets (public services aim to serve public interest
and collective goals not the amassing of private profit), but such appeals also
fail to admit that markets themselves are hardly neutral and natural but are,
on the contrary, hierarchical, human-made political configurations unequally
distributing power and control over material resources and cultural value.

The Clint Bolick of the Alliance for School Choice was also scheming to get a
foot in the door. Hopeful that the initial one-year period for vouchers in the
Bush proposal could be extended indefinitely, he said, "I think that if emergency school vouchers are passed this time they will be a routine part of future
emergency relief. I'm also hopeful that when the No Child Left Behind Act is
modified that it will be easier for Congress to add vouchers to the remedies
available under that law."[48]

The Heritage Foundation, the Alliance for School Choice, and the Heartland Institute were hardly alone, as a large number of right-wing groups committed to vouchers praised the president's plan. Gary Bauer, of the group
American Values, hailed the "rebuilding challenge as an opportunity to implement conservative ideas such as school vouchers and tax free zones."[49] The
Bush plan was praised by the Family Research Council, Rich Lowry of the *National Review*, Gary McCaleb of the Alliance Defense Fund, Marvin Olasky of

---

[47] Karla Dial, "Emergency School Vouchers Likely for Katrina Victims" *Heartland Institute School
Reform News*, November 2005, available at www.heartland.org.

[48] Ibid.

[49] People for the American Way, "Hurricane Katrina: A 'Golden Opportunity' for the Right-
Wing to Undermine Public Education," 11/14/05. available at www.pfaw.org.

World Magazine, and William Donohue of the Catholic League, among others.[50]

The Yankee Institute took a full page color advertisement in Heartland's *School Reform News* with a letter from its executive director, Lewis Andrews, who admonishes readers that when the real estate bubble bursts and public education "cost soars relative to home values" in rich communities, "savvy reformers will be prepared to make the case for school vouchers in all communities."[51] The ad begins with the expression, "Every cloud has a silver lining."

Implicit in Andrews' statements is the fact that privatizers have already been taking advantage of the historical failure to fund education properly in poor and working-class communities. Before Katrina, per pupil spending in New Orleans stood at about $5,000 ($4,986 in 1998). To put this in perspective, per pupil spending in suburban public school districts in wealthy suburbs around the nation reaches as high as roughly quadruple this amount despite the fact that they face far fewer obstacles. As the Right clearly grasps, the question of privatization is inextricably linked to matters of public funding. Vouchers, charters, and EMOs cannot make headway with well-financed public schools in richer communities. Crisis and emergency benefit privatization advocates can seize upon a situation with preformulated plans to commodify this public service. To put it differently, privatizers target those who have been denied adequate public investment in the first place. As the United Federation of Teachers' Joe Derose insists, the policy emphasis in rebuilding should be on the chronic underfunding plaguing the New Orleans public schools rather than on the schemes to privatize them.[52] As the above quotes from Bolick, Kinnan, and Andrews illustrate, the Right is eager to take advantage of crisis to subvert democratic oversight over policy matters of great public importance.

The Bush administration has long aimed to expand vouchers. In 2002 vouchers were removed from the No Child Left Behind bill at the last moment as part of an effort to secure bipartisan support.[53] Not only do the Katrina federal vouchers cover far beyond the Gulf Coast region, but they take advantage of the crisis to promote the idea of vouchers and privatization generally. For example, while select counties and parishes in Alabama, Mississippi,

---

[50] Ibid.

[51] *Heartland Institute School Reform News*, November 2005, p. 9, available at www.heartland.org.

[52] Cohen, "New Orleans' Troubled Schools Get Overhaul."

[53] George Wood, "Introduction," *Many Children Left Behind*, edited by Deborah Meier and George Wood (Boston: Beacon, 2004), ix.

Louisiana, and Florida are included in the Emergency Impact Aid, the entire state of Texas is included in the voucher scheme. While emergency funds do not permit public school rebuilding, they nonetheless give funding to schools in 49 states. What is more, the vouchers can be given to charter schools without charter schools meeting section 5210 (1) of ESEA No Child Left Behind that requires charter schools to be developed with public charter agencies. In other words, the vouchers allow public funding for charter schools that do not need to be held accountable to public oversight institutions that regulate charter schools. As a result, the Aid favors not merely the public funding of private schools but even encourages the development of charter schools unregulated by the public sector by funding them when they would otherwise be ineligible to receive federal funding for having failed to meet basic requirements.[54]

The Emergency Impact Aid is also being used to promote and publicize vouchers as a legitimate school reform. Secretary of Education Margaret Spellings made this goal of proselytizing vouchers quite explicit in her speech of April 5, 2006, in a New York church, saying that, in addition to expanding charter schools and the voucher scheme in D.C., "most importantly, we've armed the parents of 48 million public school students nationwide with the information to be smart educational consumers and become real advocates for their children."[55] Spellings notably embraces the neoliberal description of education as a business with consumers rather than as a public good crucial for the making of citizens capable of developing skills and dispositions of self-governance. In this speech Spellings explains that No Child Left Behind's provision allowing students to attend other schools and its designation of schools as "failed" are designed to expand "choice." This is how she describes both vouchers and the NCLB provision allowing students to go to any school—a measure implemented to set the stage for vouchers. And as Spellings explains, the voucher scheme in New Orleans is part of an aggressive broader attempt to use federal power to privatize public schooling:

> More than 1,700 schools around the country have failed to meet state standards for five or six years in a row. And many of these schools are in districts where public school choice isn't a real option. We're proposing a new $100 million Opportunity Scholarship Fund to help thousands of low-income students in these schools attend

---

[54] See U.S. Department of Education, Volume I, Frequently Asked Questions, Emergency Impact Aid for Displaced Students, January 12, 2006.

[55] Press Release, "Secretary Spellings Delivers Remarks on School Choice," For Release April 5, 2006, available at www.ed.gov/news/pressreleases/2006/04/04052006.html.

the private school of their choice or receive intensive one-on-one tutoring after school or during the summer.[56]

Immediately after Katrina, Secretary Spellings even sought to waive a federal law that bans educational segregation for homeless children with the obvious purpose of using public funding for private schooling even in explicitly segregated schooling.[57] What is crucial to recognize here is that disasters are being taken advantage of and produced to set the stage for educational privatization. Whether public schools are being systematically underfunded, as were the New Orleans Public Schools before Katrina and then declared "failed" (as NCLB is designed to do nationwide), or whether a storm blows them to smithereens does not matter to the privatizers—though the aftermath of Katrina indicates the Right has found just what can be accomplished through sudden massive destruction.

What goes undisclosed in the Department of Education's mandated notification is a comparison of how much money a student received in her prior public school relative to the federal funding for the private school. In fact, the vouchers give significantly less money per pupil than New Orleans students received. New Orleans students received an already very low per pupil funding of roughly $5,000 while Bush's voucher scheme pays only $750 per pupil. Clint Bolick argues that a prime reason for vouchers is to save money. Cutting funding for education certainly saves money, but it does not explain how educational services are paid for. The numbers do not appear to add up. Congress approved $645 million in the Hurricane Education Recovery Act that applies to 49 states and $496 million to the states most severely damaged to reopen schools under the Immediate Aid to Restart School Operations Program. In September 2005, Spellings stated that there were 372,000 schoolchildren displaced from Louisiana and Mississippi. Yet in March 2006, she gave a figure of 157,743 students nationwide who are eligible for a portion of the HERA money as of the first quarter of the year. That would mean HERA should pay about $4,088 per pupil, but schools will receive only $750 per pupil and $937.50 for students with disabilities. Where is the money going? Instead of going to rebuild aggressively the destroyed schools in the regions hardest hit

---

[56] Ibid.

[57] Judd Legum, Faiz Shakir, Nico Pitney, Amanda Terkel, Payson Schwin, and Christy Harvey, "Katrina: Ideology over People," ThinkProgress.Org, September 15, 2005, available online at www.americanprogressaction.org.

needing the full amount, the money is being dispersed throughout 49 states and D.C.:

> States and the District of Columbia will receive funding under this emergency, one-time program. Funds may be used to hire teachers; provide books and other classroom supplies; offer in-school or outside supplemental services such as tutoring, mentoring and counseling; and cover transportation and health costs.[58]

It would be myopic to think that this funding is merely about paying for the new burden of educating hurricane evacuees. This shifting of educational resources around the nation under the guise of emergency needs to be understood in relation to the failure of the Bush administration to pay states' federal funds as part of NCLB. As Monty Neil points out,

> Not only has the federal government failed to meet the social, economic, and health-related needs of many children, but NCLB itself does not authorize nearly enough funding to meet its new requirements. The Bush administration has sought almost no increase in ESEA expenditures for FY2005 and the coming year. The funds Congress has appropriated are about $8 billion per year less than Congress authorized. Meanwhile, states are still suffering from their worst budget crises since World War II, cutting education as well as social programs needed by low-income people.[59]

It appears that "emergency" is being used to cover failed promises that have nothing to do with emergency other than the emergencies created by an administration hostile to supporting public education in the first place. But such coverage is taking the form of privatization. Failures of a conservative executive and legislature to support public education need to be understood in relation to a conservative judicial branch that in 2002 ruled vouchers constitutional. The political Right is waging war on public education while doing all it can to force through privatization initiatives that are unpopular and difficult to win politically.

Neoliberalism and the Uses of Disaster in Public Schooling

Contemporary initiatives to privatize public schools through the use of disaster can only be understood in relation to neoliberal ideology that pres-

---

[58] Press Release, "Secretary Spellings, Gulf Coast Rebuilding Coordinator Powell Announce $1.1 Billion for Hurricane-Affected Students and Schools," March 2, 2006.

[59] Monty Neil, "Leaving No Child Behind: Overhauling NCLB," in *Many Children Left Behind*, edited by Deborah Meier and George Wood (Boston: Beacon, 2004), 102-103.

ently dominates politics.[60] As David Harvey elucidates, neoliberalism, also described as "neoclassical economics" or "market fundamentalism," brings together economic, political, and cultural policy doctrine. Neoliberalism, which originates with Frederic Von Hayek, Milton Friedman, and the "Chicago boys" at the University of Chicago in the 1950s, expresses individual and social ideals through market ideals. Within this view, individual and social values and aspirations can best be reached through the unfettered market. In its ideal forms (as opposed to how it is practically implemented) neoliberalism demands privatization of public goods and services, removal of regulation on trade, loosening of capital and labor controls by the state, and the allowance of foreign direct investment. For neoliberalism, public control over public resources should be taken from the "necessarily bureaucratic" state and placed with the "necessarily efficient" private sector. The implosion of the Soviet Union and the fall of the Berlin Wall were used by neoliberals to declare that there could be no alternative to global capitalism—Thatcher famously called this the TINA thesis, There Is No Alternative to the Market. Within the logic of capitalist triumphalism, the only thing to do would be to put into effect the dictates of the market and spread the market to places previously inaccessible.

The financial past performance of neoliberalism, as Harvey explains, is not one of accomplishment but rather one of failure having caused crises, instability, and unreconciled contradictions regarding state power.[61] However, as he shows, neoliberalism has been extremely accomplished at upwardly redistributing economic wealth and political power. Consequently, Harvey suggests understanding neoliberalism as a long-standing project of class warfare waged by the rich on everyone else. Neoliberalism has damaged welfare state protections and undermined government authority to act in the public interest. As well, these policies have brought on wide-scale disaster around the globe, including a number of countries in Latin America and the Pacific rim. Such disasters have compelled governments to reevaluate neoliberalism as it has been enjoined by the so-called "Washington consensus." In fact, recent elections

---

[60] Henry Giroux's *The Terror of Neoliberalism* (Boulder: Paradigm Press, 2004) offers a crucial analysis of the cultural pedagogy of neoliberalism. For discussion of neoliberal pedagogy in relation to school curriculum, film, and literary corporate cultural production see also Robin Truth Goodman and Kenneth J. Saltman, *Strange Love, Or How We Learn to Stop Worrying and Love the Market* (Lanham, MD: Rowman & Littlefield, 2002). An excellent mapping and analysis of these conservatisms and others can be found in Michael Apple's *Educating the Right Way* (New York: Routledge, 2001).

[61] David Harvey, *A Brief History of Neoliberalism* (Oxford: Oxford University Press, 2005).

throughout Latin America with Left victories have largely been a reaction to the neoliberal "Washington consensus" that imposes neoliberal globalization through institutional mechanisms such as the IMF and World Bank.

Initially seen as a wacky doctrine, neoliberalism was not brought into the mainstream of policy and government circles until the late 1970s and early 1980s in Thatcher's U.K. and in Reagan's U.S. As Harvey details, Chile, under brutal dictator Pinochet, was a crucial test field for the ideology, resulting in increased commercial investments in Chile alongside 30,000 citizen disappearances. The widening reception to neoliberalism had to do with the steady lobbying of Right-ring think tanks and electoral victories but also with the right conditions, including economic crises that challenged the Keynesian model and Fordist modes of economic production and social formation in the late 1970s.[62] Neoliberalism has a distinct hostility to democracy. As Harvey writes,

> Neoliberal theorists are, however, profoundly suspicious of democracy. Governance by majority rule is seen as a potential threat to individual rights and constitutional liberties. Democracy is viewed as a luxury, only possible under conditions of relative affluence coupled with a strong middle-class presence to guarantee political stability. Neoliberals therefore tend to favour governance by experts and elites. A strong preference exists for government by executive order and by judicial decision rather than democratic and parliamentary decision-making.[63]

Such opposition to democracy and preference for elite governance is ceaselessly expressed by such neoliberal education writers as those of the Koret Task Force of the Hoover Institution such as John Chubb, Terry Moe, Eric Hanuschek and company.[64] For progressive and critical educators principally concerned with the possibilities for public schooling to expand a democratic ethos and engaged critical citizenry, neoliberalism's antidemocratic tendencies appear as particularly bad.

In education, neoliberalism has pervasively infiltrated with radical implications, remaking educational practical judgment and forwarding the privatiza-

---

[62] For an excellent succinct discussion of the shift from Fordism to post-Fordism with the rise of neoliberal globalization and the concomitant shifts in social organization as well as implications for cultural theory see Nancy Fraser, "From Discipline to Flexibilization? Rereading Foucault in the Shadow of Globalization" *Constellations* 10, no. 2 (2003): 160-171.

[63] Harvey, *A Brief History of Neoliberalism*, 66-67.

[64] See, for example, Chubb and Moe's neoliberal education bible, *Politics, Markets, and America's Schools*. See also the several Koret edited collections, including *A Primer on America's Schools*.

tion and deregulation program. The steady rise of privatization and the shift to business language and logic can be understood through the extent to which neoliberal ideals have succeeded in taking over educational debates. Neoliberalism appears in the now commonsense framing of education through presumed ideals of upward individual economic mobility (the promise of cashing in knowledge for jobs) and the social ideals of global economic competition. In this view national survival hinges upon educational preparation for international economic supremacy. The preposterousness of this assumption comes as school kids rather than corporate executives are being blamed for the global economic race to the bottom. The "TINA" thesis (There Is No Alternative to the Market) that has come to dominate politics throughout much of the world has infected educational thought as omnipresent market terms such as "accountability," "choice," "efficiency," "competition," "monopoly," and "performance" frame educational debates. Nebulous terms borrowed from the business world such as "achievement," "excellence," and "best practices" conceal ongoing struggles over competing values, visions, and ideological perspectives. (Achieve what? Excel at what? Best practices for whom? And says who?) The only questions left on reform agendas appear to be how to best enforce knowledge and curriculum conducive to individual upward mobility within the economy and national economic interest as it contributes to a corporately managed model of globalization as perceived from the perspective of business. This is a dominant and now commonplace view of education propagated by such influential writers as Thomas Friedman in his books and *New York Times* columns, and such influential grant-givers as the Bill and Melinda Gates Foundation.

This neoliberal view of education dangerously eradicates the role of democratic participation and the role of public schools in preparing public democratic citizens with the intellectual and critical tools for meaningful and participatory self-governance. By reducing the politics of education to its economic functions, neoliberal educational thinking has deeply authoritarian tendencies that are incompatible with democracy. Democracy is under siege by the tendency of market fundamentalism to collapse politics with economics, thereby translating all social problems into business concerns with the possibilities for continued profit making. Yet, democracy is also under siege by a rising authoritarianism in the U.S. that eviscerates civil liberties and attacks human rights domestically and internationally through the USA Patriot Act, "extraordinary rendition" (state-sanctioned kidnapping, torture, and murder), spying on the public, and other measures that treacherously expand executive power. Internationally, this appears as what Harvey has termed "The New Imperialism" and others have called "militarized globalization" that includes the so-called "war on terror," the U.S. military presence in more than 140 countries, the encirclement of the world's oil resources with the world's most powerful military, etc. This is on top of a continued culture of militarism that educates citizens to identify with militarized solutions to social problems. In education, I have called this militarism "education as enforcement" that aims to enforce global neoliberal imperatives through a number of educational means.[65]

David Harvey offers a compelling economic argument for the rise of repression and militarization, explaining the shift from neoliberalism to neoconservatism. Neoliberal policy was coming into dire crisis already in the late 1990s as deregulation of capital was resulting in a threat to the U.S. as it lost its manufacturing base and increasingly lost service sector and financial industry to Asia.[66] For Harvey, the new militarism in foreign policy is partly about a desperate attempt to seize control of the world's oil spigot as lone superpower parity is endangered by the rise of a fast growing Asia and a unified Europe with a strong currency. Threats to the U.S. economy are posed by not only the potential loss of control over the fuel for the U.S. economy and military but also the power conferred by the dollar remaining the world currency and the increasing indebtedness of the U.S. to China and Japan as they prop up the value of the dollar for the continued export of consumer goods. For Harvey, the structural problems behind global capitalism remain the financialization of the global economy and what Marx called "the crisis of overproduction" driving down prices and wages while glutting the market and threatening profits. Capitalists and states representing capitalist interests respond to these crises through Harvey's version of what Marx called primitive accumulation, "accumulation by dispossession."

Privatization is one of the most powerful tools of accumulation by dispossession, transforming publicly owned and controlled goods and services into

---

[65] See Kenneth J. Saltman and David Gabbard (eds.), *Education as Enforcement: The Militarization and Corporatization of Schools* (New York: Routledge, 2003).

[66] Harvey offers important tools for comprehending neoliberalism and neoconservatism in both *A Brief History of Neoliberalism* and *The New Imperialism*. For a discussion of Harvey's recent work and the implications for public school privatization and theoretical limitations of this work see Kenneth J. Saltman, "Review of a *Brief History of Neoliberalism*," *Policy Futures in Education*, 2007.

private and restricted ones—the continuation of "enclosing the commons" begun in Tudor England. If neoliberalism came into crisis due to the excesses of capitalism (deregulation and liberalization yielding capital flight, deindustrialization, etc.), then the neoconservative response—emphasizing control and order and reinvigorated overt state power—makes a lot of sense. As Harvey explains in *A Brief History of Neoliberalism*, central to the crisis of neoliberalism are the contradictions of neoliberalism's antipathy to the nation and reliance on the state. Neoconservatives have responded to the neoliberal crisis by using national power to push economic competition, to pillage productive forces for continued economic growth, and also to control populations through repression as inequalities of wealth and income are radically exacerbated, resulting in the expansion of a dual society of mobile professionals on the one side and everyone else on the other.[67] The surging culture of religious right-wing populism, irrational new age mysticism, and endless conspiracy theorizing appear to symptomatize a cultural climate in which neoliberal market fundamentalism has come into crisis as both economic doctrine and ideology. Within this climate, private for-profit knowledge-making institutions, including schools and media, are institutionally incapable of providing a language and criticism that would enable rational interpretation necessary for political intervention. Irrationalism is the consequence. Not too distant history suggests that this can lead in systematically deadly directions.[68]

At the present moment there is a crucial tension between two fundamental functions of public education for the capitalist state. The first involves reproducing the conditions of production—teaching skills and know-how in ways that are ideologically compatible with the social relations of capital accumulation. Public education remains an important and necessary tool for capital to make political and economic leaders or docile workers and marginalized citizens or even for participating in sorting and sifting out those to be excluded from economy and politics completely. The second function that appears to be relatively new and growing involves the capitalist possibilities of pillaging public education for profit, in the U.S., Iraq, or elsewhere. Drawing on Harvey's explanation of accumulation by dispossession, we see that in the U.S. the nu-

---

[67] The expansion of the dual society as a result of neoliberal globalization has been importantly theorized by Zygmunt Bauman, *Globalization: The Human Consequences* (New York: Polity, 1998) and Nancy Fraser, "From Discipline to Flexibilization? Rereading Foucault in the Shadow of Globalization," *Constellations* 10, no. 2 (2003): 160-171.

[68] See Theodore Adorno, *The Stars Down to Earth and Other Essays on the Irrational Culture* (New York: Routledge, 2001).

merous strategies for privatizing public education—from voucher schemes, to for-profit charter schools, to forced for-profit remediation schemes, to dissolving public schools in poor communities and replacing them with a mix of private, charter, and experimental schools—all follow a pattern of destroying and commodifying schools where the students are redundant to reproduction processes, while maintaining public investment in the schools that have the largest reproductive role of turning out managers and leaders.

Strategies of capitalist accumulation, dispossession, and reproduction, appear to be at odds. After all, if public schooling is being pillaged and sold off, then how can it reproduce the social order for capital? Yet privatization is targeting those most marginal to capitalist reproduction, thereby making the most economically excluded into commodities for corporations. Hence, EMOs target the poor, making economically marginalized people into opportunities for capital the way that for-profit prisons do. Reproduction and dispossession feed each other in several ways: in an ideological apparatus such as education or media, privatization and decentralization exacerbate class inequality by weakening universal provision, weakening the public role of a service, putting in place reliance upon expensive equipment supplied from outside, and justifying further privatization and decentralization to remedy the deepened economic differentiation and hierarchization that has been introduced or worsened through privatization and decentralization. The obvious U.S. example is the failure of the state to properly fund public schools in poor communities and then privatizing those schools to be run by corporations.[69] Rather than addressing the funding inequalities and the intertwined dynamics at work in making poor schools or working to expand the democratic potential of public schools, the remedy is commodification.

It is crucial to emphasize that what Klein terms "disaster capitalism" and Harvey terms "accumulation by dispossession" are not just an economic project but also a cultural project and that these need to be comprehended together. What Henry Giroux has termed the "cultural pedagogy of neoliberalism"[70] is typified not merely by the language of "silver linings" and "golden opportunities" but by the turn to business language and models in thinking about the social world, including public school reform and policy. Not only have public school debates been overrun by the aforementioned neo-

---

[69] See Kenneth J. Saltman, *Collateral Damage: Corporatizing Public Schools – A Threat to Democracy*, (Lanham, MD: Rowman & Littlefield Publishers, 2000).
[70] Henry A. Giroux, *The Terror of Neoliberalism* (Boulder: Paradigm, 2004).

liberal language, but as we see in New Orleans, business "turnaround special-ists" such as Alvarez and Marsal are brought in to dictate school rebuilding while residents are dispossessed of their communities through economic ra-tionales. The state and Alvarez and Marsal invoked "supply and demand" to justify not rebuilding the New Orleans public schools (residents do not return because the schools have not been rebuilt and then the planners declare that there is no demand for school rebuilding). The idealization of choice, markets, business, deregulation, and anti-unionism is propagated in a number of ways through the cultural pedagogy of neoliberalism. It is essential to remember what Pierre Bourdieu emphasized about neoliberalism.

> Neoliberal economics ...owes a certain number of its allegedly universal characteristics to the fact that it is immersed or embedded in a particular society, that is to say, rooted in a system of beliefs and values, an ethos and a moral view of the world, in short, an *economic common sense*, linked as such to the social and cognitive structures of a particular social order. It is from this particular economy [that of the United States] that neoclassical economic theory borrows its fundamental assumptions, which it formalizes and rationalizes, thereby establishing them as the foundations of a univer-sal model. That model rests on two postulates (which their advocates regard as proven propositions): the economy is a separate domain governed by natural and universal laws with which governments must not interfere by inappropriate intervention; the market is the optimum means for organizing production and trade efficiently and eq-uitably in democratic societies.[71]

A number of educational forces in addition to schools are required to keep such premises appearing natural and hence unquestionable. Mass media is one of the most powerful pedagogical forces ongoingly educating the public to understand "the economy" as natural and inevitable whether through news programs that report stock prices like the weather or through sports that align capitalist values of numerically quantifiable progress and growth with the pos-sibilities of the human body, or through police shows (nearly half of U.S. TV content) that replace the primary role of the police (protecting private prop-erty) with the drama of seldom-committed spectacular murders, or the social Darwinist game shows that make contestants compete for scarce resources, including money, cut-throat corporate jobs, trophy spouses, and cut-face plas-tic surgery to compete all the better, or through the advertising behind it all that sells the fantasies that comprise a particular kind of radically individual-ized, cynical consumer view of the self and the social world. Such media prod-

---

[71] Pierre Bourdieu, *The Social Structures of the Economy* (Malden, MA: Polity, 2005), 10-11.

ucts function pedagogically to define what is possible to think and what is impossible to imagine for the future.

Yet, as powerful as mass media is as a pedagogical force, the traditions of critical pedagogy, critical theory, cultural studies, feminism, progressive education, and critical cultural production offer powerful tools to produce different kinds of visions—hopeful, democratic visions that articulate with growing democracy movements around the world. The neoliberal postulates that Bourdieu denaturalizes appear increasingly dubious at best as wealth and income are radically redistributed upwards in the U.S. while nation after nation in Latin America rejects the neoliberal "Washington consensus" in favor of another path that coheres generally much more with the democratic ideals of the global justice movement.[72]

The Assault on Teacher Education

Alongside the current attempts of business and the political Right to capitalize on disaster, these same forces have taken aim at teacher education in the U.S. The Carnegie Corporation through its Teachers for a New Era initiative has invoked its ominous warning from the 1983 *A Nation at Risk* report, suggesting that the present state of teacher education is akin to an act of war by a foreign power.[73] That is, teacher education in the U.S. is being described of late as, if not a disaster, then as culpable for the oft-alleged disastrous state of public education in the U.S. In the summer of 2006, the *New York Times*, which had been writing mostly favorably of charter schools for years, published an editorial that strongly criticized charter schools yet concluded the editorial by suggesting that the one big problem with public education is teacher education.[74] The World Economic Forum, in the fall of 2006, issued a press release that the United States had fallen in one year from first to sixth in rankings of global competitiveness. Of central blame for this alleged disaster: the education system. And in the fall of 2006, Arthur Levine, former president of Teachers College of Columbia University, issued a widely publicized report, "Educating School Teachers" (available at www.edschools.org), denouncing the current state of teacher education and calling for many baccalaureate and master's level programs to be simply closed. Levine's proposals

---

[72] A valuable source for entry into the literature on the global justice movement is Z Net available at zmag.org.

[73] See www.teachersforanewera.org.

[74] Editorial Desk, "Exploding the Charter School Myth," *New York Times* (August 27, 2006): Section 4, page 9.

have been criticized by the AACTE and NCATE as being "elitist" for wanting to close all but the elite teacher education programs. Levine's perspective shared with those of Carnegie, the World Economic Forum, and *The Times* both a view of teacher education as a problem and a primary responsibility of teacher education being to prepare teachers to prepare future workers for global economic competition. Levine serves on the board of DePaul University in Chicago (where I teach). DePaul signed a deal with the newly created for-profit company American College of Education (ACE) for DePaul to sell teacher education accreditation from its closed branch campus to ACE.[75] ACE had no physical site or programs when it bought the accreditation that allows it to sell as teacher education online courses paired with in-school practica in the Chicago Public Schools. Faculty in the School of Education at DePaul were not consulted. The decision sets up the for-profit ACE to compete with DePaul's own teacher education programs. The university justified the move on the basis of income generated by the sale of the accreditation. ACE's model is being developed by Reid Lyon, a Bush insider formerly of the National Institutes of Heath. Lyon's vision typifies the broad movement to remake teacher education. He advocates the end of educational theorizing, derides "philosophy" as worthless to teacher education, and calls for teacher candidates to learn "scientifically effective" instructional methods that have been empirically confirmed with hard data.   ACE board members include former Secretary of Education Rod Paige (the one who described the National Education Association as a terrorist organization) whose Texas miracle of high test scores has been revealed to be based in the fabrication of hard data. Paige, Lyon, Levine, as well as Carnegie, the World Economic Forum and many other prominent institutions and policy makers ultimately understand the role of teacher education programs through neoliberalism. That is, they view teacher education as principally preparing teachers to make competent workers who can contribute to global economic competition and whose opportunities are understood as individual capacity to negotiate an economy controlled by others. In these reports teachers and teacher educators are framed as responsible for the well-being of the economy in that the primary responsibility of schools is preparing competent workers and future consumers. Oddly, such reports and institutions do not lay a heavy onus on business schools, though business schools do

---

[75] Joshua Benton, "Tactics Spur Accreditation Debate," *The Dallas Morning News*, May 28, 2006, available at www.dallasnews.com.

prepare future managers of the economy with disproportionate power to shape economic decisions. Such a belief about business schools would expect far too much from a course of study while neglecting the ways multiple forces, structures, and institutions impact on individual and collective decision-making. Yet teacher education is being held responsible for the fate of the U.S. economy. At the same time, the neoliberal view fails to admit the democratic roles of public education in preparing students to govern themselves and others in a just and egalitarian manner by developing their capacities for engaged political interpretation and individual and collective action.

Thoroughly at odds with critical pedagogical approaches, these neoliberal views of teacher education have an accommodationist bent that views the social order as fundamentally just and do not make central the role that teachers can play in preparing democratic citizens. Perhaps most ominously, a number of these individuals and institutions advocate measuring the value of teacher education instruction by the numerical test scores of the students of teaching candidates. Such a positivist approach to knowledge both separates claims to truth from animating underlying assumptions and it insists on understanding learning as a product and knowledge as a commodity to be deposited into students so that they can "make achievement gains." Such thinking removes from consideration crucial questions about whose knowledge is worth learning and why, how knowledge relates to authority, and who designed the tests that supposedly neutrally and objectively measure knowledge that is alleged to be of universal value. These concerns are in addition to questions of who is profiting financially from test publishing, textbook sales, and the vast resources that go into such dubious "performance-based" reforms that are increasingly being extended from their destructive presence in K-12 to teacher education.

The neoliberal assault on teacher education participates in how the Right is capitalizing on disaster by producing forms of teacher education that restrict from the curriculum matters central to the making of a democratic culture. For teacher educators the most crucial matter at stake in debates over privatization and school reform generally is the possibilities for public schooling to expand a democratic ethos and foster democratic practices and social relations with regard to politics, culture, and economy. What is being done for profit and ideology in New Orleans and Iraq, in Chicago and throughout the U.S. with NCLB and the assault on teacher education does just the opposite by political dispossession, economic pillage, and cultural symbolic violence. It is incumbent upon teacher educators to develop pedagogical and material strategies to expand democratic struggles for the public to take back schools, resources, and cultural power as part of a broader democratic alternative to the antidemocratic neoliberal approaches that capitalize on disaster and imperil the public.

Bibliography

Benton, Joshua. 2006. "Tactics Spur Accreditation Debate," *The Dallas Morning News.* May 28. available at www.dallasnews.com.

Bolick, Clint. 2005. "Katrina's Displaced Students," *The Washington Times.* September 15.

Bourdieu, Pierre. 2005. *The Social Structures of the Economy.* Malden, MA: Polity.

Capchino, April. 2006. "More than 100 N.O. Schools Still Closed," *New Orleans City Business* February 27.

Chaterjee, Pratap. 2004. *Iraq, Inc.: A Profitable Occupation.* New York: Seven Stories Press.

Cohen, Sharon. 2006. "New Orleans' Troubled Schools Get Overhaul," Associated Press. March 4.

Dial, Karla. 2005. "Emergency School Vouchers Likely for Katrina Victims," *Heartland Institute School Reform News.* November. available at www.heartland.org.

Economist, The. 1999. "Reading, Writing, and Enrichment: Private Money Is Pouring into American Education—And Transforming It.," *The Economist.* January 16: 55.

Editorial Desk. 2006. "Exploding the Charter School Myth," *New York Times.* August 27: Section 4, page 9.

Editors, The. 2005. "Katrina's Lesson," *Rethinking Schools.* Fall: 4-5.

Gates Foundation, The. 2004. "Snapshot: Chicago Renaissance 2010," *Possibilities: An Education Update,* The Bill and Melinda Gates Foundation, available at http://www.gatesfoundation.org/Education/RelatedInfo/Possibilities/Possibilities2004.

Giroux, Henry A. 2004. *The Terror of Neoliberalism* Boulder: Paradigm.

Harvey, David. *A Brief History of Neoliberalism.* 2005. (Oxford: Oxford University Press.

Hill, Paul and Jane Hannaway. 2006. "The Future of Public Education in New Orleans," *After Katrina: Rebuilding Opportunity and Equity into the New New Orleans.* The Urban Institute, January.

Klein, Naomi. 2005. "The Rise of Disaster Capitalism," *The Nation.* May.

Kohn, Alfie. 2004. "NCLB and the Effort to Privatize Public Education" in *Many Children Left Behind,* Deborah Meier and George Wood (eds.), Boston: Beacon, 79-100.

Legum, Judd, Faiz Shakir, Nico Pitney, Amanda Terkel, Payson Schwin, and Christy Harvey. 2005. "Katrina: Ideology over People," ThinkProgress.Org. September 15. available online at www.americanprogressaction.org.

Lipman, Pauline. 2005. "'We're Not Blind. Just Follow the Dollar Sign,'" *Rethinking Schools Online* 19, no. 4, Summer. available at www.rethinkingschools.org.

Moore, Deb. 2004. "A New Approach in Chicago," *School Planning and Management.* July: 8.

Neil, Monty. 2004. "Leaving No Child Behind: Overhauling NCLB" in *Many Children Left Behind,* Deborah Meier and George Wood (eds.), Boston: Beacon. 102-103.

Nichols, Sharon L., Gene V. Glass, David C. Berliner. "High-Stakes Testing and Student Achievement: Problems for the No Child Left Behind Act," Educational Policy Studies Laboratory, available at http://edpolicylab.org, "Executive Summary," 3.

Online NewsHour. 2005. "Rebuilding New Orleans Schools," December 19. available at www.pbs.org/newshour/bb/education.

People for the American Way. 2005. "Hurricane Katrina: A 'Golden Opportunity' for the Right-Wing to Undermine Public Education." November 14. available at www.pfaw.org.

Press Release. 2006. "Secretary Spellings Delivers Remarks on School Choice." April 5. available at www.ed.gov/news/pressreleases/2006/04/04052006.html.

Press Release. 2006. "Secretary Spellings, Gulf Coast Rebuilding Coordinator Powell Announce $1.1 Billion for Hurricane-Affected Students and Schools." March 2.

Saltman, Kenneth J. 2006. "Creative Associates International, Inc.: Corporate Education and Democracy Promotion in Iraq," *Review of Education Pedagogy Cultural Studies* 28: 25-65.

Shipps, Dorothy. *School Reform, Corporate Style: Chicago 1880-2000.* Lawrence: The University of Kansas Press. x.

Wiley, Edward W., William J. Mathis, David R. Garcia. 2005. "The Impact of Adequate Yearly Progress Requirement of the Federal 'No Child Left Behind' Act on Schools in the Great Lakes Region," *Education Policy Studies Laboratory.* September. available at edpolicylab.org.

Wood, George. 2005. "Introduction," *Many Children Left Behind*, Deborah Meier and George Wood (eds.). Boston: Beacon. ix.

Contributors

Dennis Attick is a Ph.D. candidate in the Social Foundations of Education program in the Department of Educational Policy Studies at Georgia State University. He also works at The Bridge, a residential treatment center and alternative school for adolescents in Atlanta. His research interests include the work of John Dewey, the influence of media on students and children, and the connection between philosophy and popular culture.

Deron Boyles is Professor of Philosophy of Education in the Department of Educational Policy Studies at Georgia State University. His research interests include philosophy of education, school-business partnerships, epistemology, pragmatism and the philosophy of John Dewey, and critical pedagogy. His work has been published in such journals as *Philosophy of Education*, *Social Epistemology*, *Journal of Thought*, *Philosophical Studies in Education*, *Educational Foundations*, *History of Education Quarterly*, *Educational Studies*, and *Educational Theory*. His first book, *American Education and Corporations: The Free Market Goes to School* won the Critics' Choice Award from the American Educational Studies Association. *Schools or Markets?: Commercialism, Privatization, and School-Business Partnerships*, his second book, is an edited volume highlighting young scholars and their work on corporatism. He is a co-author, with Benjamin Baez, of *The Politics of Inquiry: Education Research and the "Culture of Science."* Boyles is a Fellow in the Philosophy of Education Society and The John Dewey Society.

Permeil Dass is a doctoral student at Georgia State University studying Educational Policy and teaches science at a local public high school. She received her bachelors degree in neuroscience from Oberlin College near her hometown of Cleveland, Ohio. The dedicated and passionate people at Citizens for Progressive Transit helped develop her interest in public transportation.

Jennifer Esposito is currently a faculty member in the Research, Measurement and Statistics program of the Department of Educational Policy Studies at Georgia State University. She teaches qualitative methods and anthropology of education. Her research interests include urban education, culturally relevant pedagogy, popular culture and race, class, and gender identity negotiation. Much of her research focuses on gender issues as they relate to schooling. In addition to book chapters, her research appears in such journals as *Educational Action Research*, *Educational Studies*, and *Teacher Education Quarterly*.

Bettina L. Love is a doctoral student at Georgia State University. Her major is Educational Policy Studies with a concentration in Social Foundations of Education. Bettina's research interests include Hip Hop culture and rap music, critical pedagogy, and urban education.

Trevor Norris is completing his doctorate at the Ontario Institute for Studies in Education with a special focus on the cultural and educational implications of consumerism. His recent work has appeared in *Educational Research*, the *Philosophy of Education Yearbook*, and *Studies in Philosophy and Education*. He is presently teaching—and troubling—Business Ethics at the Schulich School of Business.

Kenneth J. Saltman is an Associate Professor of Educational Policy Studies and Research at DePaul University in Chicago. He is the author of numerous books and articles on education, politics, and culture. His books include *Collateral Damage: Corporatizing Public Schools—a Threat to Democracy*, *Strange Love, Or How We Learn to Stop Worrying and Love the Market*, *The Edison Schools*, and most recently *Capitalizing on Disaster: Taking and Breaking Public Schools*. He is a fellow of the Educational Policy Research Unit (EPRU) located at Arizona State University.

Carly Stasko is an educator, writer, activist, artist, producer, public speaker, culture jammer and self-titled "Imagitator" (one who agitates imagination). Stasko is a contributor to various magazines and journals, and author of "Action Grrrls in the Dream Machine" in *Turbo Chicks: Talking Young Feminisms* and "(r)Evolutionary Healing: Jamming with Culture and Shifting the Power" in *New Wave Feminisms*. A former producer for CBC *Newsworld's* live political debate show *counterSpin*, Stasko has published her own zine *"uncool"* for several years. Her current interests include media literacy, reclaiming public spaces, social and environmental justice, creative healing, imagination and holistic education.

Carolyn Vander Schee is Assistant Professor of Educational Foundations at Northern Illinois University in DeKalb, IL. Her research interests include the intersections of educational policy studies, sociology of education, and school health issues.

Index

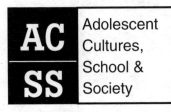

Adolescent
Cultures,
School &
Society

Joseph L. DeVitis & Linda Irwin-DeVitis
GENERAL EDITORS

As schools struggle to redefine and restructure themselves, they need to be cognizant of the new realities of adolescents. Thus, this series of monographs and textbooks is committed to depicting the variety of adolescent cultures that exist in today's post-industrial societies. It is intended to be a primarily qualitative research, practice, and policy series devoted to contextual interpretation and analysis that encompasses a broad range of interdisciplinary critique. In addition, this series will seek to provide a pragmatic, pro-active response to the current backlash of conservatism that continues to dominate political discourse, practice, and policy. This series seeks to address issues of curriculum theory and practice; multicultural education; aggression and violence; the media and arts; school dropouts; homeless and runaway youth; alienated youth; at-risk adolescent populations; family structures and parental involvement; and race, ethnicity, class, and gender studies.

Send proposals and manuscripts to the general editors at:
    Joseph L. DeVitis & Linda Irwin-DeVitis
    The John H. Lounsbury School of Education
    Georgia College & State University
    Campus Box 70
    Milledgeville, GA 31061-0490

To order other books in this series, please contact our Customer Service Department at:
    (800) 770-LANG (within the U.S.)
    (212) 647-7706 (outside the U.S.)
    (212) 647-7707 FAX

or browse online by series at:
    WWW.PETERLANG.COM